REVOLUTIONARY ROAD TRIP

HIDDEN STORIES FROM AMERICA'S FOUNDING JOURNEY

DARLEY NEWMAN

A REGALO PRESS BOOK
ISBN: 979-8-89565-731-7
ISBN (eBook): 979-8-89565-732-4

Revolutionary Road Trip:
Hidden Stories from America's Founding Journey
© 2026 by Darley Newman
All Rights Reserved

Cover Design by Jim Villaflores

Publishing Team:
Founder and Publisher – Gretchen Young
Editor—Adriana Senior
Managing Editor – Caitlin Burdette
Production Manager – Morgan Simpson
Production Editor – Rachel Paul

This is a work of nonfiction. All people, locations, events, and situations are portrayed to the best of the author's memory.

As part of the mission of Regalo Press, a donation is being made to National Park Foundation, as chosen by the author. Find out more about this organization at https://www.nationalparks.org/.

This book, as well as any other Regalo Press publications, may be purchased in bulk quantities at a special discounted rate. Contact orders@regalopress.com for more information.

Regalo Press
New York • Nashville
regalopress.com

Published in the United States of America
1 2 3 4 5 6 7 8 9 10

To the keepers of history—teachers, archivists,
re-enactors, docents, park rangers, librarians, historians,
journalists, parents and preservationists. Thank you.

National Park Foundation Charity line

From coast to coast, I've explored national parks that reveal the extraordinary diversity, beauty, and history of our nation. These sacred landscapes connect us—to nature, to one another, and to the stories that shape who we are. Preserving them is not only about protecting wild places, but about safeguarding our shared heritage for generations to come. For that reason, I'm proud to support the National Park Foundation as the charitable beneficiary for this book.

TABLE OF CONTENTS

INTRODUCTION

didn't grow up loving history. But I've always loved a good story, and it wasn't until I started traveling around this country that the "story" part of "history" came alive for me.

I've spent the last few years traveling to American Revolution sites for my television series *Travels with Darley*. From a Revolutionary-era fort hidden in plain sight in downtown Charleston to the Ivy League halls of Princeton University, to the country home of Philip Schuyler, father to Angelica, Eliza, and Peggy and father-in-law to Alexander Hamilton, I've been on a journey that's taken me to surprising places.

These travels introduced me to some amazing storytellers: the docents and descendants; the reenactors and park rangers; the history buffs spread across the thirteen original American colonies that marry a passion for history with the love of a good story. At battlefields, national parks, plantations, small museums, historic homes, and amid city streets, they are keepers of history. They passionately share a greater depth of lesser-known history and hidden gems of the American Revolution.

Like Rick Wise, a veteran who fought in Operation Desert Storm and teaches others about the dignity of remembrance at Camden Battlefield in South Carolina. Having experienced the bonds of loyalty and devotion forged in combat, Rick frames the Revolutionary experience through his respect for sacrifice beyond oneself and his experience in the fog of war. When he shares accounts of the casualties and fear accompanying battle, it hits harder.

Traveling to these sites and speaking with local experts like Rick, I've gained a true sense of place and appreciation for the complex tapestry of triumphs, emotions, sacrifices, and details that forged the founding of our nation.

Revolutionary Road Trip is a journey to destinations, places that you can visit today to experience these stories yourself. It's also a trip through time, traveling via the stories that surround the Revolution.

Not every story can make it into a history book, or even a book like mine that embraces the sharing of lesser-known stories from a traveler's journey into the Revolution. I've only written of places I visited myself and documented firsthand, places where I was able to record extensive interviews, most of which are in my digital archives. To say I feel a sense of duty to share these stories, to make them part of the public record, is absolutely true. I believe that if we take a closer look at the past, we can better understand each other and the potential of our future.

You'll learn that contributions to the founding of our nation take unexpected, lesser-known forms, like Marsh Tacky horses—who carry in their DNA resilience and fortitude. You'll discover destinations where history is woven into the background of everyday experiences, like pumping gas or stopping by the local bank in Saratoga, New York. You'll meet young reenactors and docents, like Will Krakower and Jane Pilato, who find inspiration in the smaller details that truly bring the human story of the Revolutionary era to life.

In these pages I'll take you through locations where significant events took place that shaped American history to bring an emotional and entertaining look at the past. You'll meet Baroness Frederika von Riedesel, called the original female war correspondent, who leads us into the hearts and minds of the mothers and children of the Revolution. You'll visit the John Dickinson Plantation in Delaware, where the discovery of an African burial ground has the community on the hunt for descendants.

This is not a traditional guidebook, though it does have practical purpose. Part travelogue, part historical rediscovery, *Revolutionary Road Trip* revels in lesser-known stories, while still tipping the hat to big names of the time, like Alexander Hamilton. If you travel to these sites, you may open this book to get a better sense of place. Or you might listen to the audiobook to guide your own walking tour or road trip.

As I'm hoping this book will be an evergreen tool, I purposely didn't include all the great restaurants, brewpubs, wine bars, hotels, and inns where you can stay along the way. For some of those details, you can always find my TV show, videos, podcasts, and social media posts. But I did include information about a few colonial taverns where truly intrepid travelers can still enjoy a cherry bounce or Rum Bellies Vengeance.

Above all, I hope this book sparks your curiosity and inspires you to get out there and meet the people who are safeguarding this fascinating history in the spaces and places where they continue to ensure these stories are not lost to history. When we enlist all five of our senses to experience living history, we can imprint memories and empathy that transcend any words on a page.

Plus, travel is fun! And when you explore sites off the standard tourist map there are many hidden gems waiting to be revealed. Enjoy your trip!

CHAPTER 1

New Jersey—Hamilton, Einstein, and a Pint in Princeton

Princeton University's Nassau Hall: Battles in the Halls of Learning

Fired on by artillery officer Alexander Hamilton, commemorated in a painting by artist Charles Willson Peale, and serving briefly as the United States Capitol, Princeton University's Nassau Hall is a historic American university icon. Simply getting to visit Nassau Hall is a privilege, but experiencing a guided tour inside the building is remarkable.

It was a humid, overcast mid-summer day in July when I arrived at Nassau Hall. I took a deep breath as I stepped through the imposing wrought-iron FitzRandolph Gate. Topped with eagles carved out of stone, the FitzRandolph Gate marks the official entrance to the Princeton campus. If you're standing outside, the gates also neatly frame historic Nassau Hall, which was constructed beginning in 1754. Named after Nathaniel and Rebeckah FitzRandolph, who donated the 4.5 acres on which

Nassau Hall was built, the gates were gifted to the university in 1905. They were designed by the prestigious architectural firm McKim, Mead & White, making for a fittingly impressive welcome to Princeton.

The sounds of traffic on Route 27, also known as Nassau Street—the main thoroughfare in Princeton—drowned out the sounds of birds as I walked along the granite sidewalk onto the campus of the one of the oldest institutions of higher education in the United States. Founded as the College of New Jersey in 1746, the university was one of nine colonial colleges chartered before the American Revolution. The College moved to its current location in Princeton in 1756 and later changed its name to Princeton University. Just before eight o'clock on a Tuesday morning, the campus was relatively quiet with only a few students passing by and an older man shuffling through the grass with his Pomeranian in tow, a much different scene than if I'd been walking here in July of 1783. At that time, the university had witnessed battles and plundering during the Revolutionary War. Princeton's small, war-ravaged village consisted of a few hundred people amid farmland, with the College of New Jersey housed in Nassau Hall.

During the Revolution, Princeton was a popular stagecoach layover town between Philadelphia and New York City. About halfway between the two cities, it was an ideal place for travelers and mail carriers to rest their horses. The college was also a gathering location for students who opposed British rule to foster new ideas under the leadership of the college president, John Witherspoon. That angst against Great Britain had been developed over previous decades, including in 1765 when students protested the Stamp Act and later, following the Boston Tea Party in 1773, when they staged their own tea burning.

Many people walking onto Princeton University's campus today may not know that the university grounds were once a Revolutionary War battleground and that events here would mark a pivotal turning point in the war. On Princeton's campus and at the nearby Princeton Battlefield State Park, the chaotic Battle of Princeton in 1777 saw American forces firing on Nassau Hall. Priceless art depicting George Washington and stone walls dented by cannonballs would today be part of my campus investigation into events of the past.

My goal was to uncover lesser-known stories of the American Revolution to share a more rich and personal history of the founding of America that's not always presented in textbooks. It was exciting to be at Princeton, a place that has often served as the backdrop for Hollywood films like *A Beautiful Mind* with Russell Crowe and *I.Q.* starring Meg Ryan. Though this was my first in-person visit to campus, I had seen Princeton on the big screen, which made it feel familiar and even glamourous. I didn't attend an Ivy League school, even though the college where I did study was named after one of the founders. Still, something about stepping onto Princeton's campus made the day already feel quite significant.

Some of the biggest names from the American Revolution, including Alexander Hamilton and George Washington, fought here on a frigid day in January 1777. My July visit was steamy, much as it would have been when Nassau Hall served as the United States Capitol in July of 1783. That summer was so hot that stagecoach service was impacted, and horses died from heat exhaustion on their way into Princeton village.

New Jersey is known as "The Garden State," but those who know American history may also consider it to be at the crossroads of the Revolutionary War. General George Washington and the Continental Army spent more time in New Jersey during the six years of conflict than any other state; the battles that took place in New Jersey would help direct the course of the American Revolution.

From Washington's heroic crossing of the Delaware, now preserved as a state park, to the brutally cold winter encampment at Morristown, now a national historical park, there are many sites that travelers can visit in New Jersey to relive the past. While many of these sites are preserved as parks and public spaces, others consist of taverns, homes, and university campuses, like Princeton and Rutgers, that continue to be in use today. Some have been bulldozed or gutted and refurbished into modern restaurants, homes, and shopping centers. You'd never know that history occurred at many of these locations, except for a historical marker if the location is lucky enough to have one.

I was already sweating at 8:00 a.m. in my muted silk palazzo pants and vibrant Princeton-orange sleeveless top, worn especially for the day on campus. I walked at a good clip towards Nassau Hall and spotted Dan Linke, my expert for the morning. I waved and picked up my pace to greet him at the entrance to the oldest building on the campus.

University archivist and deputy head of special collections, Dan looked very academic, wearing a light purplish-blue button-down, bowtie, and black blazer with denim jeans and black patent dress shoes. Tall and lean with a full head of graying hair and rectangular tortoiseshell glasses, I noticed his genuinely warm smile as I strode over to shake his hand.

"So, important question…the bow tie straight?" Dan gave a chuckle.

"Ha! Yes. You're good," I replied with a smile as Dan fidgeted with the keys in his pockets to make them less bulky.

I could already tell he'd be a great guide. He had an air of thoughtful ease. Having interviewed many experts, historians, and academics over the years, however, I preferred the less-is-more approach to their relaying of history. Some historians tend to send you down a rabbit hole of information. Sometimes I don't even know what the point is at the end of a conversation and ask them to please summarize in three to five sentences. This can be difficult to do when you know the full breadth of the history of any one topic but is a helpful exercise for those who want to translate history to those of us who are not experts.

I confessed to Dan that I was not an expert on the Battle of Princeton or the university's history related to the Revolutionary War, which seemed to put him even more at ease. Often, when I'm traveling, because of my busy schedule, I don't have time to do much preliminary preparation. While I strive to be prepared, I also like to let the conversation flow naturally and guide the story.

"Nassau Hall is the original campus main building opened in 1756," Dan started. "And it was everything—dormitory, classroom, chapel, library, and refectory, which is a fancy word for a commons or dining hall. And the president's house was the other original campus building," Dan pointed towards the yellow Maclean House, which was completed the same year, and is located adjacent to Nassau Hall and abutting the main road.

Today, the Maclean House serves as the home of the Alumni Association of Princeton University, but more than two hundred years ago John Witherspoon lived there while serving as a delegate to the Continental Congress. He also signed the Declaration of Independence. During the Battle of Princeton, George Washington occupied the home in 1777 and again in 1783. It was also the home to enslaved people during the eighteenth and nineteenth centuries. At least sixteen men, women, and children were once owned by the Presbyterian ministers who served as presidents of the college. A memorial plaque to the enslaved people is today displayed outside of the black iron gate in front of the Maclean House and along Nassau Street.

Dan and I walked slowly up Nassau Hall's stairs, flanked by two bronze tigers. Sculpted by Alexander Phimister Proctor, a cowboy artist who used to go big-game hunting with President Theodore Roosevelt, the tigers replaced earlier lions. They seemed a fitting greeting not only because of the Princeton Tigers team and school spirit, but also because of the rugged, enduring nature of Nassau Hall over the years.

"I wore my Princeton colors for you today, Dan," I said, as we passed the regal tigers and entered Nassau Hall through a large gray door.

The air conditioning inside the cavernous marble walled Memorial Atrium hit me like a cold bucket of water. Lined with the names of alumni who died in various American wars, Memorial Atrium was dedicated shortly after World War I and would go on to add the names of other Princeton graduates who fought in later American wars.

Like many historic buildings, the Nassau Hall we were entering today had evolved over time. Opened officially in 1756, the Georgian-Colonial style sandstone building was originally 176 feet long, which at the time, made it the largest academic building in colonial America.

Nassau Hall was designed by Robert Smith, a carpenter-architect who enlisted the help of Dr. William Shippen of Philadelphia and William Worth, a local stonemason. They started work in 1754 on the acres of land donated by Nathaniel and Rebeckah FitzRandolph. Nassau Hall was named in honor of King William III, who was a member of the House of Nassau. Like many names in the Princeton area, including Princeton itself, Nassau Hall shares a relationship to Great Britain.

Nassau Hall opened on November 28, 1756. It was constructed to house the College of New Jersey, led by the college's president, Aaron Burr, father of Aaron Burr, Jr., the third vice president of the United States and perhaps most famous for his 1804 duel with Alexander Hamilton. The building was constructed to accommodate up to 147 students who would live and study inside. Brick floors and twenty-six-inch walls would keep the three stories and basement cool in the summer and warm in the winter. It was meant to be fireproof, something that would be proven in the nineteenth century, when Nassau Hall survived two devastating fires.

Looking back at the first known image of Nassau Hall from a 1760 publication, *New American Magazine*, the exterior looked much then as it does today, with its narrow rows of windows and clock tower, except that today there's a lot more ivy growing on the exterior walls. A tradition began in 1866 among graduating students to plant ivy at the base of Nassau Hall. Students also commemorated their graduation by mounting plaques on Nassau Hall and more recently along the sidewalk in front of the building.

Dan and I continued through Nassau Hall towards the main attraction of our visit. Dan unlocked the Faculty Room, a space generally not open to the public. He unlocked the large richly colored wooden double doors, revealing a stately room lined with dark wooden walls and long wooden benches. The large room's white ceiling was accented with grand chandeliers. At the front of the room on the right was a grand portrait of King George II with a long gray curly wig of hair dragging over his velvet cloak, his hand resting beside his royal orb and scepter.

A large window separated an equally sized portrait of George Washington at the Battle of Princeton to the left, painted by Charles Willson Peale, one of the most recognized artists of the American Revolution. Peale served in the Continental Army and painted George Washington from life seven times. Between the two paintings was a glass case atop a large desk holding Princeton's ceremonial mace, symbolizing the school's interdependence and good relations between town and gown.

Modeled after the British House of Commons, the Faculty Room that we see today was conceived in 1906 by then–university President Woodrow Wilson. Wilson would go on to become the twenty-eighth president of the United States and have his name attached to many buildings and spaces at Princeton, including, until 2020, the School of Public and International Affairs. Amid a reckoning of the University's history, the board of trustees voted to remove Wilson's name from the school in light of his racist beliefs and actions.

Past university presidents' portraits line the walls of the Faculty Room, alongside paintings of George Washington and King George II of England. Prior to it being the formal Faculty Room, the two-story space was a prayer room, library, and museum for over a century. During the American Revolution and leading up to the Battle of Princeton, both British and American troops occupied Nassau Hall at various times. It served as a hospital during the war.

As we walked across the expansive checkered-tile floor towards the monumental oil paintings of George II and George Washington, Dan explained that the Battle of Princeton was fought about a mile from where we were standing.

Dan described the events immediately after the victory by American troops. Fresh from their triumph on the battlefield, American forces marched into town to confront a group of British soldiers occupying Nassau Hall and keeping American prisoners in the basement. Alexander Hamilton set up his artillery on a hill near what is now Blair Arch and fired on Nassau Hall to force the troops out.

"The story goes that a cannonball flew through a window in the chapel, which is what this space was previously, and decapitates the head of George II. This is sort of where history and myths start to mix," Dan said with a wry smile.

"That's our favorite," I exclaimed, the student in me coming out full force.

We walked over towards the eight-foot-tall portrait of Washington. The portrait showed Washington after the Battle of Princeton, looking confident following the victory with one hand on his right hip and the other resting on the muzzle of a cannon. Looking at the painting, George Washington looked massive.

"This is one of the replica pieces, which is not quite as ornate, but still quite lovely and valuable, which is why the door is locked," Dan said. "The original painting is normally on view to the public in the Princeton Art Museum."

Valuable was an understatement. In 2006, one of the replicas of Charles Willson Peale's portrait of George Washington at the Battle of Princeton set a record for the most expensive sale of an American portrait at an auction when Christie's sold it for $21.3 million.

Dan further explained that the battle took place in January 1777. When the trustees met in 1783, George Washington gave them fifty guineas in appreciation for the college's service during the Revolution, which essentially funded the cost of

Washington's portrait. The trustees then asked Charles Willson Peale to paint *Washington at the Battle of Princeton*. The trustees' meeting minutes state that Washington's portrait will hang in the frame that the King George portrait formerly held and that had been destroyed by American artillery or torn away by American artillery during the Battle of Princeton.

Dan further explained, "Some historians think that maybe artillery destroyed it, or even American soldiers damaged it coming into the building. We don't really know. But we do know it was destroyed then. And I think it's important in the greater context of what was happening. Six months earlier the Declaration of Independence was adopted, and a month after that, the British land troops in New York and push Washington out of the city and then across and out of New Jersey. But then Washington counterattacks and ends that string of losses, ultimately winning the Battle of Princeton. That turns the tide. The British thought they would come in and put down this rebellion pretty quickly, and that battle showed that they were not invincible. So, no matter what destroyed the portrait, it's portentous of what was to come."

"It's interesting that King George II is replaced by George Washington," I said, thinking about the changing tide of what would become the United States.

"Yes. Yes. And that, too, is emblematic," Dan replied. "It is really the sort of the turning point in the Revolution in the sense of the British having to rethink their strategy, and four years later, we are granted our independence. The peace treaty is signed while Congress is sitting here in Nassau Hall. That's the other piece of the story that ties into all of this, that in 1783, Congress leaves Philadelphia, and they meet here in Princeton for about four months. And Princeton becomes a capital. It is indeed, in fact, because the peace treaty is signed while they're here. Some people like to claim this hall as the first Capitol of the United States."

"So neat! So, I'm standing right now in a historic US Capitol," I reply, thinking about the irony of the 1906 renovations to make the room resemble the British House of Commons.

Tongue-in-cheek, too, that it was here that American freedom began to take hold, with young artillery officer Alexander Hamilton steps away, potentially firing on America's Nassau Hall. The dark wooden room today seems so stagnant and formal, but so many tumultuous events had occurred inside to change the course of America.

During the summer of 1783, Nassau Hall became the seat of the American government. Though many important decisions would be made during those few months, the conditions were not ideal at either Nassau Hall or in Princeton. Members of the Continental Congress used Nassau Hall as their capitol from July to October. Delegates began to arrive in June, leaving Philadelphia, then the most cosmopolitan city in the newly independent nation. They were unprepared for the conditions in the backwater village that had been ravaged by war. Further, the numerous delegates faced a lack of housing. James Madison had to share a matchbook-sized room and wrote that he was "obliged to write in a position that scarcely admits the use of any of my limbs." At just 5'4" and the smallest president on record to date, Madison's writing puts into context how truly tiny his room must have been.

It was also extremely hot that summer and food and drink were scarcer in Princeton. The town lacked the choice of better taverns found in Philadelphia. The delegates wrote home about their plight, sharing news of their suffering.

Nevertheless, despite the challenges they faced, the delegates remained in Princeton to see the end of the American Revolution. The Treaty of Paris was signed on September 3, 1783. Other significant events occurred while the Continental Congress was using Nassau Hall as their ad hoc capitol. Congress also opened diplomatic relations with the first neutral European country willing to recognize the United States: Sweden. George Washington paid a visit to Princeton, riding up Nassau Street to the cheers of citizens thanking him for his service during the war. While in Princeton, Congress also set the precedent that future states would be admitted to the Union on an equal footing with the original thirteen colonies.

If not for the Battle of Princeton, would any of these events have taken place?

The victory at Princeton had followed a set of smaller American victories over British and Hessian forces. Just eight days earlier, General Washington had crossed the Delaware on the night of December 25–26, marching on to surround the Hessian troops at Trenton in a surprise attack on the morning of December 26, capturing two-thirds of the Hessian troops. On January 2 at the Battle of the Assunpink Creek, a second battle in Trenton, the Americans would also secure a win. This helped to boost their morale in the lead-up to Princeton. Though the British thought the defeat to be minor, for the Americans, it was a pivotal win.

I asked Dan about John Witherspoon, the college president during the American Revolution, whose portrait also hangs in the Faculty Room. Dan relayed that in November of 1776, Witherspoon sent students away because the British were marching towards Princeton, which led to the college closing its doors.

The fact that the college survived through these tumultuous events is remarkable.

Since Nassau Hall wasn't spared from the cannons and artillery during the battle, I asked Dan if there are any marks on the building where the cannonball may have hit.

"Yeah. This is, again, myth and history. There is allegedly a spot that's covered in ivy. We could go try and peek," Dan offered.

"Let's investigate," the Nancy Drew in me replied with a smile.

This is what I love about looking at the history of the American Revolution. At sites across the thirteen colonies, we're still uncovering information about the past through research, archaeology, and oral histories. What we understand about the past is constantly evolving. It only proves that what we often have read in textbooks is not always the complete or final story. So much gets left out. Storytellers and experts have the opportunity to do this. I wondered if today Dan and I might uncover something new or perhaps see the past in a new light.

I took my last breath of cool air inside the hallowed Faculty Room and walked with Dan back out of the front door of Nassau Hall. We turned left towards the back of Nassau Hall, rounding the corner as Dan pointed to scaffolding about a football field away.

"That's Blair Hall, and that's allegedly, I should say allegedly, where Hamilton is reported to have set up his artillery. So, you can see its close range. What you can't see is if that building wasn't there, it's a hill. That archway is actually a staircase going down about thirty plus feet. So that would be an appropriate place to set up cannon. You want to be able to fire downhill," Dan said.

We had arrived early in the morning when the campus was just waking up. Once back outside, students and professors were moving at different speeds from class to class. I wondered how many of them had ever stopped to examine the outside of Nassau Hall to try to find where the cannonball may have dented the sandstone walls during the Battle of Princeton. How many students even knew there was once a key battle for American freedom fought right here?

We rounded the western side of Nassau Hall and moved towards the south side of the building, passing a large, abstract bronze sculpture titled *Oval with Points* by Henry Moore, which originally was created from a series of sketches of an elephant skull.

"You see the cannon sticking out of the ground ahead?" Dan asked.

"Oh," I said, looking to the center of the quadrangle known as Cannon Green to see a large cannon planted into the ground, muzzle first.

It's known as the "Big Cannon." There's a second Little Cannon on campus, too. The Big Cannon became the subject of a rivalry in the nineteenth century between Princeton and Rutgers. It traded ownership a few times, but Princeton ultimately stuck it in the ground, and it hasn't been moved since. Both were used in the American Revolution.

We stepped off the sidewalk and onto soft, wet grass. The leather on my sandals got wet and my toes squinched and slid. We moved closer to examine the ivy-covered walls on the backside of Nassau Hall, searching for any battle scars. During the battle, three cannonballs were launched at the building. One is thought to have flown through the window and taken out the head on the portrait of George II. Another was launched or directed to be fired by Alexander Hamilton. That cannonball is thought to have bounced off the south side of the building, chipping the stone.

"But now you see the ivy and why it's a challenge to see where the damage might be," Dan said, as my eyes darted around searching for pockmarks or fractures.

"I mean, if I were just guessing, I would say it was that open space right there. The first one. The first column of ivy to the left from the gutter wall," I said pointing up to the second tier of windows to an area where the ivy looked like it had been cut away. It was round and about the size of a cannonball.

"Yes, that is the alleged spot," Dan confirmed. "The myth is that the cannonball hit there and dented the wall. I wonder. You know, I would have sworn the ivy was intact when I came by a couple of weeks ago. I wonder if someone got tipped off that you were coming."

We both laughed, thinking about a groundskeeper on a ladder trimming the ivy like a topiary cannonball. Whether they did or not, for those searching for a picture of the past, this painted a clear one.

"How did we come up with this story? Is there a written account?" I asked, referring to Alexander Hamilton and the cannonball and the "off with his head" decapitation of George II. It did all seem a bit theatrical.

"There are written accounts of the cannonball," Dan said. "The first one is in a book that talks about the Battle of Princeton, but it's published in 1898. So, you know, one hundred twenty-some years after the actual events. But the trustees' minutes clearly show that the portrait was damaged, and they say torn away by American artillery. So, there's a basis to the myth, whether the cannonball actually did the deed or whether it was other things."

"So even if you can't get into Princeton, you can still come here and relive the past and be a part of it, part of our collective story," I replied.

Dan nodded. "Yes. You can. Princeton was integral to the founding of America, both in terms of ideology and soldiers and location."

"What got you interested in history?" I asked. "I always think it's interesting because everyone has a different story. Some people like history from the beginning. Some people turn the tides and get into it as we as we get wiser and older."

I think of myself in that realm. I didn't think, until recently, that I was interested in history. During the pandemic, I worked on two half-hour travel documentaries taking viewers along the Civil Rights Trail in Alabama. I interviewed women who were children during the movement, including Doris Crenshaw, a protégée of Rosa Parks, who slept on Ms. Parks's couch as a child. I spoke with Joanne Bland at the foot of the Edmund Pettus Bridge in Selma. I'm normally quite composed during my filming, but Joanne's story of how she, at eleven years old, along with her sister Linda, walked in the Selma to Montgomery March brought me to tears. It was heart wrenching. Both Joanne and Linda were badly beaten days before on "Bloody Sunday," yet they gathered the courage to march. I was blown away by their bravery, but also how personal the history seemed when someone shared it firsthand, as a story. It was powerful.

Dan went on to share how he, being the youngest child of older parents, grew up with older, wiser parents and siblings. Once in college, a professor got him interested in history and the deeper side of the past.

"It's not just facts and figures. It's about the *who* and *what* and, maybe most importantly, *why* things are the way they are.

Because when I'm talking to undergrads and showing them things in the archives, what I always say is where we are now is not predetermined. There have been decisions made going back centuries that led us to this point. And what decisions are we making now that are going to shape our future?"

"Looking at the past helps us have a better future," I said.

"Yes. Or at least understand how we got here and where we may have gone right or wrong as well, but that's a very personal answer," Dan said. "I personally think that if you study the revolutions, ideals, and where we are today, that will lead you to a certain conclusion about our government and our state as a people."

It was exactly the type of answer I was hoping for. I like it when history is personal. I believe that we all absorb and understand history better when it is relatable. I wondered if my next trip to Princeton should be on a winter day in January, so that if I stepped out on the lawn by Nassau Hall and closed my eyes, I could imagine Alexander Hamilton firing that cannon. Perhaps I'd hear the thunderous sounds and get a whiff of smoke in the air. Traveling to a place and using all our senses helps imprint it as a memory. That's why it's so important to visit places like this and hear the stories. The sacrifices made by so many before for us mean a lot, and they mean even more through the power of place.

Yankee Doodle Tap Room: Norman Rockwell, Patriotism, and a Pint

I left Dan Linke to take a walking and e-biking tour of the university and greater Princeton with Mimi Omiecinski of Princeton Tour Company. She shares the history of the area starting with the Lenni-Lenape people through the American Revolution and

Hollywood. Mimi has an infectious energy and passion for history and all things Princeton.

Mimi sort of bounced as she walked along Princeton's streets in her wide-brimmed straw hat accented by a black ribbon, with her short blonde hair tucked behind her ears sticking out from the back of her floppy hat. She wore a dusty blue button-down shirt tied at the waist with ankle-length black trousers and black ballet flats. With her high-pitched voice, she spoke quickly about the history of the land and why so many Princeton names harken back to Great Britain.

We mounted our e-bikes and whizzed through Princeton's posh neighborhoods, where trees line Colonial, Tudor, Victorian, Gothic, and New England–style clapboard houses and mansions. Mimi pointed out the simple white two-story L-shaped home of physicist Albert Einstein at 112 Mercer Street, once inhabited also by Nobel laureate Frank Wilczek and author Betsy Devine. We careened by leafy acre-sized yards where lawn keepers mowed lush green grass. We passed the former residences of Woodrow Wilson and Grover Cleveland, whose six-bedroom estate, complete with a swimming pool, recently sold for almost $6 million.

Mimi shared additional tidbits, too, about industry titans, the heads of banks and tech millionaires who lived or had second homes in Princeton. We tried not to stop too long in front of any one mansion, as after all, these homes with history were in private hands today. Our tour ended, as any good tour should, with a beer. Back in downtown Princeton, we arrived at Palmer Square's Colonial Revival-style buildings, housing shops, and restaurants. Palmer Square is located just across the street from Princeton University.

We had our sights set on a Palmer Square institution. A nod to the Revolutionary War was once again found through art at the Yankee Doodle Tap Room at the Nassau Inn. It's in this historic richly wood-paneled inn where you can belly up to the bar in the shadow of a famous Norman Rockwell painting depicting Yankee Doodle, for whom the tap room is named. Edgar Palmer, who originally built Palmer Square in the 1930s, was friends with Norman Rockwell. He commissioned Rockwell to paint the thirteen-foot mural on the wall of the taproom in 1937.

If you're sitting at the bar, this epic painting with the famous Revolutionary War song's words, "Yankee Doodle came to town, riding on a pony," is just behind a protective pane of glass and framed on the bottom by a shelf lined with bottles of liquor. The colorful mural depicts nineteen people, two dogs, one pony, and one goose frolicking along with Rockwell's signature flair for whimsical expressions. The largest work he ever painted, it was recently discovered that it's permanently attached to the plaster masonry wall.

The university owns the painting, and during renovations a few years back, they wanted to remove it to preserve it. They found they couldn't. Rockwell had painted a canvas that was attached to plaster, covering the masonry. Removing the painting would have required taking down the whole weight-bearing wall. Thus, it stays for all patrons of the tap room to enjoy.

Mimi and I grabbed an aptly named Yankee Doodle beer and perused the gastropub menu complete with Wagyu burgers and cheesy sourdough bread.

"So, Einstein came here?" I asked.

"He frequented here," Mimi said. "He had tea upstairs, where he would also be with members of the Institute for Advanced Study."

At the age of forty-two, Einstein gave a lecture at Princeton University on his theory of relativity on May 9, 1921, the same day the famous scientist was awarded an honorary degree from the university. In the 1930s, he would join the Institute for Advanced Study as faculty member and would work from an office in Princeton University's mathematics building.

"When Edgar Palmer brought the tap room here, the boys would skip class, and they'd carve their little names [on the booths]. Local folks like to say that Albert Einstein actually carved his name right there," Mimi said, pointing over to a booth across the room.

We walked over to the second booth from the left wall, located under an old black-and-white framed photograph of a Princeton basketball league from 1950. It was a dark and cozy wooden booth illuminated with a small sconce of lights under lampshades that were affixed to the back of the booth. The light helped me examine the oak-top table where loads of names were jaggedly carved into the wood. I moved back and forth to prevent reflection from the lights on the pane of protective glass from obstructing the names below, searching the table for Einstein's name.

"Okay, so I'm seeing it. I found it. It took me a second," I said.

"There are a lot of names carved in here…Dr. Einstein," Mimi said, pointing to the block-letter signature.

"So, while we don't know if this was legitimately carved by Albert Einstein, we do know that Einstein was here. Sort of feeling like this beer is making me smarter," I winked.

"Cheers," Mimi said, clinking pint glasses with me, the caramel-colored lager spilling over the rim just slightly.

It was another instance where fact and myth may have combined in Princeton, and I thought it was just grand. I took a sip of beer, starring at Dr. Einstein's name.

The Nassau Inn also hosted members of the Continental Congress when they were meeting at Nassau Hall and has been popular with students over the decades. I took some time to pick out famous faces of Princeton alumni lining the walls in old black-and-white yearbook photos and spotted Brooke Shields, Michelle Obama, and Steve Forbes.

This was all in preparation for my next adventure with Princeton University. We were invited to see Peale's original oil painting *George Washington at the Battle of Princeton.*

Princeton University's Grand Art Collection: Art of a New Nation

Normally on display in the Princeton University Art Museum, because of renovations, Peale's original painting *George Washington at the Battle of Princeton* was being stored at an offsite facility. We were given rare insight into the famous painting with Princeton University Art Museum Director James Steward. We arrived at a sort of series of warehouse buildings. A staff member met us at our vehicle outside and directed us to a large empty all-white art-storage room.

The interior reminded me of the Library of Congress's Packard Campus in Culpeper, Virginia, a state-of-the-art facility where audio and visual works that are copyrighted are stored, including priceless films from the silent era and beyond. The larger-than-life Charles Willson Peale painting *George Washington at the Battle of Princeton* was set on a substantial gray dolly on wheels in a large, chilly, white room.

Wearing light khaki pants, a seersucker blazer, striped bow-tie, and glasses, James Steward looked the part of a Princeton academic and scholar. Steward specializes in eighteenth-century art, with a focus on the art and culture of Britain, France, and Italy from 1700 to 1830. Originally from outside of Charlottesville, Virginia, the land of Washington and Jefferson, Steward's first "museum" job was as a summer tour guide at Monticello. James Steward's tenacity has led him to great things in the museum and art world, including managing the vast collections at Princeton University.

I was struck immediately by the subtle differences between this original painting and the variant that's now in Nassau Hall. In this work, George Washington stands, not with his hand on a cannon, but brandishing a sword. An American flag sways in the breeze above him and three men flank the rear to his right, one of whom is Hugh Mercer. Born in Scotland, Mercer came to America in 1747 and was appointed to Congress in June of 1776. He would be just one of the many immigrants to fight for American independence. He was also a friend of George Washington.

Mercer would die from wounds he received during the Battle of Princeton at the Thomas Clarke House on what is now the grounds of Princeton Battlefield State Park. In this first Peale painting, George Washington is wearing a dark blue coat and saffron yellow uniform. His cheeks are a rosy red, likely from the cool of the January battle day. I was interested to hear about this historical piece from James.

We moved in to examine the painting. I was close enough to reach out my hand and touch it with the tips of my fingers, which I dared not do. The room was chilly, and now I immediately wished that I'd brought in my white linen jacket to cover my arms, though the Princeton orange did stand out against the room's stark white interiors.

"This is considered not only the original of this particular painting, but one of the great documents in the whole of American art history," James pronounced. "It's one of the most important representations of George Washington painted from the life, unlike many others that were not."

"Painted from the life" means that Washington was in the room with Peale as his model for the painting. Princeton University, formerly called the College of New Jersey, has always collected important art, starting in the 1750s. During the American Revolution, that collection was destroyed during the Battle of Princeton, when a stray cannonball caused Nassau Hall to catch fire.

"So, after the end of the war, the trustees of the College commissioned the then–most prominent American painter, Charles Willson Peale, to come to Princeton and paint the General," Steward said. "Peale had fought with Washington in the Battle of Princeton, so Peale painted this work as if it's literally taking place during the unfolding of the battle."

The painting depicts Washington standing confidently with his sword lifted. General Hugh Mercer has been wounded on the battlefield, and in the distance, a mounted rider is coming out with a white flag from Nassau Hall.

"That seems to be a portent of the British and their imminent surrender. There was a sense the nation, as it was coming into being, needed statements like this that could become the equivalent of the paintings of British monarchs," James said. "In this case, for over two hundred years, this painting was hung in Nassau Hall, the space for which it was created. There are very few works of art in American history about which something like that can be said."

Peale had fought in the Battle of Princeton, so he had first-hand familiarity with the environment of the battle.

"What is so arresting about this is the way it functions as a document of American history by contrast with the later painting that was reproduced a number of times as a kind of piece of political propaganda of the new nation surging forward," James said.

"It's interesting that during the American Revolution, the College already had the foresight to say, 'Let's start an art collection,' and now you have these amazing works," I remarked to James. "What does it mean to Princeton University to keep hold of this history?"

"In 1755, the college started acquiring art objects, and it did so saying that it was going to be a way of bringing the world to this little backwater hamlet in central New Jersey when the population would have been tiny and the men of the College, because they were only men at that time, would have had very little likelihood of travel, of being able to go to Europe on the grand tour or other things that well-born individuals might have done," James continued. "And so, it was understood as a way of advancing the education of these young men that they should have access to objects that spoke to history and to the high points of culture. When that collection was then destroyed, including a painting that once inhabited this very frame, the College had to start over again. I like to invoke that history because it's a kind of portent of how we understand art collecting even in the twenty-first century, as a way of bringing the world together under one roof and helping our students and visitors from all over the globe have access indirectly to experiences of a kind they'd never otherwise have."

That's why I value museums so much. They show so many artifacts, art, and pieces that are valuable and from which we can learn. The oil painting by Peale had been our focus so far, but its frame was also significant. It was the frame that originally held a portrait of George II, the portrait that was possibly damaged by cannon fire from Alexander Hamilton. I asked James about its story.

"This is widely considered to be one of the most important historical frames in the United States," James said. "What we know from firsthand evidence of the Battle of Princeton is that during the battle a cannonball flew through the window of what's now the faculty room in Nassau Hall and was reputed to have destroyed the painting [of George II]. It was said that it decapitated the coronet that once surmounted the frame. That sounds too perfect to be true, but I like that story. We have examined the frame, so we can see it was sawn off intentionally. It was clearly not blown off by a cannonball."

I looked to the top of the ornate gold frame to see if I could tell that it was hacked off. I could. So many myths and legends were being showcased and dispelled during my visit to Princeton. In all my travels documenting stories, I like to understand the more personal side of famous figures, so I probed James a little more, asking him why George Washington was reluctant to have his portrait painted. James shared that Washington felt his appearance, and more specifically his bad teeth, were awkward.

"It is essentially why he was never depicted smiling. If Instagram had been around, he was not going to be a selfie taker," James said with a smile.

"I suspect not," I chuckled.

At six feet two inches, George Washington was unusually tall for the eighteenth century, as was fellow future President Thomas

Jefferson. This height would have physically conveyed power to so many, at a time when average height was shorter than today.

"This portrait absolutely gives us a sense of his height," James said. "The fact that inevitably, however, the painting might have been hung or will be hung in the future, we're always looking up at his face. He's not at our level."

It is amazing that this painting, an artistic document of a turning point in American history, survived more than two hundred years. It's also remarkable that Nassau Hall survived through the Revolutionary War and subsequent fires. It's fortunate to have scholars and historians like James Steward and Dan Linke who care enough to help safeguard this history and share it with the world.

Leaving James, I traveled to another site of importance during colonial times, the Peacock Inn, where I would spend the night. Albert Einstein and F. Scott Fitzgerald once slept in this historic inn owned in the 1700s by Jonathan Deare, a member of the Continental Congress. He purchased the property from Thomas Stockton, a signatory to the Declaration of Independence who lived just down the street in a home that is today the Morven Museum & Garden, another site travelers can visit.

Stockton is unique in that he's one of the few signers who was captured by the British during the Revolution. It was early in the war and after signing his allegiance back to the king, Stockton was pardoned. He eventually signed his allegiance back to the Colonies and went on to crusade for independence.

This sophisticated, colonial-style Peacock Inn is within walking distance of downtown Princeton and the University. For those who like a good cocktail, you'll find it here, along with menu items like seared sea scallops with purple cauliflower puree and bok choy. For those who want to see the famous Peale painting of Washington, it's now back at the Princeton University Art Museum, anchoring the new museum's galleries of American art, on display for the world.

Princeton Battlefield State Park: Ordinary People in Extraordinary Circumstances

Nearby the downtown is Princeton Battlefield State Park, where the former home of a Quaker family caught up in the war is open to the public. The American win at Princeton was the third surprising and significant victory to cap off what many historians often refer to as the Ten Crucial Days to describe a series of events that helped to turn the tide of the Revolution and rebuild confidence for the Americans.

Costumed interpreters at Princeton Battlefield State Park share the story of Thomas Clarke, a farmer who lived in the house that's now a museum on the property. Thomas, along with his sister and an enslaved woman owned by the Clarke family named Susannah, worked the two-hundred-acre farm which would be at the center of activity during the battle.

The white clapboard house dates to 1772 and has been neatly restored, painted a crisp white with bright green doors. A cannon stands upright on the back brick-bottomed porch with a plaque from the Sons of the American Revolution, commemorating the death of Brigadier General Hugh Mercer in this very home on January 12, 1777, nine days after the battle.

I stepped inside to view maps, dioramas, and timelines of the battles, laid out in a small museum. One case displayed firearms and musket balls; another showed a British bayonet and a musket's pick-and-brush tool. Multiple rooms downstairs are staged to look as they might have been when the Clarke family took in soldiers injured in the battle, making their home a hospital.

Farming the land that Thomas Clarke purchased from his brother would have been a year-round pursuit, using horses and oxen and then human power to till the fields and cultivate various crops. Though by the end of the eighteenth century most Quakers opposed slavery, the Clarke family's location in the Stony Brook region meant that many of their neighbors still held enslaved people. Thomas Clarke, his sister Sarah, and their five siblings owned Susannah up until her thirtieth birthday in 1779, two years after the battle. It is thought that she was purchased by Thomas's father and willed to him, along with the farmland.

Resource Interpretive Specialist Will Krakower greeted me in the Clarke family living room. Dressed to look like an eighteenth-century Quaker, Will was wearing a blue jacket with black knee breeches, blue stockings, and buckle shoes. With a distinctive wide-brimmed hat, he also donned a simple white cravat around his neck, a folded piece of linen that acts as a neckband and that was in fashion during the time of the Revolution. Thirty-year old Krakower, a self-described cat lover and history buff, is an example of a younger steward of history, passionately working to keep vibrant the only structure that survived the battle at this locale.

The room where we conducted our interview was furnished with a large table draped in a white tablecloth and set with reproductions of medical instruments. It's rare to see eighteenth-century medical instruments that aren't reproductions, as they were expensive and therefore saved by individuals. I examined a large thin-bladed saw resting in the middle of the table beside a pewter candlestick and could only imagine the horrors of post-battle medicine and treatment, like limb amputation.

Behind the table was a large fireplace where a variety of long and short cooking pots and spoons, a kettle, and other tools to stoke a fire lined a light greenish-gray painted hearth. Officers' uniforms were draped over chairs.

"The three of them, the Clarkes and Susannah, were here in this house with, obviously, shrapnel shot and shell coming through the building. They hid below our feet in the basement of this house," Will said. "During and after the battle, this room would have been lined with wounded British and American troops."

I felt a chill run down my spine as I surveyed the small room, imaging the grisly and cramped conditions. Will explained that since the Clarkes were Quakers, they were also pacifists, and consequently their loyalty would have been questioned by both the American and British forces. In this period, it would not have been uncommon for Quakers to be arrested for not signing a loyalty oath or for refusing to give service to one side or the other in their attempt to remain neutral.

Processing this information, I commented, "Many people had problems choosing sides. And then you think, oh, they're neutral. They're just not choosing anything, but it's still a problem for them."

I thought about the Clarkes' predicament and realized that for many in the area, no matter what they did, war might end up on your doorstep.

"A lot of people were killed. A lot of people's homes were burned or destroyed or confiscated, because they chose not to pick a side," Will replied.

"You're damned if you do. You're damned if you don't," I said.

"You certainly are in the American Revolution," Will replied.

Will continued to share that after the battle, when the Continental Army had moved away and into town, people like the Clarkes would have opened their doors to find that their yards and farms had been taken over by the dead and wounded. While not wanting to take part in the war, the Clarkes determined to help those who needed it, taking in both British and American soldiers and turning their house into a makeshift hospital.

"That's very much like a modern hospital," I observed. "They're supposed to take anyone in who needs medical attention."

"And this is one of those times where it's very similar to something today that you might see. You know, do no harm, help everyone you can. And that's exactly the mindset that people here had in the aftermath of the fighting," Will said, agreeing with my observation.

A lot of what we know about what happened in the Clarke home during this time is from Dr. Benjamin Rush, who arrived at the battlefield the day after the battle in his capacity as chief surgeon to the Continental Army. Dr. Rush was a member of the Continental Congress and yet another signatory to the Declaration of Independence. Like the Quakers and Susannah, Dr. Rush also treated soldiers on both sides.

I thought back to the original Peale portrait depicting Wahington at the Battle of Princeton and General Hugh Mercer dying in the arms of surgeon Benjamin Rush.

Will explained that General Mercer was at the front of the American attack, leading his troops and exposing himself to deadly bayonet wounds when British troops pushed back with a charge into an apple orchard.

The apple orchard where this all happened was located just about two hundred yards from the Clarke house and where

Will and I were standing. To get there, one would have had to walk through farm fields, over the crest of a hill, and then through a gully.

I looked from Will to the right to survey the room where General Mercer was taken after. It was furnished with a simple bed to recreate what it might have looked like at the time when Mercer spent the last nine days of his life there. When he died, he was the second highest-ranking Continental Army officer killed in the war.

The room next to where Mercer lay dying was a pantry and housed a wounded British officer in the aftermath of the battle. How strange it must have been for these enemies to lay dying essentially next to each other. It must have felt unreal, too, for Thomas, Sarah, and Susannah, who couldn't hide from the carnage but were thrust into the chaos.

Susannah was thirty years old on February 10, 1779, when the Quakers finally granted her freedom, along with a place to live and an education. Not entirely surprisingly, Susannah chose to flee the Clarke family and the Princeton area and disappears from historical records. Not much more is known about what became of Susannah. Like many of the enslaved persons, documentation is scarce. We do know that she was thrust into the crux of the American Revolution and played a crucial role aiding soldiers during and after the battle.

"We have this battle happening on the tenth day of what is called the Ten Crucial Days," I said.

Will noted that a contemporary colonist was said to observe that the American victory at Princeton bolstered Patriot tenacity, rekindling hope that the Revolution could be won. While the war would continue for another six years, those ten days were the first step towards victory.

A battle at Princeton was not planned that early in the morning, but the Continental troops were moving north to Princeton just as the British were traveling south to attack Trenton. The area where Princeton Battlefield State Park is today was at that time farmland, including the Clarke family farm. The troops may have strode through crop residues of perhaps winter wheat growing as the two armies suddenly confronted each other on the morning of January 3, 1777. General George Washington's Continental Army clashed with British forces under Lieutenant Colonel Charles Mawhood.

I walked outside amid the open fields of what had been the Clarke farm. A light rain started to fall, and the sky looked like one unbroken gray cloud. In the distance were a few scattered trees, including the Mercer Tree, a large white oak tree replanted in 2000 to replace a tree that had been there previously. It was protected with a brown wooden fence today, noteworthy as General Mercer was laid against the original tree after being wounded.

Outside I would learn more about the battle from author Larry Kidder, a Navy veteran who went on to teach highschool history for forty years and now volunteers as a historian, interpreter, and draft horse teamster at various historical sites in New Jersey. He's the author of several books including *Revolutionary Princeton* and *Ten Crucial Days* and a contributor to *The American Revolution in New Jersey*.

I thought about his work in driving horses as I looked at his tan and blue baseball cap, embroidered with a team of horses. He was wearing a light blue short-sleeved polo shirt, left untucked, with navy blue cargo pants and gray sneakers. The grass was dewy as we walked past the front of the house to a set of interpretive signs on the battlefield. Larry was prepared for more rain with a small umbrella cradled in his left hand.

"What did this land look like during the time of the battle?" I asked as we walked slowly towards a marker in the distance.

Larry explained that during the battle, the land was farmland, but the fences that had been on the property had likely been torn down because the British had stationed troops at Princeton for about a month before the battle. The British troops confiscated goods and animals from the local farmers. They also sought out any wood that they could get, including fencing and outbuildings, to burn for heat and for cooking. Many farms were devastated.

I looked across the undulating grassy battlefield out to the distance toward Mercer Road, where an occasional car whizzed past. Across from where we were standing and beyond Mercer Road, a colonnade rose up amid another area of grass spotted with a few trees. It marked hallowed ground: the grave of twenty-one British and sixteen American soldiers killed in the battle.

Larry explained that this part of the battle occurred over several hours down in the valley below us towards Mercer Road and the colonnade.

"When did the fighting move onto the college's campus and Nassau Hall?" I inquired.

"After everything was done here and the British troops were defeated and left the battlefield or were captured. Some were captured and some left. Washington then continued up to Princeton. That's when the last gunshots, the last interactions were around Nassau Hall. So, they kind of pushed their way to Nassau Hall to reclaim that," Larry said as we stopped by a sign entitled Site of Moulder's Battery.

We were standing in the very spot where, on January 3, 1777, after the British had forced the Americans to fall back, the Americans took a stand around a small artillery battery. Today near the entrance to Princeton Battlefield State Park, we were a little more than a mile and a half away from Nassau Hall. Captain Joseph Moulder, with only two guns and twenty troops, bravely fired and prevented the British from advancing. By delaying the British, Washington had time to organize a counterattack.

"Before the Battle of Princeton was the time that Thomas Payne referred to when he said, 'These are the times that try men's souls,'" Kidder said. "The revolution was essentially envisioned as being close to over by both sides, and the Americans obviously losing. By the end of the Battle of Princeton, and the Ten Crucial Days, everything had turned around, and the Americans had a new lease on life, and the British were saying 'Uh, oh, we got a long thing going here.'"

"Why is it important for people to visit Princeton Battlefield State Park?" I asked Larry.

"The battlefield has been preserved and is now a park, but it's important for people to realize that battles didn't take place in parks. They took place on land that was used for other purposes and in this case farming. Visiting the battlefield, one can learn about the ordinary people who suffered because of the battles taking place. They can learn about the way in which the people before the battle, during the battle, and then after the battle participated in many ways that just never make it into the books. In addition, understanding the significance of the actions of the British and American armies here that changed the course of the war," Kidder replied.

While many people do utilize Princeton Battlefield State Park for recreational purposes, walking their dogs or cross-country skiing in the colder months, many others come to experience a battle site where ordinary people had to act extraordinarily and heroically to survive. Princeton is one of many destinations in New Jersey where significant battles and decisions would create waves of change that greatly affected the outcome of the American Revolution and founding of the American nation.

I took my final walk past the Clarke house towards our rented SUV by myself. I thought about the many students and scholars who have been able to walk the campus to learn in a higher institution where America and American ideals took shape. I thought about the families who visit Princeton Battlefield State Park or grab a bite at Yankee Doodle Tap Room and learn something unexpected.

Princeton has a complicated history. Being here sharpened my vision and understanding of the extraordinary events that occurred. Leaving Princeton, the echoes of cannons and the cries of soldiers resonated along with the stories of heroism and patriotism, of standing up for something greater than oneself. Thanks to the knowledge and generosity of Will, Larry, Dan, and James, I could now picture famous figures like Peale, Washington, and Hamilton alongside those who died within the Clarke house, taken care of by the farming families and an enslaved woman thrust into a scarring conflict they had tried to avoid. I was reminded of how life sometimes can be more than unfair, unfortunate, and just plain sad, but also how often people who care and help others can make such difficult times more bearable.

CHAPTER II

South Carolina— Dungeons, Monasteries, and Hidden Fortresses in Charleston

Marion Square: Searching for Charleston's Secret Fortress

How did I find myself in a Charleston city park searching for an American Revolution fortress that was nowhere to be found? I had heard that the remnants of a "hidden" fortress were in Marion Square, a public park located in the center of Charleston's downtown. On a late September midday, the time of year when it can still be quite warm in Charleston, South Carolina, the sun beat down from overhead as I strode across the wide-open grassy lawn in the center of the park on a second lap, searching for the vestiges of this fortress.

Living in New York City for the past few years, I'm often on the hunt for speakeasies, the best of which are usually the hardest to find. This so-called hidden fortress was reminding me of that search. This quest for American Revolution hidden gems had nonetheless landed me in the center of one of my favorite cities on the planet: Charleston. What I'd find in and around Charleston, including dungeons, monasteries, and a tabby fortress, would surprise me.

I grew up in Myrtle Beach and frequented Charleston as a child. I also have visited often as an adult, staying at charming historic inns and hotels throughout the city and eating well, a must in a foodie city like Charleston. The top restaurant scene is well known, as are photogenic historic sites, like Rainbow Row. As many times as I'd visited Charleston, I'd never heard of this remnant of the Revolution called the Horn Work as part of Charleston's history before. It was a good thing I had an expert meeting me in the park to share more.

As I continued my search, I gazed out across the large plot of beautiful open grass in the center of this ten-acre park, which often plays host to farmers' markets and performances. My eyes were drawn to the tall steeple of the Citadel Square Church, a Romanesque Revival–style church located directly across from the park on upper Meeting Street. The park is surrounded by pretty and notable architecture, including well-known hotels like the Francis Marion Hotel, across from the park on Meeting Street. Though it doesn't date back to Revolutionary Times, it is historic, dating back to 1924. Beside this hotel is St. Matthew's Lutheran Church, which dates to 1840 and was founded by Germans who wanted to worship in German.

I was meeting Dr. Nic Butler in the park, and I definitely needed him to help me find the Horn Work. I knew that this would be a great start to my walking tour of downtown Charleston, where history is around every turn and step.

Charleston is a city well known as a bastion of American history and well-preserved architecture. You'd think in a city as popular as this that every nook and cranny of significance would have been overturned, yet I was about to discover the remains of a massive fortress hidden in plain sight that few locals knew about.

I recognized the man waving at me in the distance as Dr. Nic Butler from the photo I'd looked up online. His long hair was pulled back, and he was wearing his signature bowtie. Tall and with long legs, he took big strides as he walked down a sidewalk and across the grass to see me, greeting me with his gentile southern accent. Wearing a light blue button-down shirt, mustard yellow bow tie, and maroon pants, his more preppy look was offset by his long salt-and-pepper hair and hip sunglasses placed on top of his head. Gray sideburns creeped down the sides of his face.

A historian, podcast host, and the special collections manager at the Charleston County Public Library, Dr. Butler was a South Carolina native who'd gone near and far to uncover history, including as far away as London, diving into archives to find out more about Charleston's past. He was about to show me what remained of a huge eighteenth-century fortress that straddled what is today busy King Street during the American Revolution.

To get a better sense of Charleston's role in the Southern Campaign during the Revolutionary War, Marion Square is a great place to start. Named after Francis Marion, a Revolutionary War hero nicknamed the "Swamp Fox," partly for his guerrilla warfare tactics in the swamps of South Carolina, this public park is located between King and Meeting Streets in the heart of Charleston. Standing in Marion Square, you can spot beautiful architecture and notable landmarks all around. Francis Marion's escapades were fictionalized in movies like *The Patriot* with Mel

Gibson. Bring up *The Patriot* in historical circles, and you'll have a lively discussion of how this movie is filled with fallacies.

Dr. Butler led me towards Meeting Street, traveling from the sidewalk back into the grass to reach an area with wood chips as footing. In front of me was an uneven finger-shaped mass of rough concrete, about the size of a vending machine.

Dr. Butler said that this was the Horn Work, and at the time of the American Revolution, it was an approximately ten-acre fort. Half of that, the eastern flank of it, was right where we were standing in Marion Square. The other half of it was on the other side of King Street, a historic thoroughfare named after King Charles II of England and today a busy shopping and dining street.

As I looked at the craggy gray mass, my mind was blown. I still couldn't fathom what exactly it was that I was seeing. An iron fence circled the concrete mass, whose uneven texture included oyster shells. It was a mixture called tabby. From the late 1500s to the 1850s, this type of concrete was used for construction throughout the coastal South. Made from burning oyster shells to create lime, which is then mixed with water, sand, ash, and pieces of oyster shells, it would be used to construct homes, buildings, and forts, like the Horn Work.

King Street was the only path in and out of Charleston at that time. The Horn Work straddled that main path and was constructed to control traffic in and out of the town. Dr. Butler told me that's why it was created. It helped to control access to the back part of Charleston in case the enemy sailed up the Cooper River or the Ashley River, disembarked and marched back down, which is exactly what the British did in 1780 during the Siege of Charleston.

"British military engineers in the 1750s during the French and Indian war came to Charleston and said, well, you've done a good job of protecting the southern part of the town. If someone came into the harbor and attacked the city, you'd be fine, but we need to protect the back part of the town," Dr. Butler said. "And that was why the Horn Work was started in 1757."

Measuring at about six feet high and ten feet long, this Revolutionary War remnant was significant, yet most people walked by it all the time and had no idea it was here. There was a historical marker nearby that you could spot if you were a curious traveler or local. It shared that at the time of the Revolution, the town gates were just across "Broad Path," the busy throughway now known as King Street. By 1780, the gates would be surrounded by the protective Horn Work, so named because of its two half-bastions which looked like the horns of a bull. We were walking across the foundation of the historic fortress.

"It's shaped like what you'd see in many other European or even American cities where there's a fortification that's designed to protect the entrance of a town from the countryside," Dr. Butler said.

We only had a small portion of the fortress to see today, but it was still remarkable that even that had survived, given that we were right in the middle of downtown Charleston. I asked Dr. Butler how it had come to remain here after all these centuries.

"In 1784, the newly incorporated City of Charleston said we don't need that Horn Work anymore. It's blocking traffic into Charleston, so it was knocked down," Dr. Butler said.

If I didn't hit the palm of my hand against my forehead like Homer Simpson, that's what I was thinking. I knew that everything from the past couldn't be saved. We needed progress and new construction for many reasons, but how cool would it be to see this fortress in downtown Charleston today?

"Enslaved people with sledgehammers were paid to knock this stuff down, except this one part that appears to have been used as some kind of a garden fence, like a partition fence," Dr. Butler said, pointing towards the tabby form. "What we now call Marion Square, this park, was once subdivided into rental lots by the city of Charleston. There were several houses built here in the late eighteenth and early nineteenth century, so this was part of somebody's garden back in the day, and that's the only reason it survived."

Often things survive because they are necessary or well used. Someone needed a fence, and so a piece of this fortress survived. It was remarkable and funny. Perhaps it was serving its purpose now and we just didn't realize what that would be. It was a teacher for those who took the time to stop and wonder.

The Horn Work was pockmarked with a myriad of divots and holes, some of which may have been part of the construction technique and others perhaps from bullet holes or cannon shot from the siege of 1780. History was all around in Charleston, even when it was hidden in plain sight.

Dr. Butler told me that the fence had been around the Horn Work since the 1880s, but there hasn't been great signage. It was something that Charleston and outside groups like the American Battlefield Trust were working to change, making its presence in the park more educational. The new signage at the site of the Horn Work stands a few feet away and calls out the Horn Work as a location on The Liberty Trail, a travel route that includes Revolutionary War sites throughout the South and East Coast. It was a road-trip route that I'd follow, too, in South Carolina, taking me up to Camden and then the Upcountry in the state. On this trip though, I'd just be walking through Charleston and then driving out to Berkeley County to explore, where more surprises would be revealed.

I knew that oysters were a popular food item during the American Revolution but wondered why this fortress would have been constructed with oyster shells. In South Carolina, there was no natural stone. Bricks took a long time to make and were expensive. At the time, oyster shells were abundant. Oysters were a staple food during colonial times—cooked up, raw, or pickled, they were eaten by all social classes. In fact, they'd lead me to discover my next location, located along Charleston's Battery.

South of Broad: Walking Charleston's Living Museum

Alphonso Brown of Gullah Tours was leading me on the rest of my walking tour of historic Charleston, starting in the beloved White Point Garden, part of Charleston's iconic Battery, located just a mile from Marion Square. Several people were out walking their dogs as I entered White Point Garden from South Battery Street and walked toward the big white gazebo. A popular place for engagement and wedding photos, you may see couples taking photos here, where there are also reminders of this location's rocky past.

I read the inscription on a monument to Stede Bonnet, a pirate who was hanged in the park in the fall of 1718, along with a slew of his men. The park was a site where more than a few outlaws and pirates met their demise. Rumors swirl that this area is haunted. I could understand why that might be so, given the eccentric nature of what happened here over the centuries.

Under the shade of stunning oak and palmetto trees, a tree you may recognize from South Carolina's state flag, I scanned around for Alphonso. A South Carolina native, Alphonso's resume is extensive, with accolades ranging from lecturer on Gullah language and the Black history of Charleston to a member of All Negro Spiritual Concert in the Piccolo Spoleto Festival of Churches.

The Gullah Geechee people are descendants of West and Central Africans who were enslaved on the coastal islands and mainland of the southeastern United States, mostly in South Carolina and Georgia. They have a unique culture, food, and history that you can discover today as you travel through various places in the South.

Alphonso was wearing black pants and a black, short-sleeved button-down shirt with a collar and button stand embellished with purple and black African patterns. With a clean-shaven head and bright, white-toothed smile, he exuded warmth and confidence as he quickly hurried me along towards the water and the cannons. We had a lot to see today.

At first, I thought he was in a rush, but then realized that Alphonso just spoke quickly, in fact sometimes so fast that I had to take a few seconds to process back what he had said. He knew so much about Charleston's history that I figured it was hard for his lips to keep up with what his brain was downloading. We headed through the park along sandy trails towards the water to check out two cannons, one from the Revolutionary War and another that was Civil War-era. I noticed the crunch of little bits of oyster shells under my feet that were embedded within the sandy trail.

European colonists forming the Charles Town settlement in the seventeenth century coined the name Oyster Point for this area because of the mounds of oyster shells left there by the early indigenous peoples. Later, because these banks of oyster shells would get bleached by the sun and become stark white, Oyster Point's name would morph into White Point. I could imagine the dry white shells almost radiating a sort of spotlight up to the sky on a hot, sunny day. It was formally named White Point Garden when the park was formed in 1837.

This waterside location had been a location of strategic military importance throughout time, including during the American Revolution, War of 1812, and Civil War. Down by the water, the Ashley and Cooper Rivers collided, and Alphonso and I looked out at vast Charleston Harbor. In the distance, we could spot Fort Sumter, whose bombing in 1861 would mark the start of the Civil War.

Alphonso also pointed out Sullivan's Island, home to Fort Moultrie, a national park site of relevance to the American Revolution. The first fort on Sullivan's Island was made from palmetto logs and sand and was attacked by the British on June 28, 1776. In White Point Gardens, there are monuments to Major General William Moultrie and Fort Moultrie. Alphonso also pointed to Morris Island.

"Have you ever seen the movie *Glory*?" he asked.

I hadn't. It was based on the 54th Massachusetts Infantry Regiment, one of the Union Army's earliest African American regiments in the American Civil War. It starred Matthew Broderick and Denzel Washington.

"They're trying to take Fort Wagner in that film," Alphonso said, referring to the Fifty-Fourth in their attempt to gain command over the Charleston Harbor. "The actual battle took place out there off Morris Island, where the first shot of the Civil War was fired."

These first shots were cannon fire from cadets at The Citadel, a military college dating back to 1842. In January of 1861, they took aim at the *Star of the West*, a ship hired by the government to resupply Fort Sumter. Months later in April of 1861, the first attack of the war would occur.

We walked along the promenade, known as the Battery. Flanked by Charleston Harbor and colorful antebellum homes, the Battery is a seawall and promenade so named after a defense artillery battery at the site during the Civil War.

Charleston has some of the prettiest homes in the world. Being a fan of pastel colors and having grown up in a Southern home with paintings from local Charleston artists lining my walls, I could spend a good amount of time admiring this beautiful architecture.

As Alphonso and I walked along East Battery Street, I paused to take a photograph of the pretty pink Edmondston-Alston House at 21 East Battery. It was built by Scottish shipping merchant Charles Edmondston and dated back to 1825. It was remarkably intact, having survived the Civil War, 1886 earthquake, and numerous hurricanes, including the devastating Hurricane Hugo in 1989. I was living in Myrtle Beach at the time and witnessed the destruction firsthand, so knew how truly remarkable this was. I read a sign about house tours and marked it down to double back to later in my trip.

We walked in the direction of downtown and Marion Square, meandering amid the vibrant homes and mansions. Many had historical markers, and a few had the prestigious Carolopolis Award plaque, which was given by the Preservation Society of Charleston and honored outstanding historic preservation, restoration, or rehabilitation. Having grown up with parents who restored a historic home along Maryland's Eastern Shore, turning it into a bed and breakfast, I understood the work and care that would go into restoring a home like each one that we were passing. It wasn't for the faint of heart.

Less than two blocks away on King Street, Alphonso stopped by a red brick mansion with remarkable white columns and multi-level portico balconies. The Miles Brewton House was special as a colonial-era "double house." The home was split equally inside by a central hallway with double rooms on each side and was a popular architectural design in Charleston. It was also distinguished in Charleston from the tall, slender row homes. Although today in private hands and not available for tours, the building's exterior brought Charleston's history to life, from the Colonial Era to the American Revolution and into the Civil War. It's a National Historic Landmark that is considered one of the most outstanding examples of American Palladian architecture.

On the left, I noticed a stone marker hanging on the gateway, detailing the home's history. Although it carried Miles Brewton's namesake, he did not live in the Charleston mansion for long. Miles Brewton, a local merchant, slave trader, and rice plantation owner, constructed the home in the 1760s. After being elected to the Second Provincial Congress in 1775, Brewton left Charleston to support the American Revolution in Philadelphia, but he never made it. He and his family got lost at sea during their voyage to the north. Brewton's sister, Rebecca Brewton Motte, took over the Charleston home.

When the British Army captured the city of Charleston in 1780 during the American Revolution, the Miles Brewton home became the headquarters of British officer Sir Henry Clinton and Lords Rawdon and Cornwallis for about two years. After the officers left, the home was restored as a residential property. The well-restored home today remains in the ownership of descendants of the Brewton family.

I noticed the iron fence and gate outside were topped with thick black iron spikes, sort of like a medieval-looking barbed wire. Alphonso shared that in Charleston in the 1820s, many families installed those spiked fences after learning about Denmark Vesey's insurrection plot.

Denmark Vesey was a free Black man in Charleston in the 1820s. He was born in St. Thomas in the Caribbean and brought to the United States in the 1760s, where he was enslaved. He was freed during a lottery in 1799 and became a carpenter and churchgoer at a prominent Charleston Black church. Denmark Vesey would eventually rally enslaved people for the cause of freedom. His plan spread to thousands, assembling them to escape or kill their enslavers and sail to freedom in Haiti. His plot was leaked and Vesey was hanged along with thirty-four other enslaved men.

Hearing about Denmark Vesey while looking at these spikes made me feel a bit ill. Wealthy or comfortable families in Charleston chose to install pain-inflicting spikes outside of their homes to keep in potential freedom seekers or keep themselves safe from those who might stop by, all the while holding them hostage and profiting off their lives and labor. Many of these same families were at the same time fighting for the Patriot cause, for their own freedom from Great Britain. It didn't sound very American to me.

It was interesting to look at this home with Alphonso. Had I walked by it alone, I might have simply thought it was a beautiful, historical home, but in hearing more about its legacy, I was a bit shocked. Alphonso pointed to the large slave quarters beyond the house and shared that the home's original owner,

Miles Brewton, made his fortune from the slave trade. He profited greatly from the enslaved people he brought in on ships and traded. That wealth was used to build this mansion. It was the dichotomy of beauty and tragedy that existed in Charleston and in history in general. It was another example of how knowing the history makes you digest and internalize what you see differently.

Charleston had a lot of fires, but the area where we were walking wasn't as affected, so we saw many homes from the eighteenth century. I took a closer look at one dating to 1746, the John Prue House, which at last listing had sold for over $4.2 million. I was sure there was nothing under a million, probably two million, nearby. In recent years, Charleston's real estate market has boomed, with people moving in from across the nation and world, buying up these historic homes, causing the inventory to shrink and prices to soar.

The John Prue home had stucco on the outside in a yellow, beige color. You could see how old some of the homes were by looking at the bricks, and for those with stucco, the historical markers would normally reveal dates. We walked further along, hearing the clip-clop of a horse-drawn carriage passing by on the road. It was filled with tourists on a guided tour, probably venturing by some of these same homes.

Our walk continued along tree-lined Tradd Street to the gray clapboard, Georgian-style John Stuart House. Alphonso shared that this home was the centerpiece for legendary stories related to the iconic Revolutionary War figure Francis Marion.

The story goes that Marion was at a party in the home. According to some, he had too much to drink and literally fell out of a second-story window. In other stories, he leapt out of the window to escape the British. Either way, Marion did hurt his ankle in Charleston, an accident that led him to travel back to a plantation in inland South Carolina to heal. He thus missed being captured by the British when they took Charleston a few weeks later in the Siege of Charleston.

This is another home that isn't open for tours, but is one you can walk by and admire, including reading information about the house on a wooden sign set on a gray brick fence along the sidewalk. I briefly met one of the owners outside of the home on my visit. She welcomed us to take photographs, and as she and I spoke, we discovered that we'd attended the same high school!

The home was built in 1772 and is a National Historic Landmark. Its architecture is notable in that it is a colonial side-passage plan. The home's original owner and its namesake, John Stuart, hailed from Scotland. He was also a Loyalist who fled Charleston during the Revolution, spending his final years in West Florida. His home was confiscated.

It was wild to me that so many stories swirled amid the spiked fences and second-story windows of the homes located all within walking distance in historic Charleston, and Alphonso and I hadn't even scratched the surface. Seeing these mansions from the outside did make me want to go inside to see an interior, which we were able to do on my next stop.

Heyward–Washington House: Echoes of the Enslaved

While homes like the Miles Brewton House remind us that it was money made from the enslaved people who allowed wealthy slave owners to build mansions, for those who want to see what life was like for the enslaved here in the city, the Heyward-Washington House offers a peek behind the curtain. Charleston's first historic house museum, the Heyward-Washington House is a historic Georgian style double home built in 1772. It was the home of Thomas Heyward, Jr., one of the four South Carolina signers of the Declaration of Independence. George Washington stayed here for a week while visiting Charleston in 1791, and today this remarkably well-preserved three-story brick home is open to tour.

I said good-bye to Alphonso as I walked inside to meet Carl Borick, the director of the Charleston Museum, which owns and interprets this historic property. Carl has published several books on the history of Charleston during the American Revolution, and he and his staff have worked to collect and preserve artifacts related to the time, including at the Heyward-Washington House. Being a wealth of knowledge related to Charleston history, Carl doesn't always lead tours but did agree to give special insight into this home and the life of the enslaved here for my visit.

Carl was wearing a meticulously pressed blue-gray suit with a red checkered tie, his short, straight, silver hair neatly arranged. We had walked through the main home and out to the back formal gardens, budding with plants and herbs that you might have seen in late-eighteenth-century Charleston gardens, like tulips, lemon balm, and hyssop. These gardens are just as beautiful from above as they are on the ground. Designed as a "parterre" garden, flowers and plants in enclosed beds are meant to be artistic when seen from the second or third stories of a house. Here you can examine and go inside the outbuildings where the enslaved people would have lived and worked.

Carl led me into the kitchen building, which dates to the 1740s and has light, worn exposed brick walls. On the left was a washroom where laundry would have been done. There was a large copper tub, wooden chair, and wood tub for washing. Laundry was a hot and labor-intensive endeavor during colonial times. A fire bellows was beside the fireplace, which would have been used to stoke the fire heating solid iron and cast-iron pots in which the laundry would be cooked clean, perhaps using lemon slices and pearl ash to remove stains and grease.

Down the hallway, the kitchen would be used for cooking and preparing food, but also for sleeping. The table today was set with fake food items, common in these historic homes with recreated aspects. There were lemons, eggs, potatoes, carrots, and other staple items, along with a large rolling pin and big ceramic pitcher. Off another fireplace, a set of stairs led to an upstairs area.

"A 1790 census indicates there were about twelve or thirteen people that were here living in the kitchen building," Carl said.

He continued to relay that a lot of what is known about this building and the main house comes from archeology, including a major project in the 1970s. An archaeologist by the name of Elaine Herold recovered approximately eighty-eight thousand artifacts related to the history of the house. Game pieces, wine bottles, cooking implements, porcelain bowls, dining room tableware, sea-grass basket fragments, buckles, buttons, scissors, and keys would reveal more about what life was like for the people who lived here, including the Heyward family and the enslaved people. Inside the main home, travelers can view some of these items, enclosed in glass cases, to get a better sense of the tools that were used for daily life.

I always think about enslaved people being on vast plantations, but they were here in the city of Charleston, too. In fact, at the time of the Revolutionary War, about half of the twelve thousand people in Charleston would have been enslaved. The enslaved people served the households, acting as butchers, craftsmen, assistants to furniture makers, silversmiths, and other urban trades.

After the Heywards sold the home in the 1790s, it would be owned by several families and eventually become a bakery in the 1880s, before being taken over by the Charleston Museum.

Thomas Heyward is known for being a signer of the Declaration of Independence, but he was also a militia captain. He served and was captured in the Siege of Charleston. His wife stayed in the main house, while he was sent as a prisoner to St. Augustine, Florida. Carl shared that while many people know the hard facts about the Siege and what happened in Charleston, they don't always think about what happened to the women and families who were caught in the crossfire.

He shared a story about the Heyward family that struck a chord with me. After the British had taken over the city, they asked the local inhabitants to put candles in their window to commemorate the Fall of Charleston the previous year. Mrs. Heyward refused to do so. A mob of Loyalists attacked the home, throwing bricks and trash at the front of the house, frightening her and her sister, who had just given birth. Vulnerable, there with her sister, a newborn, and with her husband hundreds of miles away, I could only imagine how tense and frightened Mrs. Heyward must have been. That's the thing about the American Revolution. It wasn't fought just on battlefields, but in cities, farmsteads, and inside private homes. Even in places where people believed they might be out of the fray, the war often reached them.

The Heyward-Washington House tells this and many other stories, including that of George Washington's visit in May of 1791. Inside, in addition to artifacts, you can explore period furniture and learn about the home's later years when Revolutionary

War officer John F. Grimké, father of abolitionists and women's rights activists Sarah and Angelina Grimké, lived there.

Sarah was in the home, living with enslaved people as a child from the age of two to eleven. Her sister Angelina would be born in 1805 when the family had already moved out. In reading about their life's story, I wondered about how the home had shaped the sisters' later life.

The two sisters would go on to stand up for the rights of women and African Americans. Perhaps what they had seen or heard in their own homes would have influenced them to speak out. They, along with Angelina's husband, abolitionist Theodore Dwight Weld, would write *American Slavery as It Is*. It was published in 1839, became a bestseller, and served as some inspiration for Harriet Beecher Stowe's *Uncle Tom's Cabin*. The home where the sisters later lived together is also nearby, the Blake-Grimké House at 321 East Bay Street.

It's remarkable what you can learn about a place through its architecture, artifacts, documents, and even oral histories passed down through the generations. Even more outstanding when travelers can step inside these places and hear, read, and see the past through physical objects and accounts. In the 1920s, the Heyward-Washington House was turned into Charleston's first historic house museum. Inside, a complicated and compelling history is shared that sheds light on the history of America.

Leaving Carl and the Heyward-Washington House, I walked just another block and landed in one of the most iconic and photographed places in Charleston, Rainbow Row. Thirteen pastel-colored row homes share a fascinating transformation of Charleston over time. Built in the eighteenth century, the homes on Rainbow Row were occupied by merchants who lived on the top floor while running their businesses on the ground floor. The area was a center for commerce. Ships moored right along East Bay Street. By the end of the Civil War, the neighborhood fell into ruin with many of the houses abandoned.

In 1931, Dorothy Porcher Legge and her husband purchased a Georgian-style home on what is today called Rainbow Row. Hoping to beautify the area, Dorothy decided to paint her East Bay Street home a bright shade of pink, a homage to Charleston's Caribbean Colonial history. Other homeowners on the block decided to as well, covering their homes in vivid pastel colors. This would become what is called Rainbow Row.

Legge and Susan Pringle Frost would go on to found the Society for the Preservation of Old Dwellings in 1920. Today, it's the Preservation Society of Charleston, which safeguards many of the buildings we were passing today.

For fans of literature and theatre, it's fun to note that DuBose Heyward, author of the novel *Porgy*, which later became the musical *Porgy and Bess*, lived nearby between 1919 and 1924. The novel's Catfish Row was based on Cabbage Row, referring to cabbage once grown in the windowsills of the poor tenants in this area prior to its rise to a quite expensive real estate location.

While the homes on Rainbow Row are stunning to view altogether, each has its own unique features. Rainbow Row begins with house Number 79–81. The final house on Rainbow Row is Number 107. Known as the John Blake Building, this home dates to the American Revolution. Its visible alterations demonstrate the changing architectural techniques and culture of Charleston over the years.

Old Exchange and Provost Dungeon: Grandeur, Tragedy and George Washington Parties

My next Charleston American Revolution location couldn't be more different than the outwardly splendid homes I'd just visited with Carl and Alphonso. Stepping into a dark, dank dungeon with Marshall Willis, I was taken into another Revolutionary War realm—captivity.

"Definitely not a place that you would want to be incarcerated," I said, as I looked around the dark, brick-lined dungeon and over to costumed figures in shackles and chains. Their faces looked pained—those that I could see. Two were positioned as keeled over, in desperation or pain or both, their long, ragged hair hiding their faces. It was a total juxtaposition to the beautiful, colorful homes on nearby Rainbow Row that I'd admired just steps away.

"Very crowded. Disease breaking out," Marshall said. "People did die down here. It was a terrible place to be."

I was in the Old Exchange and Provost Dungeon, with tour guide Marshall Willis, who was charged with knowing the ins and outs of this building and its 250 years of history, ghost stories included. Leading many lives, the Old Exchange and Provost Dungeon was once used as a commercial exchange, an old dungeon and jail, post office, customs house, a site for slave auctions, and more, representing the richness and complexity of American history that's waiting for curious travelers at every turn in Charleston. As a bonus, George Washington made a stop here. During World War II, it was a military site for the army and the coast guard, and now it's a museum displaying that history. It was a place of dichotomy, mixing grandeur with grit and tragedy.

The brick-lined space was dry where we explored, but I walked over to see an area that looked like a moat and realized there was visible water in the dungeon, too. I wondered about the overall climate down here for the prisoners, where lack of sanitation bred further disease. Marshall said that some ghost stories say that the dungeon would flood, drowning those who were locked and shackled inside, but that's not true. There was no way for a large amount of water to enter the cellar. The primary danger was disease and assaults. Still…not ideal. It was totally different here in the dungeon than amid the upscale mansions just outside and just upstairs, where business, parties, and events would take place in a grand ballroom.

Constructed in 1771 as a commercial exchange and custom house, this Georgian-style building with Palladian windows had many uses over time. Prior to British occupation, it was used for trade and as a social hub with the cellar used for storage. During British occupation of the American colonies, it was used as a prison until their evacuation in December of 1782. The British called it the provost, which has a nicer ring to it than dungeon or jail. It was also the site of many important events and decisions, like South Carolina's ratification of the United States Constitution on May 23, 1788.

Following the Siege of Charleston, British occupied the city starting on May 12, 1780, and they needed a prison. The cellar of the Exchange building became just that. Marshall went on to explain more about the conditions and circumstances. We were walking under the brick archways past wooden storage boxes and by another batch of colonial costumed figures representing the many prisoners who had been held here.

"The first prisoners were actually British soldiers that were found drinking on duty or maybe associating with some of the elements of the local population they shouldn't have," Marshall said. "But then they started throwing criminals down here, then political prisoners and men, women— enslaved or free.

"One of the prisoners, Dr. David Ramsay, wrote that one of the cruelest things the guards could do was to turn their backs and just allow what happened down here to happen," Marshall said.

I didn't even want to imagine that. The lighting was dim, and it was eerie in the dungeon, which was used as a prison until the winter of 1782, when the British abandoned Charles Town. During the Colonial and Revolutionary time periods, Charleston was called Charles Town.

Of course, I had to ask about the ghosts. Charleston is known as a very haunted city, and I had already heard that the Old Exchange and this very dungeon were reputed to be haunted. Marshall confirmed just that and a lot more.

He shared a firsthand experience of being in the Old Exchange one night, upstairs in the room named after Patriot Colonel Isaac Hayne. He was cleaning up after a party all alone when one of the doors shut completely on its own. I could imagine the fear he must have felt as he called to see if anyone was there, perhaps feeling that someone or something was. Upon getting no reply, he quickly did what he had to do to finish cleaning up and fled the Old Exchange. While he would normally take about an hour to tidy things and set the security alarms, that night he said that he got out in a record fifteen minutes.

Just to my right a thick chain lay stretched across two poles, stopping people from entering an exhibit space. Marshall said that he had also once looked over to see the heavy chain swinging on its own and that others have had the same experience. Perhaps the ghosts of prisoners past were letting Marshall and others know that they were still around, haunting the halls of the Old Exchange and Provost Dungeon. Many had reason to do so.

We walked upstairs from the dungeon to the Great Hall. Shiny, dark wood floors skated into a large, stately ballroom dotted with elegant white Ionic columns, light gray paneled walls, and a dramatic Caribbean blue ceiling. It was a room that George Washington may have danced in. He'd attended several meetings and parties in this building, including a ball, two banquets, and a concert on his visit in May of 1791.

"While a lot of places have signs that say George Washington slept here, we should put up a sign that said George Washington partied here while he was in town," Marshall laughed.

Post–Revolutionary War in 1791, George Washington toured the South and spent time in Charleston, coming to the Old Exchange for meetings and parties. Marshall shared that the space wasn't just used for parties and events. British Redcoats were reported to have camped on the floor of this building, and auctions of enslaved people were also held in and around the building. It was quite the contrast of events. Enslaved people were sold in many downtown Charleston spaces, including inside this building and in an open space just north of the Exchange building. In 2022, Lauren Davila, a graduate student at the College of Charleston, discovered the largest known slave auction in the United States happened on the north side of the Exchange building in 1835. An advertisement claimed six hundred enslaved individuals would be auctioned off.

It wouldn't be until 1856 that public slave auctions would be banned in Charleston. Once they were, Marshall relayed that they moved into a building only one block away.

There were numerous auction houses in the blocks to the northwest of the Exchange building. A large auction complex was Ryan's Mart at 6 Chalmers Street. The Old Slave Mart Museum is there today. The complex spanned from Chalmers to Queen Street and featured a four-story barracoon, or jail for enslaved people.

"Here in Charleston, you do have some grandly beautiful things," Marshall said. "But you have some very tragic things that happen in this city, and often they occupy the very same space."

I left the Old Exchange feeling that irony settling in even more, as I walked another few blocks to the Historic Charleston City Market, one of the oldest markets in the country. It dates to 1788, when South Carolina political leader Charles Cotesworth Pinckney donated the land to the city of Charleston for use as a public market. Stalls were built between 1804 and the 1830s, and vendors rented booths selling meats, vegetables, and fish. Later, in 1841, the market that still stands today was completed in the Greek Revival style, with striking use of brownstone stucco, red sandstone, and green ironwork. Inside, I savored the mix of everything, from the beauty of sweetgrass backets woven by Gullah artists to homemade candles and Lowcountry food.

The market is located adjacent to Charleston's Powder Magazine, the oldest building in the Carolinas. Built in 1713, the structure was constructed to safely store gunpowder from 1713 to 1770 and during the American Revolution. From then on, the Powder Magazine has been adapted to fit city life, being used as a stable, print shop, wine cellar, carriage house, and a blacksmith shop.

Though I had visited Charleston numerous times in my life, I really hadn't understood both the charms and chaotic history of the city until this visit, when I took the time to walk with historians and guides to more closely examine the fabric of the city and its hidden history. Did it make me think of Charleston differently? It did.

For all its flaws, beauty, turmoil, and juxtapositions, I realized that the city continued to stand and share its stories, for better or worse, through preserved spaces and landmarks. Its journey and survival over time was fascinating. The beautiful homes didn't always have a beautiful past, but they did share a legacy worth discovering.

My walk was leading me back to where I'd started my day at Marion Square, and I knew oysters were likely on the evening menu. There are many restaurants to choose from for oysters and fresh seafood in Charleston. Oysters are a dish one must eat on a visit, but next time I eat one, the Battery's oyster-strewn gardens and a Revolutionary-era fortress may come to mind.

Middleton Place: Revolutionary Gardens and Enslaved Horticulturalists

In my travels to discover Revolutionary War history, I've learned that history doesn't just live on through museums, buildings, and artifacts, but also through living, breathing things. In Camden, South Carolina, I'd meet animals with roots in Revolutionary times, including Marsh Tacky horses and heritage chickens. There were also people descended from Revolutionary heroes— families and soldiers who kept the spirit of the past alive through oral histories, like the many visitors I met at Kings Mountain in South Carolina who were related to veterans of the past.

At my next two locations, I'd see the plants and the gardens of the time, tended to in colonial times by enslaved people and carefully preserved today through the work of master gardeners. I'd also meet the chief of a lesser-known tribe, presenting an oral history not well documented related to the role of indigenous peoples in America's founding. These were all in Berkeley County, just a short drive from downtown Charleston.

Middleton Place is a National Historic Landmark that is home to America's oldest landscaped gardens. Amid historic beauty lay a bigger story about the enslaved people who toiled here as America's first horticulturalists. To hear that story, I was meeting the "King of Camellias," Sidney Frazier, who had been tending to the gardens at Middleton Place as the vice president of horticulture for over fifty years. He was wearing a dusty blue short sleeved button-down shirt with a brown belt and khakis. I met him at the entrance to the gardens at Middleton Place, less than a thirty-minute drive from Charleston.

"You know, people don't think about it, but when they walk through this garden, they walk out on the very path that the Middletons walked on, and the guests walked on, and the enslaved Africans walked on," Sidney said as we strolled beside a large green hedge on a path in the shade of live oak trees laden with Spanish moss.

We were on the allées or walkways leading to those formal gardens. Characterized by symmetrical order, geometry, vista points, and formal design, the designs for the gardens here followed the principles of the designer who laid out the gardens at the Palace of Versailles. Of particular note, the thousands of camellias at Middleton Place are descendants of those brought over by French botanist André Michaux in 1786. Depending on the season, you can also walk among azaleas, magnolias, terraced gardens, and ponds shaped like butterfly wings. A stroll here is altogether peaceful and magical.

Many of the plants you'll find were cultivated here during the American Revolution. Middleton Place is working to ensure these heritage varieties survive by paying close attention to propagating them in-house. They want to sustain these older varieties that can't be found on the market anymore. They are saving these living pieces of history. Though this living history is beautiful, it didn't take root without serious human costs.

"Everything is laid out in a formal control condition. The more control you demonstrate in your landscaping, the more power you demonstrate. It was the planters demonstrating power against one another. 'I have a larger plantation than you do. I have more slaves than you do,'" Sidney said as we strolled down a shady dirt lane with a giant hedge on one side and the formal gardens on the other. "So that's where the power demonstration came in. But you know something we never think about? The first horticulturists were the enslaved Africans. And they were brought for the knowledge that they had. Everything that we see out here is the bones of the garden, all done by enslaved Africans."

It was the plantation owners who were showing off their power to their neighbors, guests, and friends. With more slaves, more manicured gardens, and land came more power and, perhaps more importantly, the perception of more power. Looking at the bones of the garden, Sidney told me that this is what I would have seen in 1741 when Middleton Place was planned and created through work performed by enslaved Africans. They had a knowledge of rice cultivation brought over from Africa on how to water, maintain, and cultivate. It was used here on Middleton Place.

I had also seen this at Hampton Plantation, a state historic site located north of the charming fishing town of McClellanville in South Carolina. On a visit there, I heard another Francis Marion tale. Assistant Park Manager Jayson Sellers shared that he escaped from a trap door inside of the home to evade capture by Lieutenant Colonel Banastre Tarleton and the British.

Hampton Plantation was a refuge for women and children during the American Revolution, primarily around 1780 when the British captured Charleston. It is also a place that intensive Carolina Gold rice was grown by over three hundred enslaved West Africans at the height of its prominence. Hampton Plantation is another site travelers can add to their list when combining travel and history in South Carolina and along The Liberty Trail, a road trip to discover sites of the American Revolution throughout South Carolina and along the East Coast.

Back with Sidney, I listened to the birds singing and watched the Spanish moss swaying in the light of morning. I walked over to one of the butterfly ponds, where I spotted a heron in the distance. I may be biased, having grown up in the state, but the light at various times of day in South Carolina is truly enchanting. It was peaceful by the water, but if I were here during the American Revolution, where I now saw a heron, I may have instead spotted enslaved people toiling away at this man-made environment. I felt conflicted about these well-cultivated gardens. It was yet another instance in Charleston of beauty built on the backs of those who were enslaved. It was Sidney's job to create and tend to this great beauty, but he couldn't do so without knowledge learned from the past.

At Middleton Place, a staff of scholars has worked for a decade to piece together more about life here, cataloging the names of 3200 enslaved persons. Home to generations of the Middleton family, who played prominent roles in South Carolina during Colonial times, it's remarkable that Middleton Place survived the American Revolution and the Civil War, when the home was burned by Union troops in February of 1865. What's open as the

House Museum today for the public to tour dates to 1755 when it was used as an office and gentleman's guest quarters. It was one of three buildings to survive the Civil War fire. Middleton Place is yet another Charleston area location where beauty and tragedy collide, but where people are working to share as much of this history as they can.

Moncks Corner: "Swamp Fox" Swamps and Oral Histories

From Middleton Place, I drove along quieter roads to Moncks Corner. This small South Carolina town is the kind of place where if you blink twice while driving through, you may miss it. It's exactly the type of place where you should park downtown by the historic train station along Behrman Street and take a walk. The hundred-plus-year-old train station depot reminds travelers of so many towns that grew up around depots. No longer serving train travelers, it's still in the heart of this small Southern town. Historical markers outside include information on the Battle of Moncks Corner on April 14, 1780, a British victory, which ultimately helped lead to the Siege of Charleston.

Moncks Corner is home to the Berkeley County Museum and Old Santee Canal Park: the site of the first true canal built in America and around 150 acres of cypress swamps. It was raining when I arrived at this park and nature area that has both outdoor trails and an Interpretive Center. The four miles of boardwalk trails are beautiful to discover on foot. There are also canoe rentals.

Even in the rain, I decided to explore. I made sure not to slip on the wooden boardwalk after noticing a sign cautioning that it was slippery when wet. I was here to meet up with Park

Director Brad Sale to hear about the history of this canal, which opened in 1800 to connect the Santee River with the Cooper River, allowing for travel by water from the Charleston Harbor further inland.

Prior to the canal's construction, merchants and farmers transporting goods from inland South Carolina to the Port of Charleston had a convoluted and rough route of travel, involving rivers, deltas, and oceans. The twenty-two-mile canal, complete with locks, gave a direct route from the Santee River to the Cooper River and allowed travelers from further afield, including North Carolina, to reach the Charleston Harbor by boat. Plans for the canal project dated back to the 1770s, but the American Revolution put plans on hold for decades. The canal operated into the 1850s.

Brad Sale was dressed in a short-sleeved button-down shirt embroidered with "Old Santee Canal Park" above his pocket. I donned a khaki baseball hat to brave the rain and ended up using an umbrella. It was raining hard as Brad and I ventured past bald cypress trees, laurel oak, and red maples, listening to the sounds of pig frogs brought out by the rain. We carried binoculars so we could potentially spot birds and frogs.

"In the park business, we call it rinse and refresh," Brad said. "Fill the swamp up with water. Water the flowers, wash the pollen off. There are lots of frogs that come out. There are some with some funny names, banjo frogs that sound like a detuned banjo string being plucked, pig frogs that kind of snort around. If you come out to the swamp and you hear a pig, it's actually a frog. This warm, wet rain activates their activity."

In addition to the beauty of the wetlands, I was on the lookout for snakes, alligators, and all those treacherous things that we think about inhabiting swamps, as we walked along the Osprey

Loop. It was terrain that General Francis Marion, also known as the Swamp Fox, might have also traversed—of course, not on the raised wooden boardwalk we enjoyed today. Francis Marion garnered his moniker for his abilities to navigate the swampy terrain and outsmart the British, using early guerilla warfare. He would go on to be one of the directors of the incorporated company for opening the Santee Canal as an inland navigation route. His firsthand knowledge of the swamps and rivers must have made him an apt person for this endeavor.

Old Santee Canal Park is also home to educational programs for kids and resources for adults, like the Interpretive Center and Museum and Heritage Center, which chronicle South Carolina's nature and history, including the many American Indian tribes who lived along the coast and further inland in South Carolina.

While there is some documentation of tribal activity, I was fortunate on my visit to the Old Santee Canal Park to meet Lisa Collins, the chief of the Wassamasaw Tribe of Varnertown Indians. I had never heard of this tribe, so was interested to learn about their role in American history.

Lisa's long dark hair stood out against her bright red blouse as we strolled along a dirt trail outside of the Old Santee Canal Park and Berkeley County Museum, also located adjacent to the Canal Park.

"We are an assimilation of different native lines—eight, in fact," Lisa said with her Southern accent. "Two of those came from the coastal region, which is the Edisto Indian line and the Etiwan, so our ancestors are descendants of those Native people."

The Wassamasaw Tribe is active in Berkeley County, also tracing their bloodlines to the Catawba, Cherokee, and other Settlement Indians, a phrase coined by the English to describe Indigenous tribes that settled among the colonists in South

Carolina, even though it was the other way around. There are many other tribes in South Carolina including the Beaver Creek Indians, Pee Dee Indian Tribe, Sumter Tribe of Cheraw Indians, Waccamaw Indian People, and more. I asked Lisa about the role that her ancestors played in the American Revolution.

"Native American people didn't think it was our fight," Lisa said. "We have those that sided with the Loyalists and those that sided with the Patriots. That's how we fought. And it was more for our ancestral land protection than believing in a cause. We did have a loss with the American Revolution and the forming of our independence here because we lost our ancestral lands."

Despite losing their ancestral lands, indigenous tribes played a role in the American Revolution, including serving in Francis Marion's brigade. Now, Lisa is working on an oral history project to record tribe elders.

Lisa shared her tribe's history related to the American Revolution. Virginian William Dangerfield, who fought in the American Revolution at Camden and Cowpens, had a son, John Dangerfield, who married the last Edisto Indian from Edisto Island, Hannah Eddings. They had children and were part of the community. On the Driggers line, another Native American lineage, the families provided beef to Francis Marion during the war.

"You can't change the past, and you can't change history," Lisa said as we neared the museum, "but you sure can make a better direction for your community and your descendants. That's what our people are trying to do. To make sure that generations to come will have access to our history, to our culture, and be proud of the people they descend from."

Inside the Berkeley County Museum, travelers can learn about the history of the American Revolution in Berkeley County, including the Native peoples who once lived in South

Carolina and those who are still active today. It's a history that's still unfolding but becoming more fully understood thanks to people like Lisa Collins.

Mepkin Abbey: A Trappist Monastery with Hamilton Ties

Another unexpected history stop is Mepkin Abbey, a Trappist monastery just a fifteen-minute drive from the Old Santee Canal Park and Berkeley County Museum, located on the grounds of the historic Mepkin Plantation. This plantation was owned by Henry Laurens, a wealthy merchant and slave trader who became a leader during the Revolutionary War. His son's name, John Laurens, may be familiar to those who've seen the hit Broadway show *Hamilton*, where John Laurens is portrayed as Alexander Hamilton's closest friend, as he was in real life.

Today, Mepkin Abbey comprises three thousand acres of gardens, trails, and the Abbey, where monks lead a life of contemplation, study, and work. They produce products sold on site and locally, including mushrooms, fruitcakes, creamed honey, and preserves. They also welcome travelers. The grounds are a popular place for locals and travelers to walk the trails and explore sites including the Nancy Bryan Luce Gardens and Mepkin Abbey Church. For those who want a deeper dive, there are guided tours of the Abbey Church.

Henry Laurens is notable as the only Founding Father imprisoned in the Tower of London in 1780. He also served as fifth president of the Continental Congress and was later vice president of South Carolina.

Henry Laurens's son John Laurens was indeed good friends with Alexander Hamilton, as evidenced through their letters and correspondence. During the American Revolution, John Laurens was outspoken about wanting enslaved people to be able to fight alongside the Patriots and eventually gain their freedom. At one point, he even offered to give up his inheritance to form a regiment that included enslaved people if they would then be granted their freedom. He brought the idea to the attention of the Continental Congress, who voted it down, and also to the State Legislature General Assembly in South Carolina. It was voted down there, too.

His father, Henry, didn't agree and thought John was moving too quickly with his ideas. He famously said "haste would make havoc" to John, telling his son to slow down, that it would come, but let's not do it all at once. It was common—an elder telling someone decades younger to take things slowly. It was something to which I think we all could relate: both the inclination to tell someone to take it slow and the inclination of a younger person to want to move things along. It was also that divide that comes with generations, when the ideas and ideals of those who are younger normally tend to be more progressive.

The Laurens family owned hundreds of enslaved persons, many of whom worked the plantation where Mepkin Abbey now stands. Henry Laurens also was a partner at one of the largest slave-trading houses of the time. Enslaved peoples were an important part of his wealth.

I was hearing about this history while walking the stunning grounds of Mepkin Abbey with historian, attorney, and battlefield preservationist David Reuwer. David is a kind-hearted person who is so passionate and knowledgeable about history that he'll take you down a circuitous rabbit hole of information. He knows so many details that it can be hard for the layperson to follow. On my visit with him to Mepkin Abbey, I was happy to report that I learned a lot, but my brain was extra full when we left each other.

"It's a concept of the American Revolution," David said in his gravelly Southern voice. "They viewed themselves moving as English colonists to America, and so the concept was not just independence and freedom, but the concept of their rights as liberty, and the way that John Laurens and Henry Laurens saw it, including Alexander Hamilton in a different way, was liberty was freedom coupled with responsibility. You had to do something for your country."

When I think about Henry and John Laurens and people like Alexander Hamilton, it leads me to ponder the diversity of people who were involved with the American Revolution. In many instances, people were forced to be involved, while others chose to not only be involved but also strived to take major roles. Some people did choose to fight to get hot meals or because they somewhat believed in the cause. Henry and John Laurens were the elite, upper class and had much to lose in the war, yet John Laurens still fought for the Patriots. That's why it's interesting to visit sites like Mepkin Abbey—it's not just about battles and battle sites, but plantations, homes, and even gardens where the effects of the Revolution were felt.

David was wearing a bright blue cotton polo shirt with khaki pants and a wide-brimmed sun hat, emblazoned with a blue patch embroidered with a white South Carolina crescent moon, like the one on South Carolina's state flag, and the word *Liberty*. It represented his work on The Liberty Trail project. We were walking along this soft, verdant patch of grass on a bluff overlooking the Cooper River in the shade of giant oak trees, once again dangling with beautiful Spanish moss. David said that I could think of Mepkin Abbey sort of like the Mount Vernon of South Carolina.

Henry Laurens had purchased the property from John Coleton. The original plantation had three main bluffs and a valley. David was pointing in the distance to where the crops, including hundreds of acres of rice fields, would have been on the other side of the Cooper River. The historic wharf today was under the water. Behind us was the residential home, and on past that was another vale where they did shipbuilding and repairs. Atop the northern bluff was the location of the family cemetery. David shared that Mepkin would have been a huge working operation during the American Revolution.

David wanted to take me to the site where John Laurens and his father are buried in their family cemetery on the grounds of Mepkin Abbey. John Laurens died before his father did at the age of twenty-seven during the August 1782 Revolutionary War Battle of the Combahee River. He was shot on horseback as he boldly and somewhat impetuously went on the attack against the British instead of waiting for backup.

We walked across a wooden bridge amid the palmetto fronds and greenery of thicker trees and vegetation growing up from a large ravine. A painting by artist Charles Fraser of Mepkin shows a simple cabin of an enslaved person in a ravine. I looked down and imagined this painting could have been done on this very spot.

We walked up a long set of wooden stairs to reach the cemetery. It was nestled within the walls of a thick five-foot-high brick fence with an iron gate at the entrance. David and I walked through the gate to see headstones of different sizes. The graves of Henry and John Laurens rested beside each other along with the graves of Henry's wife, Eleanor, and their grandchildren and children, including their daughter Martha Laurens. I read a Latin phrase on John Laurens's gravestone, which David loosely translated to mean, "sweet and proper it is to die for your country." At the bottom of John's headstone, three small American flags were stuck into the sandy ground.

Hamilton sent a letter to General Nathanael Greene following John Laurens's death expressing his dismay: "I feel the deepest affliction at the news we have just received of the loss of our dear and (inesti)mable friend Laurens. His career of virtue is at an end. How strangely are human affairs conducted, that so many excellent qualities could not ensure a happier fate? The world will feel the loss of a man who has left few like him behind, and America of a citizen whose heart realized that patriotism of which others only talk. I feel the loss of a friend I truly and most tenderly loved, and one of a very small number."

A sign outside of the cemetery shared a story that I thought quite wild. It was apparently Henry's wish that he should be cremated. This was because his daughter Martha was almost buried alive. They thought that she had passed away from smallpox, but while prepping her for burial realized that she was in fact alive. Taphophobia, or the fear of being buried alive, was a real worry in the eighteenth century. People were normally buried within twenty-four hours, on the day following their death. At a time when doctors weren't as prevalent, it was usually whoever was nearby who proclaimed the person dead.

In the case of little Martha Laurens, we don't know if it was just Henry and Eleanor Laurens or if a doctor was also consulted, as the Laurens would have been able to afford and access a doctor. Either way, young Martha was laid out on her bed by a window so family and friends could pay their respects before her burial. It wasn't until one of these guests, Dr. John Moultrie, noticed Martha move that they realized that she was still alive. Thus, Martha was spared. Martha went on to live, get married to a doctor, and pass away many, many years later in 1811.

Following that incident, it's said that Henry put into his last will and testament that upon his death, they should "wrap him in twelve yards of tow cloth and set him on fire." He was set ablaze upon his death, which made for one of the first cremations of a political figure recorded in the United States.

On my visit, I also met with Father Joe Tedesco, who walked with me by the Tower of the Seven Spirits, a landmark on the property dedicated to the seven groups of people who have been of the Mepkin land over the centuries, including the Kusabo tribe. Seven is also significant, as the monks pray seven times a day, starting at four in the morning. For each time of prayer, the bell tower rings.

Father Tedesco wore a habit: a white tunic layered with a black cloak and scapular and a brown leather belt. Amid the buzz of the cicadas outside, I noticed a definite Northern accent from the father. Born in Philadelphia, Father Tedesco had come to Mepkin Abbey in the 1960s after he quit high school. He later was able to attend college and became a priest in Trenton, New Jersey, for twenty-nine years before returning to Mepkin Abbey on a retreat. He said it was like God sent him a telegram that said, "Joe, you're home."

He decided to enter the Trappist monastery in 2008. He would become a monk in 2014. I had watched an interview from Father Tedesco on YouTube on a show called Catholic Corner right before he left Trenton for Mepkin and could tell he had led a long life of service to others. Now, he was serving the land and its heritage and history at Mepkin Abbey.

The word *Mepkin* comes from the Native American word meaning serene. Friar Tedesco shared that they still today find arrowheads and other artifacts on the property, strewn amid the monastic property's church, dining room, infirmary, library, guest houses and farm.

Father Tedesco was aware of the magnitude of history on the property, revealing that hundreds of acres of what had been rice plantations where the enslaved toiled were now submerged under the Cooper River. He also explained how following his fifteen-month imprisonment in the Tower of London, Henry Laurens would return home after being exchanged for the freedom of General Charles Cornwallis of Great Britain, who had been captured after surrendering at Yorktown—all significant events.

In 1936, the Mepkin property was purchased by media magnate Henry Luce, who, along with his wife Clare Booth Luce, can be thanked for the stunning gardens still onsite today. Mrs. Luce had converted to Roman Catholicism and donated the property upon her death to a group of Trappist monks, who set up a monastery in the 1960s.

For those wondering about the monastic life, programs at Mepkin Abbey offer stays for a month, or up to a year, to participate in daily life, complete with study and work. Having stayed at a few monasteries and temples myself, I found it intriguing, though also a personal challenge. I also knew from my short stay at Monastery of Christ in the Desert along the Rio Chama and near Ghost Ranch in New Mexico, that the silence was hard for me. I was shushed a few times on that adventure. On my visit to a temple in South Korea made famous by Jeong Kwan from Netflix's *Chef's Table*, I broke from the vegetarian diet with a secret stash of Cheez-Its and was taken back to my days at summer camp, when illegal M&M's stashed in my laundry bag were a personal treat. I guess I was still flawed but had seen the good that retreats like this did for me and others, clearing my scattered mind a bit and immersing me in nature and a less distracted existence—albeit briefly. While Trappist monks don't take a vow of silence, they do maintain a quieter lifestyle.

I asked Father Tedesco more about those who stay here for a month, living the life of a monk. I was curious to know how it affected them and how many went on to become monks. He said that amid all the prayer and contemplation, they must work, too, cooking, cleaning and making a living. One man who thought he might like to be a monk left after a forty-eight-hour stay when he realized just how much work the monks do. He said that for many who enter the life of quiet prayer and self-reflection, it can be life changing.

It was quite the property to contemplate life, both our own and the past lives of people like John Laurens. While he didn't have to do so, he gave his life for something bigger than himself and stood up for those he believed were treated unjustly. So many heroes of the American Revolution, both written about and unsung, had.

Francis Marion's Gravesite: Larger than Life Legacies

With so many locations in South Carolina, and across the United States, named after Francis Marion, from Marion Square in downtown Charleston, the site of the hidden fortress, to the historic hotel alongside it, and the Francis Marion National Forest, the legacy of the Swamp Fox runs deep. At just a forty-minute drive from Mepkin Abbey, I felt I had to visit Marion's gravesite. Perhaps it would be the swan song to this Charleston adventure.

A visit to the Marion family gravesite in a rural outpost amid a forest might be a simple homage for those who don't know his story. Had I not met Francis Marion researcher Keith Gourdin at the site, I may have quickly visited, photographed, and left, not understanding why this site and its history is another South Carolina hidden gem.

Indicated by a readily identifiable entranceway by two historical markers and a State Parks sign on Highway 45, the Marion gravesite and tomb are located at 1 General Francis Marion Avenue four miles west of the village of Pineville, South Carolina, on what was once Francis Marion's older brother Gabriel's plantation, Belle Isle. It's about a thirty-minute drive from Moncks Corner, forty minutes from Mepkin Abbey, and just over an hour from downtown Charleston. The site is surrounded by forest woodland. There is no guide to take you to this remote location, which is free to visit, but there is a one-mile-long paved road leading to small parking lot, which is just a few steps from the gravesite. There's also interpretive signage onsite. A historical marker details more about Marion at the entrance of a large open fenced-in lawn.

The descendent of French Huguenot emigrants, Marion was born and laid to rest in Berkeley County. He's thought to have been born in 1732, though no one knows the exact birth date. He passed away in Berkely County on his own plantation, Pond Bluff, following an illness on February 27, 1795, and would be buried at this brother's Belle Isle Plantation family cemetery.

Keith Gourdin, who has spent years studying Francis Marion and Berkeley County Revolutionary War action sites got out of his pickup truck wearing light blue jeans, a tan baseball cap, sneakers, and a long button-down shirt embroidered with "Berkeley Soil & Water Conservation District" on the chest pocket. It is one of the many nonprofits he serves on. He is president and founder of the Berkeley North Historical & Cultural Association, historian with the Berkeley 250 Francis Marion Commission, a commissioner with Berkeley Conservation and Greenbelt Commission, and many others, keeping him quite busy.

Growing up on a farm in Berkeley County, Keith has been dedicated to the area's environment and history. He has a husky Southern, sort of subdued voice. Some of his words seem to dance out with a whistle of air. Very serious in his demeanor, he told me that he was eighty-six, and I was taken aback. He moved and acted no more than late sixties. If we could all be so blessed.

We walked across the open grass towards Marion's grave, which is covered by a huge granite monument provided by the state of South Carolina and unveiled on May 22, 1893. It has beautiful bronze markers attached to its sides. Marion's wife's grave is next to his, on the north side of the monument.

Gourdin talked about the unveiling of the monument. The stonecutter, a Mr. Reynolds, reported that it took ten mules to haul the granite blocks and bronzes from the depot in Saint Stephen, as well as having to strengthen several bridges along the way. There were over a thousand people that traveled from far and wide to attend, including military regiments and clergy. Gourdin shared that many had come a distance by train to get here, traveling to Pineville and then on wagons and buggies along what was then the old dirt River Road. At that time, Marion's brother's home was still on the plantation, though uninhabited and in disrepair. Keith described the scene of people peering out from every window, porch, and every nook and cranny, to get a glimpse of the ceremony.

As we walked towards the tomb, which was surrounded by an iron fence, I noticed two interpretive signs. One explained Marion's guerrilla combat techniques and the despondency people felt following American defeats in the war at Charleston and Camden in 1780, both of which attributed to the heroic stature he would receive as a Revolutionary War icon. Marion would rally an ill-trained group of troops to fight in the swamps and rugged backcountry of South Carolina for more than two years.

Unlike George Washington and other more traditional commanders, there are no known paintings created of Marion during his lifetime, but a description by a fellow soldier and paintings made later help us to picture him. William Dobbin James, a teenaged soldier in his brigade, described him as of "middle stature, swarthy…with badly formed knees and ankles, a limp, a projecting chin and piercing black eyed forty-eight-year-old." Quite the description!

Francis Marion was born on a farm in Berkeley County and had malformed legs. He nonetheless went on to crew a schooner bound for the West Indies as a teen and later join the South Carolina militia in the French and Indian War. Some think that this is where Marion may have learned the guerrilla ambush techniques that he would later employ during the Revolutionary War.

The name "the Swamp Fox" is said to have been coined by British Lieutenant Colonel Banastre Tarleton. On one occasion after Francis Marion had managed to evade capture by British cavalrymen for many hours and miles, escaping once again into the swamps, Tarleton exclaimed, "as for this damned old fox, the Devil himself could not catch him." This story and the name, "the Swamp Fox," circulated and stuck after the war. It was one of the many legends that would swirl around Francis Marion during the Revolution and well into the twenty-first century.

In the Berkeley County Museum, an exhibition shares information about the 1959 Walt Disney Production of *The Swamp Fox* series starring Leslie Nielsen. In 2000, a movie with Mel Gibson, *The Patriot*, would fictionalize Marion's exploits. Heath Ledger is also in that film, which was a success at the box office. Prior to that, a book by Mason Locke Weems based on the memoirs of soldier Peter Henry brought the Swamp Fox to the American attention. Weems is known for writing the fictionalized story about George Washington chopping down the cherry tree and uttering, "I cannot tell a lie." Again, Marion's life is sensationalized in these more mainstream media works. It's no wonder that his legacy has lived on through so many years.

Keith and I passed another interpretive sign that spoke to Marion's enduring fame. I was trying to listen to Keith, but a bug decided to nip quite viciously at the back of my arm. I slapped myself and then reached into my pocket for the small orange bottle of bug spray. I'd learned to keep things like this on my person during some of these deep forest treks in South Carolina. Keith somewhat proudly told me that he is also French Huguenot. His immigrant ancestor, Louis Gourdin, came over on the same boat as Francis Marion's grandfather.

We reached Marion's tomb and that of his wife, which were enclosed by an iron fence held up by a series of square brick pillars. Just outside of it, there were other family graves. I read a few markers. One was for George Porcher, son of Dr. John and Anna Porcher, who passed in 1859. There was another for Gabriella De Veaux, who passed in 1908.

On the brick pillars that held up the iron gate surrounding Marion's tomb, there were two plaques. One said that Francis Marion and his wife, Mary Esther Marion, were buried inside. The other side's plaque read that Daughters of the American

Revolution South Carolina had erected this in 1931 "in grateful appreciation to the services of the Swamp Fox during the American Revolution."

I asked Keith more about what he had learned about Marion's personality over his years of research and reading. Keith relayed that Marion was very strong toward education and was a real people person.

"He was one of the greatest American patriots ever," Keith said resolutely.

Keith told me he's been keeping a list of all the sites named after Francis Marion, and he's up to seventy or more scattered all over the United States. Submarines, schools, colleges, counties, cities, and communities are named after Francis Marion.

Since it's not clear as to the exact day that Marion was born, the annual Francis Marion Day is commemorated on February 27, the date of his death. Past commemorations have seen people from all over six or seven states gather at his tomb and gravesite in the woods in Pineville. In 2025, Francis Marion Day was met with quite the fanfare with the South Carolina Air National Guard 169th Swamp Fox Fighter Wing flyover, with the Washington Light Infantry Color Guard posting the colors.

I took a few minutes to read the inscription on Marion's tomb: "History will record his worth and rising generations embalm his memory as one of the most distinguished patriots and heroes of the American Revolution."

Keith told me he wanted to share something with me. We walked back to the parking lot. He uncovered his trunk bed, where he had set a framed map of American Revolution action sites in Berkeley County. Keith said he also has a book about all the Berkeley County action sites. I thought it was nice that he had taken such an interest in both the site of Francis Marion's grave and the local history, perhaps because some of his own family was also part of the story. Perhaps because he has spent his entire life right here, from farmer to protector of the land.

As I drove off down the rural, forested road back to Charleston, I thought about how my final Revolutionary stop had perhaps been the quietest, yet another where I'd met a devoted keeper of history. Keith Gourdin and so many others shared and documented stories of heroes and unsung heroes, and in doing so, brought the past alive. Often, they shared offbeat stories and color commentary that didn't capture the headlines or make it into classroom history books.

CHAPTER III

New York—Turning the Tide in Saratoga

Stewart's Shops: History at the Corner Store

You may have heard the phrase that history is all around us. This was never more evident than in Schuylerville, New York, in Saratoga County. We'd been filming in and around Saratoga Springs at the beautiful and powerful Saratoga National Historical Park, the monumental Saratoga Sword Surrender Site and the Saratoga Inn, a historic women-owned property with much fodder for history enthusiasts. We were filming at these sites to continue to document lesser-known stories of the American Revolution, but we didn't expect to learn anything about the Revolution in the parking lot of a convenience store and gas station. Stewart's Shops had been recommended for a few reasons. It's known for its ice cream. I'm a huge fan of ice cream. I also needed to fuel up my rental car occasionally on this travel adventure. But I was surprised to discover that Stewart's location and the family-run business both had ties to the American Revolution. In fact, I was in for a Revolutionary triple treat at Stewart's Shops.

Next to the sidewalk leading into the store sat a stone marker with a plaque stating, "Here on Retreat from Bemis Heights night October 10, 1777, British Army Parked Artillery." Part of the Battles of Saratoga, the Battle of Bemis Heights is one of two battles between the British Army led by General John Burgoyne and the Continental Army led by General Horatio Gates. Burgoyne would be defeated within a week and surrender on October 17, 1777.

Just across Broad Street rests a second New York State Historical Marker erected in 1927 in front of a middle-class single-family home. The marker explains that this was the site where General Burgoyne camped from October 10 to 17, 1777. In fact, this area has several markers within walking distance, giving it a sort of outdoor-museum feel for the more intrepid strollers or drivers.

Today, looking around the mixed-use neighborhood, consisting of family homes, offices, the Saratoga Town Justice Office, and Stewart's Shops, it can be hard to visualize the once-bucolic farms that were here prior to the American Revolution. It's even more of a stretch to think about thousands of tents, pack animals, soldiers, and their camp followers milling through areas where cars now whizz by and people live and work in tidy homes and offices.

I adjusted my eyes looking from the marker to the cars parked behind it at a series of gas pumps under a carport. It was quite the juxtaposition. I looked over to the one-story beige and white clapboard-style convenience store, noting that it was much nicer than a typical chain store. In fact, Stewart's Shops consists of over 350 convenience stores in New York and Vermont. This one was one of their newer, well-appointed locations featuring stone accents around its foundation, befitting of a more upscale roadside stop.

Oftentimes, sites in the United States that date back to Revolutionary times have changed a lot over the years. Many have been paved over numerous times to make way for modern homes, shops, offices, restaurants, and bus depots. We don't always even see the markers that tell us something historical took place there. I love these historical markers for giving ordinary, modern, and historic places more meaning. Even though new construction is often built over historic sites, a marker's existence shows that people and communities take the initiative to commemorate what was there before. These simple signs give us a window into the past and the people living nearby who are keepers of that history. My trip to Saratoga would reveal a lot about those safeguarding history in this area located about a forty-minute drive north from New York State's capital city of Albany.

I walked down the sidewalk past the marker and stepped inside what looked like a typical convenience store to order ice cream. I had to try what some locals said was rich, creamy, and delicious. Inside I met CEO Bill Dake, who is among the second generation of the Dake family to run Stewart's Shops. Dating back to 1917 when Charles V. Dake and Percy W. Dake took over the Dake family dairy farm in Middle Grove, New York, the family has been in the ice cream business since the 1920s. Through expansions, and the hard times signaled by the stock market crash of 1929, the Dake family eventually amassed a collection of sixty-five locations by 1975. A longtime family enterprise, Stewart's Shops has served up not only a lot of ice cream but has also served our nation.

I would have pegged Bill Dake as much younger than his age, being part of the so-called Silent Generation. He was ordering a double scoop of butter pecan ice cream on a sugar cone from the store's counter, where guests can order milkshakes, ice cream floats, brownie sundaes, and banana splits with enticing flavors like death by chocolate, mint cookie crumble, raspberry fudge torte yogurt, and "brew ha ha." I opted for a double cup of peanut butter pie, which the server told me was "amazing." Being an ice cream connoisseur, I was a bit skeptical of this convenience-store ice cream, but upon first lick, I agreed it was pretty good.

"That has too many inclusions in it," Bill said to me as he took a bite of his butter pecan. "You lose the real flavor of the ice cream."

"I think it's pretty good!"

We both laughed.

"All of the dairy is sourced locally for the ice cream?" I asked.

Bill nodded. "We have twenty-some-odd farms and three thousand cows that are giving milk to our ice cream.

"That's a lot of cows," I remarked.

"And we've got sixty-five thousand chickens making eggs from the various farmers we buy from, so a significant part of the problem is making sure it's all fresh and local."

I hadn't heard of a convenience store chain as vast as this one that worked so hard to source fresh and local, but I started to realize that Stewart's was just a little different.

Bill was wearing a steel blue blazer that accentuated his baby blue eyes and light gray hair swept back on his head. He wore a light stone-colored sweater vest and white button-down with gray khaki pants.

We went outside to talk more, away from the door's dinging and the sounds of kids and families going in and out of the store.

We rounded the corner to sit at a red picnic table under an awning adjacent to the historical marker across the road and next to the stone marker onsite. My ice cream was already beginning to melt, as I ate it in a measured manner, wanting to savor each bite. I asked Bill how his family got into this business.

Bill explained that his brother, who was much older, was a veteran of the Second World War. During the war, many products were rationed both for consumers and businesses. Sugar was the first item rationed and the last to have its rationing lifted. When Bill's brother came home, he started making ice cream. As so much of the country had gone without sweets during the war, the family was able to sell all the ice cream it could make.

Bill's brother had caught onto something: at seven cents for a single scoop, the family was making a profit. Bill continued his story, with only one scoop of ice cream remaining in his cone.

The Dake family first came to the United States in the early 1700s and eventually settled in White Creek, New York, in the mid-1750s. The family experienced the Revolutionary War first-hand, as the Battle of Bennington took place near the family homestead. Whether they wanted to or not, the Dake family witnessed and participated in part of the Revolutionary War.

I'd heard similar stories at sites up and down the Eastern Seaboard. Everyday people were thrust into a war without the luxury of choice, because it literally ended up in their yards.

"The Battle of Bennington was important because it was the turning point of the Saratoga Battles which were the turning point of the entire Revolution. And it wasn't just because the French got involved. All the Americans were not sold on this revolution at that time," Bill said. "So, because of participating in the war, we got a land grant. It's just a few miles from where the dairy is now. My father and uncle were working the farm there, had extra milk, they started making ice cream and built an ice cream plant," Bill said.

"So, the dairy farm has its roots in the American Revolution?" I asked.

"Yes," Bill replied. "With my son, there'll be three generations."

Bill took a big bite of his cone before sharing more about the family's expansion over the years with ice cream, a dairy, specialty products, and, eventually, convenience stores. In the 1970s, this business rooted in Revolutionary-era farming initiated an employee profit-sharing plan. The family later converted the profit-sharing plan to an employee stock-ownership plan in the early 2000s. Today, employees own 40 percent of the company. The family also runs several foundations, donating millions of dollars annually. In 2025, the Dakes donated over $12 million to charitable organizations.

"The long-term role, we're seeing, is as Big Box stores kill most small businesses, we have a very efficient distribution system, warehouse, and plan, and we are the surviving local fresh player that is filling that role," Bill said. "It's a lot of things that were just good luck that turned out to be positive socially but also turned out to be positive financially."

An employee on her work break sitting at a table next to ours piped up to share that Stewart's employee plans also have helped with educational pursuits. Her daughter's college tuition was partially paid for by a company benefit because she worked at Stewart's. Had I been wary of Bill and what he told me about Stewart's Shops, I might have thought that this woman was a plant, but she seemed more like an eager-beaver employee—and one who actually owns part of the company.

I noted that from the American Revolution to modern times, Stewart's has been a story of innovation and transformation from a small dairy farm to a much larger regional business, with employees having a stake in both the business and their community.

Bill went on to explain that his son will be the third generation to run the business but that probably, over time, the family will turn the bulk of Stewart's ownership over to the employees because there won't be additional family members still in the business.

It was amazing to hear how Stewart's started and expanded its business during tumultuous times in American history and has continued to thrive today, led by the Dake family but also through partnering and sharing with the greater regional community.

It was an interesting place to sit for ice cream outside a convenience store by a busy road where most people, truckers included, raced by to get to their next appointment in life. I wondered how many had stopped to read these historic markers or how many had even noticed them during their idle time pumping gas. Maybe if they stopped to grab an ice cream, they'd see that where they were going about their daily business had deep historical roots. Maybe they'd feel the same sense of surprise that I felt at the magnitude and significance of what took place in this seemingly ordinary location.

Downtown Saratoga Springs:
Cannonballs and Carousels

In downtown Saratoga Springs a Beaux-Arts-style bank building was my next stop, with banking joining with a history lesson for those who step inside. The Adirondack Trust Company is located on Broadway in the heart of Saratoga Springs, a charming, even picture-perfect little downtown with independently owned shops, restaurants, hotels, and historic Congress Park with its celebrated wooden carousel. The bank, which is built of marble and was designed to look like a Greek temple, stands out amid neighboring three- and four-story colorful brick buildings. Stepping inside is a feast for the eyes.

Charles Wait was being called down to see me in the main area where tellers and representatives meet with clients for regular banking needs. As I waited, I looked around at the opulent interior. The Adirondack Trust Company was founded in 1902 at this very site. In 1916, as the company had surpassed a few million in deposits, they built the current bank building out of marble at a cost of $100,000. The bank has been preserved pretty much as it was when originally constructed. The front doors, cast in bronze, were made by Tiffany and Company; beneath the words "The Adirondack Trust Company," doors depict scenes of nature from the Adirondacks. Inside, the original 1902 bank vault rests below elaborate gold chandeliers accented with signs of the zodiac around the bottom and topped with statues of bucks with full sets of antlers. The marble bank walls are lined with oil paintings of the generations of the Wait family who have stood at the helm of this powerful community bank.

Charles Wait is the chairman of the board of the Adirondack Trust Company, an independent bank that helped rebuild many of the landmark buildings in downtown Saratoga Springs. Charles walked down the stairs from his office wearing a navy blazer with gold buttons, a navy-and-red-striped tie, dark-rimmed Clark Kent-style glasses, and khaki pants—the epitome of preppy. By contrast, I was casually dressed in jeans and a bright yellow sweater layered with a three-quarter lime green base layer from my previous rail-biking adventure.

I hadn't ventured to this building to hear about banking. I'd come to discover another unusual place to learn about history; right in front of me in the lobby was a long glass case holding a series of armaments with descriptive cards, like what you'd see in a museum. It rested against a short wall in front of the original bank vault.

Charles explained that the musket in the glass case was a British musket that was surrendered at the Battle of Saratoga. Also in the case were several cannonballs that had been buried at the site where the Hessian troops had their artillery positioned near Saratoga. Great Britain had hired Hessian soldiers from several German states in the fight against the American colonies.

I looked closely at the descriptions. There was a Brown Bess musket, surrendered at the Battle of Saratoga along with period sabers on loan from the Masons' Unity Lodge 22 in Greenfield, New York. Two cannonballs rested in one corner of the case, including a Revolutionary War six-pounder Hessian cannonball, apparently not fired and recovered on top of Mill Creek Hill, the site of Hessian Captain Georg Päusch's artillery company.

The cannonballs were part of Charles Wait's personal collection, and he explained that they were found long ago when a farmer's plow hit them. The farmer's widow had collected and saved them. Charles purchased the cannonballs from the widow, which is how they ended up being safeguarded in this case in the bank.

"It's like you're banking with a bonus. You have a little museum in the bank," I exclaimed, not having seen anything exactly like this before.

Charles replied, "We do; we do! Anybody can walk in. You don't have to be a customer to walk in. You do have to be a customer to get money out!"

Around the corner from the lobby was a waiting area and hallway where more artifacts were on display. Charles and I rounded the bend to see the presentation silver service, which was used aboard two different ships named the USS *Saratoga*, after the Battles of Saratoga. The community came together to purchase this set now on display at the bank. Individuals gave as little as twenty-five cents in the late 1920's. When the last one was decommissioned in 1994, this silver treasure came home to the community.

I asked Charles how it feels to be working in the same bank where his father and grandfather and now his son also work—a bank that is so intertwined with the Saratoga community, both past and present.

"We try our best to be very supportive of the community because it's a symbiotic relationship where you have to help each other," Charles said. "It's not unique, but it's rare and people appreciate it. You mentioned Hattie's Restaurant earlier in our conversation. You know, there's any number of businesses that have been around for multiple generations in Saratoga, and it's because of that feeling of community and that feeling that we need to support each other. I mean, you don't find that everywhere."

I nodded in agreement. I was thinking about the many places we have visited, where communities come together to help each other, which made me feel pretty good.

Mixed in with the artifacts housed in this museum within the bank is artwork created by local artists, sharing history and creativity in a space that could just be a bank—but is so much more.

Outside the bank, I walked along Broadway to find other reminders of history mixed with modern surroundings. Saratoga Springs emerged in the early 1800s because of its mineral springs, which were thought to provide health benefits. In Congress Park, a few blocks from the Adirondack Trust Bank, you can see and taste those very springs that made the town so famous. I stopped at a fountain under a gazebo that still gurgles next to historic Canfield Casino. Horses and healing waters are a big part of Saratoga's past and present. Home to one of the oldest horse-racing venues in the nation, the Saratoga Race Course has been hosting races since 1864 and is still drawing large numbers of visitors to the city.

I used a cup to try a small amount of the famous waters, which tasted metallic and a bit minerally to me. The tastes vary by spring, but they can all be unusual to those who aren't quite used to them.

My next adventures in Saratoga would reveal more hidden gems. At the Saratoga Sword Surrender Site, I'd get to know Lauren Roberts, Saratoga County's historian. With a community so centered on preserving its history, I wasn't surprised to find that the Saratoga County historian wasn't just preserving the past, she was actively digging it up to find forgotten stories. Lauren would shed light on a woman of the past whose story is another Revolutionary tale that's lesser known.

Saratoga Sword Surrender Site:
Lady Riedesel's Witness

While many stories of American Revolution battles, triumphs, and defeats center around the logistics of what happened, I am always interested to learn how we even know the many details related to these events. They occurred so long ago. How were the various details from this history pieced together—and what didn't make it into the history books? The untold stories often reveal a more detailed and nuanced account and provide texture and additional context that further explain what happened, why it happened, and how it affected ordinary people.

Lauren Roberts met me at the Saratoga Sword Surrender Site. It was here that on October 17, 1777, British General John Burgoyne handed over his sword to American General Horatio Gates. This British surrender sent shock waves around the world. Benjamin Franklin was one of many notable people who celebrated the victory in France as evidence of American staying power in the fight for independence. This surrender at Saratoga was a turning point that would help to persuade French King Louis XVI to make a landmark commitment to ally with the American states, providing financial support, manpower, and munitions—critical in the road to American independence.

If you ask a local in Saratoga, they will tell you that the Battles of Saratoga were the crucial turning point in the American Revolution. Having filmed up and down the East Coast and discussed the American Revolution with locals and historians for many years now, I can tell you that many people believe that their region lays claim to the "turning point." It's a bit of a competitive topic, but I am convinced that the Battles of Saratoga and the surrender by the British most definitely changed the course of the Revolution and the world.

I parked near a series of interpretive signs at the Saratoga Sword Surrender Site to meet with Saratoga County Historian Lauren Roberts, who I thought could pass for my sister. With thick, long red hair and a smattering of freckles on her face and hands, this young mother and historian has a striking appearance and even more noticeably, a poised demeanor. Lauren has made waves and grabbed headlines as a historian, podcaster, and researcher. She met me at the Surrender Site wearing a maroon wool jacket and colorful yet muted patterned scarf. Her autumnal look was complete with a knee-length jean skirt and high brown leather boots, with her wavy red hair tied back halfway.

I looked over to see Lauren's finely put-together fall ensemble and grabbed a hat that I'd just purchased from the downtown and women-owned Hatsational shop to spice up my fall look. Often when I'm traveling, my schedule is tight. I'm hopping from rail biking to a James Beard restaurant in a matter of minutes. Having attended an all-girls boarding school, I was trained early on to be a quick-change artist, but spending almost two decades on the road filmmaking has made me even faster.

The parking lot at this site is easily accessible for those seeking to make their way to the monument's overlook with a paved sidewalk that curves through the memorial park and passes a bronze bas-relief of artist John Trumbull's painting *The Surrender of General Burgoyne*. The oil painting *The Surrender of General Burgoyne* hangs in the Rotunda of the United States Capitol. The bronze relief at the Surrender Site overlooks the Hudson River and Route 4, just one mile south of Schuylerville, and about a four-minute drive straight down Route 4 from Stewart's Shops on Broad Street.

The Surrender Site also has two reproduction six-pounder cannons, the type that General Burgoyne surrendered. Thirty bronze artillery pieces were captured by the Continental Army, including twelve light six-pounders. The Continental Army would turn this artillery against the British for the rest of the war.

Lauren and I walked down the sidewalk towards the cannons and overlook, passing a large marble marker with a bronze plaque recognizing many of those in the community who preserved the site.

The Saratoga Sword Surrender Site was privately owned until the early 2000s when it was listed for sale. In 2006, New York state Senator Roy McDonald and New York state Assemblyman Steven Englebright sponsored efforts to have the state of New York fund and help preserve the site with the Open Space Institute, an organization that has worked since the 1970s on preservation and conservation efforts with the mission of making lands also more open to the public to enjoy. Locals in Saratoga once again banded together to fundraise and secure grants to establish the monument and Saratoga Sword Surrender Site, which is now part of Saratoga National Historical Park.

The victory at Saratoga was decisive, and it greatly impacted the morale of the British. With it came Louis XVI recognizing the United States as an independent nation and coming aboard as an ally, providing military support with troops who played a major role in the eventual victory of the United States.

Lauren explained that the Convention of Saratoga was the formal agreement that specified the terms of surrender by the British forces. The Continental Congress in Philadelphia didn't ratify the agreement, fearing the British wouldn't honor it. They wanted the British to recognize the independence of the United States, but the British were not ready to enter into this formal agreement. Thus, Burgoyne's army became prisoners. For years, they were shuffled to different areas in the states as prisoners of war. They were referred to as the Convention Army.

Lauren noted that tens of thousands of observers saw the surrender of almost six thousand British and German troops. Much of what we know about what happened comes from journals and letters, including a journal from a baroness who wrote an account of the surrender. As we approached the monument, I began to read the quotations lining the memorial. There was one from a Massachusetts militiaman, another from Major General Horatio Gates, and another from a British lieutenant, but one stood out to me.

"I was comforted to notice that nobody glanced at us insultingly…and some of them even looked with pity to see a woman with small children there. I confess that I was afraid to go to the enemy, as it was an entirely new experience for me." Lady Frederika Riedesel, wife of Burgoyne's German commander.

Lauren told me that we are lucky to have Lady Frederika Riedesel's firsthand account of the surrender memorialized in her own words. Frederika Charlotte Louise Riedesel was, perhaps by her very upbringing, somewhat prepared for being on the sidelines and frontlines of the war in America. She had grown up in Germany where her father was a lieutenant general in the Prussian Army. In 1762, she married Baron Friedrich Adolph Riedesel. He was an officer. Wishing to keep her family together following the birth of a third daughter, she traveled to Britain, where she learned English. She hoped to join her husband across the ocean, but her mother disapproved of her plan. She eventually made it to Canada with her children in tow and was reunited with her husband in June of 1777. She would then, in her simple carriage, join General Burgoyne's army in their trek towards Albany, ending up in the Saratoga area in the middle of the war's chaos.

Lauren explained that Lady Riedesel had to hide in a house that still stands in Schuylerville. The Baroness, then about thirty years old, and her three children—all under the age of six—hid in the basement of the house. Her writings provide a firsthand account of the horrors of war, including hearing cannonballs hitting the house and witnessing wounded soldiers being brought inside.

The Baroness wrote a very detailed account of her time leading up to and in Saratoga and throughout the war. They included letters that she would eventually publish more than a decade after returning home to Germany. A translated version of Frederika's journal was published as *Baroness von Riedesel and the American Revolution: Journal and Correspondence of a Tour of Duty, 1776–1783* by the University of North Carolina Press, who called it "the most detailed account of the Revolutionary era by a woman reporter." Other reviews also called out the great value of Riedesel's accounts.

This is the only known account of the war by the wife of a German soldier. More than one-third of the British fighting force at Saratoga was made up of Germans. These trained troops were hired and paid for by the British and hailed from Braunschweig and Hessen-Hanau.

Lauren expressed that reading the Baroness's letters in her own words made the story relatable as a mother. It made her internalize what she had to endure keeping her three young children safe amid the mayhem, all the while missing and worrying about her husband out on the battlefield.

"In her diary, she talks about how worried she was for her husband's safety. I'm sure you can imagine. You know, what would she do if he died?" Lauren asked. "And she was here in a foreign country with three young kids. So, her story is really important. That's one of those underrepresented stories, but from a female perspective—she can be thought of as an early female war correspondent. It's nice to have these stories that she was able to tell in her own words, so that nobody else must tell her story for her."

I found it fascinating that we have these detailed firsthand accounts from so long ago. Lauren agreed and told me that the Baroness was better off than other women who were traveling with the British and Hessian forces. She apparently had a calash, or small carriage, and maid servants. Lauren explained that many of the other women and children traveling with British Army were out in the cold and starving from a lack of rations. I know how cold it can be in October in upstate New York; being at the Surrender Site with Lauren and seeing the Baroness's words immortalized on the monument gave me goose bumps.

Between three thousand and five thousand women are believed to have traveled with British forces at one point or another during the War of Independence, and perhaps twenty thousand women and children followed the American troops over the course of the war. Exact counts are hard to pinpoint. These women were known as camp followers and often nursed the wounded and sick, washed clothes and cleaned, and cooked meals—necessities of daily life and life at war. Written accounts depict the hardships these women faced.

I like to think the Baroness followed her husband for love, and scholars have conjectured this to be true based on her correspondence. Given the period, it also highly likely that she followed from a sense of duty, necessity, and the drive to keep her family united during times of uncertainty. Regardless, we often think of soldiers and their great courage during war. Women like Lady Riedesel also displayed leadership, bravery, and tenacity in the face of war's cruel injustices.

> *At 2 o'clock, we heard again a report of muskets and cannon, and there was much alarm and bustle among our troops. My husband sent me word, that I should immediately retire into a house which was not far off. I got into my calash with my children, and when we were near the house, I saw, on the opposite bank of the Hudson, five or six men, who aimed at us with their guns. Without knowing what I did, I threw my children into the back part of the vehicle, and laid myself upon them.*

Lauren provided additional details about the end of the Baroness's story, which would lead me to our next location with more Saratoga surprises.

Baroness Riedesel wrote about coming to the Surrender Site and how afraid she was to travel through the American camp. There she met Philip J. Schuyler, a distinguished Revolutionary War general, and he helped her children down from the carriage. Her writings noted that he must have been a father because he was very kind to them and she really was surprised how friendly the Americans were when she finally met them.

Saratoga National Historical Park: Unlikely Heroes and Villains

Lady Riedesel led me to another unlikely hero of the American Revolution at the Schuyler House in Schuylerville, New York. Part of Saratoga National Historical Park and east of Saratoga

Springs, the Schuyler House was the country home of Philip Schuyler, the prominent American general and member of the first United States Senate. The Schuyler house dates to 1777 and was built to replace the one that the British had burned during their retreat following the Battles of Saratoga.

Had the home not been burned, it might have been the location that General Schuyler opened to General Burgoyne, the Baroness, and three children following their surrender. Instead, General Schuyler invited them to his home in Albany and the family obliged. The Baroness wrote that she was surprised at this hospitality, given the circumstances.

Rebuilt in 1777 in only thirty-seven days, today the Schuyler House rests on a large lawn surrounded by a smattering of trees. You can tour this house on your visit to this national park site. It's a peaceful, quiet setting, much different than it would have been in the late eighteenth century. It seemed a good place to learn more about Schuyler's personality and daily life in a home in New York state during Revolutionary times. This, though, was no ordinary country home, having been visited by many famous figures, including George Washington, the Marquis de Lafayette, and Alexander Hamilton, who married General Schuyler's daughter Elizabeth Schuyler on December 14, 1780, at the Schuyler family home in Albany, New York.

I was lucky to have Ranger Garrett Cloer guide me on my visit. His account of life at this working estate paints a greater picture of those who served during the war. Ranger Cloer led me to the Schuyler family kitchen, the center of life for the enslaved people who lived on the estate. Attached to the main house today, it was previously one of the outbuildings. Ranger Cloer was wearing his National Park Service uniform with its gray shirt, gold badge and arrowhead patch, and olive drab trousers as he guided me into the kitchen with its large fireplace and low wood-beam ceiling.

Like many families at this time, the Schuyler family depended on enslaved people to help run their estate. The enslaved cleared land, harvested crops, fished, worked in the mills and fields, and milked cows. In 1790, the Schuyler family reported having fourteen enslaved persons on their country estate in addition to another thirteen held at their mansion house in Albany.

Though there were free Blacks in New York state at the time of the Revolution, they comprised only 2.4 percent of the overall population and about 10 percent of the African-descended population. As the American Revolution forged on, the numbers of enslaved people in New York multiplied. Many men of African descent also served as soldiers on both sides, fighting in racially integrated armies. Enslaved people were sometimes drafted to fight as substitutes for their owners, while free Black men also enlisted. Indeed, slavery was not abolished in the state until 1827.

"It's important to remember or to understand that all people of African descent in the colonies and here in New York were not enslaved. The estate here has a very close tie with one of those people. His English name was Louis Cook," said Ranger Cloer.

Joseph Louis Cook was born to an African American father and a Saint-François Abenaki mother in Saratoga. At a young age, he and his mother were taken captive during a French-Mohawk raid and taken to Canada, where Cook grew up with a Mohawk family. He would go on to fight with the Mohawk, becoming a leader in the French and Indian War on the side of the French, who were at war with Great Britain. During the American Revolution, Cook would join the fight siding with the Americans. He would travel and meet multiple times with

George Washington, as well as Philip Schuyler and John Adams, in addition to traveling to Québec with Benedict Arnold. He would also venture to Valley Forge in the winter of 1777. Stories recount his fierceness as a fighter and his ability to speak fluent French, as well as English and Oneida. In 1779, Congress awarded Cook with a commission as a colonel in the Continental Army, the only person of African descent to get such an honor and one of the highest-ranking officers of native descent.

Ranger Cloer noted that at the time, Louis Cook would have viewed himself, as did others, as a Native American ally. Only later did we learn of his mixed background. In his time, he understood how to work the levers of power with the Revolutionary authorities; his military rank testified to his drive and intelligence.

I agreed and wanted to know more about Cook. He surely must have been a charismatic and interesting man.

"I think anywhere you look in American history, you can find characters like that who would be hugely popular if their stories were told," Ranger Cloer said.

These are the stories that you don't get to hear or read about every day. That's why coming to a historical site like this and being able to speak with people who have done the research and know the history well is so rewarding. If we are all able to see more of ourselves and each other in America's founding, perhaps we will feel more invested in a shared future.

Inside the Schuyler House's first-floor hallway, there's a copy of *The Death of General Montgomery in the Attack on Quebec, December 31, 1775* by artist John Trumbull hanging on the wall. This painting features General Richard Montgomery at the Battle of Quebec along with Louis Cook, Colonel Louis, with a tomahawk raised in a depiction of the Revolutionary War event. Trumbull also penciled a sketch portrait of Cook in 1785.

I went to the Schuyler House to learn more about General Schuyler's personality and left knowing more about a hero, Louis Cook, whose name isn't as recognizable as Schuyler's, but has great meaning for our nation. Americans come from all over the world, and the story of America's founding is influenced by that tapestry of peoples.

Ranger Cloer would also take me into the area of Saratoga National Historical Park where the Battles of Saratoga were fought. This is about a fifteen-minute drive from the Schuyler House. It's here that you can see and learn about the landscapes where two major Revolutionary War battles occurred and where American troops would secure a significant victory against the British Army.

The visitor's center at the northwest corner of the Saratoga Battlefield welcomes travelers. I was ready to hike through the park, wearing jeans, hiking boots, and a button-down long-sleeved shirt. I walked from the parking lot to meet Ranger Cloer inside, where he was to point out several of the more interesting artifacts on display. This included artillery surrendered by the British at the Battles, including one of three surviving six-pounder cannons. These cannons are so named because they could shoot a solid iron cannonball that weighed six pounds. A glass case also housed two trophy cannons weighing 2,400 pounds and engraved with the words "Surrendered by the Convention." I couldn't imagine an artillery crew trying to pull one of these massive cannons through the ravines and rugged terrain just outside.

The visitors center had an exhibition entitled *Warrior Children*, sharing information about the required militia service for teenagers, starting at age fifteen or sixteen. I learned about twelve-year-old George Williams, who was commissioned as an ensign, the most junior commissioned officer rank, under General John Burgoyne. He went on to be a prisoner of war and later became a lieutenant. As an adult, he became a member of Parliament in Great Britain. Other young militiamen weren't so lucky.

Following a tour of the visitor center, we stepped outside onto the battlefield. Walking to an open spot not far away to view the terrain, I noticed a grave marker amid the grass dated September 1987 "in memory of unknown soldiers reinterred here."

Noticing me looking at the grave marker, Ranger Cloer explained, "We consider most of the areas that we're going to go hallowed ground. Soldiers were not typically moved to cemeteries; they were buried where they fell or nearby."

We also saw a plaque mounted on a rock memorializing Brigadier General Simon Fraser, a British officer killed at the Battle of Bemis Heights, also known as the second Battle of Saratoga, which occurred on the morning of October 7, 1777. Ranger Cloer told me that there have been numerous archaeological digs here to learn more about the past through recovered artifacts.

We walked past a cannon to look over at the edge of the hill to see where the Battles of Saratoga took place. It was an overcast day and, in the distance, the leaves on a few trees were just starting to turn red. Yellow wildflowers lined the top of the hill, and I could imagine that at peak fall season the colors here would be beautiful. In the distance, we could see the mountains of Vermont. A group of vocal geese flew by, reminding me that it would be winter soon.

"Standing here, I think you can get a really good idea of why the battle took place in this location…. The high ground is on the far side of the river," Ranger Cloer said, pointing to the distance. "That's what forced General Burgoyne to bring his soldiers over to this side of the river in the first place. They crossed about eight miles north of here. If you look through that gap in the trees, that's Freeman's Farm. That's where the first Battle of Saratoga took place and where the British would build their largest fortification after the first battle at the top of the hill. Off to the left, that is where the Germans built their camp."

The two battles were fought on September 19 and October 7. Ranger Cloer explained that the cold weather and hard rain were factors in the October battle, but the topography, too, played a large role in the military strategy and outcome. While the American forces may have not had the training that the Germans and British did, they had the elements on their side.

I knew this to be true from my time in the South, where the swamps and rugged interior of South Carolina in particular proved difficult for the British soldiers. The Americans had home-turf advantage, with many knowing their terrain, the insects, and other obstacles that could be challenges but also could work to their advantage.

"When we fast-forward to the second Battle of Saratoga on October 7, we have that location falling to a group of American soldiers led by Benedict Arnold," said Ranger Cloer, mentioning a name that is infamous for most Americans, even for those who know little about history. "He went around the side of the defense and got behind them, forcing the Germans to run away. Once the Americans held that position, the British forces here could not stay on the battlefield. And that's what led to them beginning to try to retreat to the north a couple of days later."

There are many stories to uncover at Saratoga National Historical Park, but I was curious about Benedict Arnold. I had already heard about a monument that I would need to visit while here, but first we would take a five-minute drive to another section of the park to see the Neilson House, Benedict Arnold's divisional headquarters and Enoch Poor's brigade headquarters during the battles. The house would serve as the nerve center for their planning and operations to defeat the British soldiers.

The small red wooden home is the oldest and only surviving structure on the battlefield, dating from 1775, though it has since been restored. It was the family home of a young couple, John and Lydia Neilson, before they evacuated after hearing that the British were coming down the valley towards them. Ranger Cloer described it as the setting for drama with its location at the western end of the American defensive line. From the porch, you could look out and see stakes of the western end of the American defensive line, which ran down to the river to Bemis Heights.

We stepped from the gray wood plank flooring on the covered porch through the front door of the one-room farmhouse with its attic loft. Inside, the room is set up to look as it did when used as a command center, with a portable wooden writing desk topped with quill pens and an ink bottle for documents that would have relayed vital military communications and decisions. Soldiers' cots line the walls next to a stone fireplace. The headquarters would have been surrounded by thousands of American soldiers encamped in the area. With the small interior and crowded setting, it surely would have made for a tense environment.

Further on we ventured to a monument in the park which has an unusual story and one that people vie to see: the Boot Monument. At the end of the Battles of Saratoga, Benedict Arnold was badly wounded, suffering from a shot through his leg. Having had an ankle injury and surgery myself following a train accident in Hungary (a story for another time), I can tell you that it can be quite painful. I couldn't imagine the pain Arnold faced from a musket ball shattering his leg. Arnold was on horseback, and his horse was killed in the incident. Arnold lay pinned under this dying horse. In similar cases, Arnold's leg would have been amputated, but the general refused this treatment. He recuperated, but the devastating injury would plague him thereafter.

We were walking along the path where Arnold was wounded by a musket ball and looked over the gate at the stone monument with the outline of a tall boot wrapped in a laurel-leaf wreath lying over a howitzer barrel. The monument, which does not mention Arnold by name, symbolizes that a major general was wounded in the leg, right above his left ankle, in this area.

The reverse of the monument is inscribed with the following quote: "In memory of the most brilliant soldier of the Continental Army who was desperately wounded on this spot, the sally port of Burgoyne's great [western] redoubt 7th October 1777 winning for his countrymen the decisive battle of the American Revolution and for himself the rank of Major General."

Ranger Cloer went on to tell me the rest of Arnold's story that he is now better known for.

Following Saratoga, Arnold was sent to Philadelphia to stabilize the city after British occupation. Soured from his experiences, Arnold ultimately became a turncoat and sided with the British. He eventually led British forces against the American militia.

"He gets injured here, sent to Philadelphia, and then goes on to conspire against the army. He gets a choice. General Washington, who loves Benedict Arnold, said, 'You can have any command you want, any field army that you'd like to command,' and he says, 'I'd like to have West Point,' which I think should have sent up some red flags for this aggressive field commander who had made his reputation taking chances on the battlefield to decide he wanted to command a fort," Cloer says. "A lot of people have said they wished that Benedict Arnold would have died instead of only having been wounded here because he would have gone down as one of the great American heroes."

But then history wouldn't be the same, I thought. It was interesting to me that the Boot Monument was erected in 1887 without Benedict Arnold's name. It was as if 110 years later, people were conflicted, wanting to honor his valor and significance in winning at Saratoga, a defining turning point, but knowing the end of the story would be an "about face."

It's another instance of how examining not just monuments, but their conception and context, tells us more about history. What people were thinking at the time they conceived and erect a monument tells us a lot about that period. This thought was brought home once again in Saratoga National Historical Park at Saratoga Monument, just a short drive away from the Boot Monument.

Saratoga Monument: Truth and Storytelling in Stone

Saratoga Monument is located at the site where General Burgoyne surrendered his army numbering six thousand soldiers. The monument rests on a bluff about eight miles from the battlefield in the town of Victory and just a few minutes' drive from General Schuyler's home. After the Battles of Saratoga, British and American soldiers camped in the area and fired on each other numerous times before Burgoyne finally surrendered. The monument was completed in 1883, before the Boot Monument, which would be erected four years later.

Ranger Cloer explained how the monument came to be, as we walked among gravestones on a wooded path in Prospect Hill Cemetery.

"The Civil War had just happened. There's this great interest in commemorating the American Revolution and the heroes that had won American independence. This is partially a project to heal some of those wounds from the end of the war. This monument, I think, really shows the efforts that those nineteenth-century Americans were making to honor people."

I noticed the bronze statues nestled in porticos of the imposing granite obelisk. There were three statues honoring prominent American commanders: Colonel Daniel Morgan, General Philip Schuyler, and General Horatio Gates. We were looking up at the outside of the almost 155-foot monument with its various Gothic and Egyptian elements. Saratoga Monument stands on a higher patch of grassy land, not far from the road or parking lot. Sidewalks lead up to and around the obelisk.

There was an empty portico on the side of the monument, where a statue to Benedict Arnold would have been placed. But here, Arnold was snubbed and scrubbed from the historical record. This monument came to fruition from a community effort in Saratoga, a running theme of this community where, throughout history, people have valued examining and commemorating the past.

In 1859, residents created the Saratoga Monument Association. It wasn't until 1872, following the Civil War, that they would decide to create the unusual Saratoga Monument to commemorate the centennial of Burgoyne's surrender. Designed by architect Jared C. Markham and the Booth Brothers of New York

City, they laid the cornerstone on the one hundredth anniversary of the American victory at Saratoga, but it would take many years and a lot of fundraising and partners to bring the monument to fruition.

The timing of the initial thought to build the monument made sense. As anniversaries come up, people tend to think about and reflect on moments of the past. Ranger Cloer provided some additional reasons that the monument was commissioned in the 1870s.

"We have immigration picking up and some of these groups thinking it's very important to reinforce American values for new folks who are coming into the country. And this idea of not just commemorating the battles, but also really pointing out the American Revolution as the beginning of all of this, as sort of a wellspring of these American values that they felt should be perpetuated."

"It's such a striking monument," I said. "It actually reminds me a bit of the Washington Monument."

Ranger Cloer agreed, explaining that nineteenth-century Americans loved obelisks and saw themselves as heirs to these ancient Roman and ancient Greek political ideals. This same admiration for their political ideas also applied to architecture, and that view was infused in the early years of our country as well.

It was a blue-bird-sky fall day as we stood in the grass under the shade of trees and surrounded by Revolutionary-era gravesites, examining the monument erected over a hundred years after the war ended. In recent years, we've seen an onslaught of monuments coming down across the nation with other monuments topping lists of the most controversial for various reasons. Mount Rushmore was designed by an artist with ties to the Ku Klux Klan on lands seized from the Sioux tribe in South Dakota. Atlanta's

Stone Mountain commemorates Confederate President Jefferson Davis and generals Robert E. Lee and Stonewall Jackson.

I wondered what we could learn from the Saratoga Monument, conspicuously missing one major general of the Battles of Saratoga.

"What can monuments like this teach us about how we might want to look at times of history like the American Revolution?" I asked Ranger Cloer.

"On one level, they do remind us of the sacrifices of people at the time and of their accomplishments, but they also tell us even more about the people who made them. This is not an eighteenth-century artifact. This is a nineteenth-century artifact. You can go inside and find depictions of events from the American Revolution that didn't happen, but they were chosen to tell a particular story about what those later Americans thought was important about the earlier period and what they thought their contemporaries and the future folks who would come here would take away from it."

It took me a minute to process what Ranger Cloer was saying. I stood staring at the monument, nodding, and then asked:

"But okay, so what's inside that's not accurate?"

Ranger Cloer laughed as he motioned me inside. It seemed a strange response to my question, but inside the monument, I would come to understand.

Travelers can go inside the Saratoga Monument and climb 188 steps to a viewing platform at the top, looking out to the Hudson River, area homes, and Victory Woods. From the ground floor and second-story platform, you can view bronze bas relief plaques of various scenes along with text describing each one.

Walking into the Saratoga Monument, I was taken aback by the elaborate interiors. I looked up to the rounded brick ceiling above to a colorful tiny red, blue, and orange stained-glass window and terracotta cornices. There were sixteen bronze bas relief plaques with various intricate scenes.

I homed in on one entitled "Women of the Revolution" that depicted a woman holding a rifle at the forefront and the following description: "industrious, self-denying, frugal: clothing and feeding themselves and their families and giving aid and comfort to an army of defense."

Wow, I thought. These Revolutionary women were no slouches!

Another plaque showed Catherine Schuyler, Philip Schuyler's wife, burning their wheat crops to keep them from being harvested by the British. This event didn't happen. The couple was in Albany before the British even arrived in Saratoga. There were also depictions of some fanciful causes of the Revolution. Those reasons were not true but were perhaps included because they better resonated with nineteenth-century Americans.

"Why," I asked, looking sideways at Ranger Cloer, "did they do that?"

"In some ways, the made-up stories are a lot more fun," Ranger Cloer said. "We have idle British ladies making their husbands tax the poor colonies. You have industrious American women sacrificing for their defense. We have Mrs. Schuyler over in the corner burning down the family's wheat fields. These stories illustrate American ideals of sacrifice to the cause—that people in the nineteenth century considered to be of utmost importance."

He was right. Good stories and storytelling are often the best way to get across a point or message. The Saratoga Monument Association, though potentially well-intentioned, was basically lying about the past.

I just hope that travelers and people today who decide to step inside Saratoga Monument understand that some of these Revolutionary War scenes are not accurate!

As I speak with experts, historians and scholars, I find it valuable to hear their broader thoughts on historic occurrences of the time, so I asked Ranger Cloer for his perspective.

"What can we learn from looking back at the American Revolution?"

"I think we can see sacrifice, the value of personal sacrifice, the value of collective sacrifice. We can see people working together to create something larger than them. We can see people arguing about what the meaning of what they were building was going to be and what that was going to look like. These were people that had very, very different opinions and they argued and they fought about them. They came up with compromises that enabled the country to take off. And nobody got everything they wanted out of it. They had to give things up. But they were able to do that. They were willing to work together to build something."

It was like so many things in life related to careers, relationships, and family. The choices we make individually and with others aren't always perfect. To make it all work requires compromise. This was how America was built. It is how the United States grew despite our imperfections on the way to create a more perfect union.

CHAPTER IV

South Carolina—Echoes Beneath the Pines in Camden

Camden Battlefield: The Fallen Found Again

"**W**hen you look at the trees out here at this battlefield, every one of them represents an unmarked grave," said Rick Wise. "This is hallowed ground."

Former soldier and military historian Rick Wise and I had stopped walking to stare at the tall, thin longleaf pine trees at Camden Battlefield, located in the woods by South Carolina's oldest inland city, Camden. My cowboy boots sunk into the sandy trail, which was lined with a carpet of brown pine needles and dotted with pinecones the size of a large, outstretched hand. Mosquitoes buzzed annoyingly under the brim of my light blue baseball cap. They were like tiny missiles aiming for the whites of my eyes.

Over the past year, I had been navigating the interior of the Carolinas at wooded battlefields, swamps, and small towns as I documented historical sites related to the American Revolution. Growing up in South Carolina, I was well attuned to life in the state along the coast, but not the interior. I was finding the muggy swamps and buggy forests that Francis Marion, otherwise known as the Swamp Fox, trudged through were much harsher than the breezy beaches I remember from my childhood. You may remember Francis Marion, the Patriot hero of the American Revolution, known for his knowledge of South Carolina's terrain and guerrilla warfare tactics, from my Charleston chapter. It had been a long time since I'd lived at the beach or in South Carolina, as I had traded the ocean for New York City's skyscrapers years ago.

We felt far from downtown Camden at the battlefield, though sounds of traffic and the buzz of mosquitoes occasionally interrupted this seemingly quiet, wooded location. While the traffic noise and bugs were not ideal, their annoyances paled in comparison to the day of the battle, when intense smoke filled the air at dawn as General Horatio Gates's 3,700 American soldiers and more than 2,200 British forces under General Charles Cornwallis met head-to-head in Camden. The August 16, 1780 battle was a decisive British win and was riddled with American causalities.

Rick and I were walking down a sandy path not far from the interpretive entrance signs, which are located by a wooden split-rail fence lining Flat Rock Road. The same road saw British troops moving along at a quick pace on August 15. American soldiers made their way towards the British troops more slowly, many tired and ill from eating poor rations and a mixture of molasses, bad bread, and raw meat, which did them no favors, and bogged down by a miles-long trail of baggage wagons behind them. Their journey took them along part of the Great Wagon

Road. During the chaotic retreat after the battle on the 16th, the road north of the battle was choked with American wagons, which added to the drama.

Rick was dressed for the great outdoors, wearing old hiking boots, khaki tactical pants, and a black short-sleeved button-down shirt, made of that moisture-wicking fabric that also included sunscreen and bug repellant. It was late May in South Carolina, when the weather is not brutally hot, but humid enough that it can cause you to sweat after spending a few minutes outside. Rick's black baseball cap was embroidered with a Camden Burials emblem, honoring what many call America's First Veterans. Wearing all black on his top half accentuated his large blue eyes, which seemed to pierce through the still air.

Rick pointed to small white flags protruding from the ground on thin metal rods. They marked burial sites. They blew in the breeze among the sandy soil, interspersed with a sprinkling of pine needles and patches of small white wildflowers.

"Over here are the graves of five Continental soldiers who were buried together. I can envision these guys probably back-to-back, protecting each other as they tried to fight off the British attack, until they all went down. And then they were buried in a common grave. The sacrifice they made was remarkable," Rick said. "A lot of our independence and liberty that we have today was the result of the sacrifice of these five men that were recovered here at the battlefield at Camden."

Rick spoke with conviction, but occasionally his voice seemed to quiver. I couldn't tell at first if it was his natural voice or if he was getting emotional. I quickly realized that it was the latter.

Recent archaeological excavations at Camden Battlefield have revealed more about the hundreds of soldiers buried here. Major General Horatio Gates commanded the American troops. He had also been called a hero for winning the Battles of Saratoga. It was Gates's effort to try to push the British troops under General Cornwallis's command back into Charleston. Part of what's called the Southern Campaign, the British thought that if they could take the South, it would give them the rich agricultural colonies and isolate the middle colonies and the northeast. They hadn't fully appreciated the harsh conditions of South Carolina's backcountry, the areas fifty miles and further inland from the coast. Though the difficult terrain would eventually cause the British soldiers much turmoil, it was the Americans who would be badly defeated. In fact, the Battle of Camden would be one of the worst tactical defeats of an American army during the American Revolution.

Some of the most significant battles during the American Revolution were fought in South Carolina, including the battle near Camden, which was established as a town in 1732. Originally called Pine Tree Hill in 1733, it was later renamed to honor Charles Pratt, the First Earl Camden, who was a British supporter of the American colonialists.

Following the siege and capture of Charleston in the spring of 1780, General Cornwallis marched his soldiers to Camden to establish their main supply headquarters. Located about thirty-five miles northeast of the state's capital city of Columbia, during the American Revolution Camden became a garrison for the British.

"We're trying to return this battlefield to the longleaf pine forest that was native to this area," Rick explained. "A lot of the undergrowth you see here is not what was here at the battlefield. At the time of the battle, you had these tall, unbelievably majestic longleaf pine trees that were over one hundred feet tall."

I looked up the reddish, scaly bark of a tall tree to its canopy topped with long needles. The longleaf pine is native to the Southeastern United States, growing in sandy, dry soil like that found in the Camden area. Camden is home to a longleaf pine preserve, where growth of these endangered trees is being fostered. Once covering almost ninety million acres from southeastern Virginia to Florida, these special pines now cover less than 3 percent of their original land according to the National Wildlife Federation. This fact reminded me of the vast Midwest prairies in Illinois, which are now just a fraction of their original size. In the case of longleaf pines, their value as a resource along with a lack of conservation would lead to their near demise as early settlers clear-cut areas for agriculture and farming, and loggers harvested the trees to use as lumber to build ships and railroads.

Rick and I walked toward the large gray monument honoring Baron DeKalb. one of the most influential foreign officers who fought on behalf of the Americans during the war. The monument is located amid landscaping covered with small stones lining a granite frame in which a small American flag was placed. The etching noted: "Baron DeKalb, mortally wounded on this spot at the Battle of Camden August 16, 1780."

The Daughters of the American Revolution are active historical preservationists. Their Hobkirk Chapter placed the monument there in the early 1900s. They also held the original few acres that would go on to form the preserved battlefield, which now is around eight hundred acres in size.

Rick shared the story of DeKalb, a German by birth who had fought for the French and accompanied the Marquis de Lafayette on his journey to America. At the Battle of Camden, DeKalb commanded the Maryland Division, troops from Delaware and

Maryland. He was mortally wounded here, along with his horse, who was shot from under him early in the battle.

"All the firsthand accounts said that Baron DeKalb was the bravest of the brave," Rick explained. "He had a saber wound on his head that was dressed, and he fought on foot with his sword in hand. Some reports say he killed as many as three British soldiers. On that day, Baron DeKalb was mortally wounded. He had a total of eleven wounds. He had three gunshot wounds and eight bayonet or saber wounds."

The memorial, placed by the Daughters of the American Revolution in 1909, marks the spot where a tree once stood that the wounded Baron DeKalb was laid against before being taken prisoner by the British. As Rick recounted the stories of individual soldiers who fought at Camden Battlefield, I could tell he'd personally studied each of their lives, poring over as much source material as he was able to find.

I didn't have to wonder why Rick was so invested in learning the history of these men. He could see himself in these stories and those of his fellow soldiers. Rick served over twenty-three years in the United States Army Field Artillery and fought in Desert Storm and Operation Iraqi Freedom. Rick is airborne and air assault qualified and was awarded the Bronze Star with Oak Leaf Cluster for his heroic service in a combat zone. Though modern combat is not the same as it was in 1780, Rick shared that there are similarities. His fellow soldiers were not just brothers in arms, but in life.

"The rocks you see on top of the memorial," Rick said under his breath. "That is a tribute that people are paying by putting them up there. When we had the ceremony here, we had the road closed, so you didn't have all the road noise and didn't get people running over."

On April 23, 2023, Rick participated in a ceremony to honor and to reinter the remains of fourteen soldiers found at Camden Battlefield—twelve Patriots, one Loyalist, and one British soldier of the Seventy-First Regiment of Foot, Fraser's Highlanders. Their gravesites had been discovered years before by various people, but mainly by the archaeologists from the South Carolina Institute for Archaeology and Anthropology at the University of South Carolina. However, some identified gravesites were threatened by further degradation unless mitigation was done to protect them.

In the fall of 2022, the late Doug Bostick, executive director and CEO of the South Carolina Battleground Preservation Trust, in cooperation with the Historic Camden Foundation, coordinated the effort to recover remains from six known gravesites. That plan would lead to another discovery.

After their recovery, forensic studies were conducted with the hope of discovering as much as possible about who these soldiers were and perhaps even identifying them. The remains would then be buried on the battlefield with honors in April 2023. Archaeologists had studied the battleground for decades, but this was a unique unearthing of human remains. The remains were sent on to a lab where scientists used forensic DNA analysis to learn more about the fallen men. The initial intent was for them to be reinterred at the original locations where they had been found.

However, with the US Army and other entities involved, that plan changed as a ceremony was planned that would honor all those, recovered and lost, who were hastily buried in shallow graves on hallowed ground.

The project did not simply recover six soldiers. The archaeologists found more. "We recovered fourteen soldiers here. And so those soldiers…they're kind of representative of the approximately four hundred that are out here," Rick explained. "And that's a pretty sobering thought."

I remembered Rick's previous statement about the trees representing unmarked graves on this battlefield. I scanned the forested landscape to see if I could even count the trees. I couldn't. Around me was a maze of thin trees with spindly pine needles rising up to a muddy gray sky. I closed my eyes and imagined the trees as men, some standing and others lying fallen or propped against tree trunks, the jagged bark catching on their red, blue, or brown coats, tattered from use and soaked in blood.

"A lot of trees out there," I said, suddenly feeling chilly.

My father was a US Army captain and my grandfather, Richard Love Tedrow, served in the navy during World War II. I also have a great-uncle who saw active duty in the navy and was buried at Arlington National Cemetery with full military honors. Though these family members served, they didn't often open up about their experiences. Over the years, in meeting veterans with post-traumatic stress disorder who use horses for therapy, I've had the opportunity to hear from other veterans who have witnessed the many horrors of war. Still, being on an actual battlefield with a soldier who'd seen combat sharing his story and the history that happened here had a whole different cadence. It got my mind churning and wondering what had occurred with my own family during these struggles. I wished I'd taken the time to ask more questions.

By connecting with Rick, I was tied more personally to what happened to the men at Camden Battlefield. Without Rick's insights, I would have walked this forested area and read the historical markers by the split-rail fence alongside the road at the battlefield and gotten the facts. The signage here does relay some of the drama, gore, and turmoil of what occurred, but being on this battlefield with Rick, a former combat soldier, made my experience hit home differently.

Most of us know someone who has served for our nation, their bravery tested in various ways. Rick was not only brave enough to serve in combat, but he was also brave and humble enough to share his own vulnerable emotions, making my time on the battlefield that day even more poignant.

"There's a site here where there are five Continental soldiers, and out of those five Continental soldiers, two of them are teenagers," Rick said. "They paid the ultimate sacrifice on this battlefield. It was their fate to remain here, but their sacrifice allowed others to be able to escape the battlefield. And those soldiers were the ones who fought the Battle of Cowpens, Guilford Courthouse, Hobkirk Hill, Ninety Six, Eutaw Springs, and then the Surrender at Charleston."

Rick was listing battles fought in North and South Carolina that were significant to the Southern Campaign. If you speak with historical experts from the Carolinas, many will tell you that the Revolutionary War was really won in the South. Of course, everywhere I travel to learn more about Revolutionary history, I've heard of many battles being described as a or "the turning point." There were clearly many pivotal battles across the colonies throughout the Revolutionary War.

"So, their sacrifice allowed those other folks to be where they needed to be. I was a soldier for twenty-three years. And when I come out here, I commune with these guys…. What took place here is very humbling to me when I think about the soldiers and the sacrifices they made," Rick said.

I didn't know how to respond. I only nodded, seeing a sort of agony channeling through Rick's eyes and his pursed-lip silence.

It was like what you might experience when you don't know what to say to someone who tells you that their mom or dad or grandmother has passed. When a touch on the shoulder or a hug if you're with them is the sorrowful reply. If you're on the phone, there's that pause or hopefully the immediate *I'm so sorry*. All the while, you feel a little helpless for the person and situation. While I felt a sense of sorrow being on the battlefield, I felt that Rick was channeling it more intensely. In a sense, he'd walked in these soldiers' boots, and his empathy was on full display.

A loaded logging truck passed by as Rick and I stood facing each other in the middle of a sandy path. We decided to move back further into the woods away from the road, passing the area where the white flags protruded from the ground, signifying a burial area for soldiers. I wondered how much more we would be able to learn about these men. Forensic experts were working to create a family tree for descendants of the soldiers uncovered at Camden. The project has been called the longest-spanning John Doe investigation ever attempted. I asked Rick more about these nameless soldiers as our feet crunched on a blanket of dry pine needles peppered with pinecones.

"Do we know anything about these men, their ages, where they came from?" I asked, referring to the soldiers they recovered.

"You know, Darley, one of the interesting things is that out of the twelve Continental soldiers, five of them were teenagers. One as young as fifteen years old. So, fifteen- to nineteen-year-olds were fighting on this battlefield," Rick said.

It took a minute for his response to sink in with me. Some of the soldiers had been too young to even drive a car by today's standards, let alone order a beer. I thought about myself at that age and how naive I had been about the world. While I had known that teenaged boys would have fought, knowing that they were buried just a few steps away made me sad and a bit anxious. What else was directly beneath the ground where I was walking? Who else was buried here? There were many, many more men and boys whose stories would remain unknown.

Rick shared that there were two additional men buried nearby that were around thirty and forty years old. He referred to the forty-year-old as "the old man."

"And we can kind of think that maybe he was their sergeant, and he fought with them and led them until they all went down. This took place on the battlefield after Lord Cornwallis had committed his reserves to include the Seventy-First Highlanders," Rick said.

I could imagine the scene on a hot, misty, August morning at daybreak, with smoke hanging close to the ground from cannons and muskets. In the gloom of the gun smoke and early morning light, the soldiers would have struggled to see each other. The fighting started and was over in forty-five minutes. It was brutal. I looked down at my cowboy boots and moved my square toe in the sand just a bit, thinking about how much of this sandy footing would have been soaked in blood. It was an obscene thought.

"The bloodshed was unbelievable," Rick said.

"Uh," I muttered. I literally had no words.

"And we've got to remember; the musket was not really the killing mechanism. It was the bayonet. And those bayonets were horrendous. Baron DeKalb suffered eight bayonet or saber wounds. He died three days later. Because those triangular bayonets made wounds that were really—you couldn't stop the bleeding."

"Just gruesome," I said.

In some books and movies, war is romanticized to be heroic. Taking a life, no matter why, is traumatizing for those with a moral compass. Having personally witnessed some of my own family members pass away, I know it's something that you can never unsee. It's a reason I don't even watch scary or dramatic movies or TV shows. Yet here I was trudging through a battlefield, internalizing the personal losses that changed individuals and families—that changed American history.

Camden was a horrific battle, and though it was one of the worst of the American Revolution, it was also just one of over a few hundred battles and skirmishes in South Carolina alone during the Revolutionary War. At Cowpens National Battlefield, where the Patriots under Daniel Morgan defeated Banastre Tarleton's nine hundred British troops, my guide ranger Paul Cothren spoke about the South during the American Revolution, making sure not to downplay the region's importance. There were many people I met on my travels in the South who shared the view that the war was all but won due to the Patriots' hard-fought battles during the Southern Campaign.

The exact number of battles and skirmishes depends on how you count, but conservatively there were over two hundred. According to *Parker's Guide to the Revolutionary War in South Carolina*, the number of battles, skirmishes, and murders in South Carolina alone was over four hundred.

"I've studied military history my whole life, and recovering these men here has given it a different persona because these guys are not excerpts from history. They're real and they're right here with us.... Most people, when they read history, it's words on the page. But history is people and their stories and what happened to them."

I thought about the many soldiers who fought in the Battle of Camden, some of whom marched over 750 miles from Morristown, New Jersey, only to arrive in South Carolina in the heat of August. Having grown up in South Carolina myself, I remember that August heat. It's humid and sticky and sometimes a bit suffocating just trying to breathe.

At fifteen, when I was in high school, I got my first car for $500. I needed it to get to my summer job at a Western Steer steakhouse, where I was a line girl handing people warm, soft yeast rolls. My job consisted of going to a hot oven to get fresh rolls to refill the buffet line. I was soon bored by the work. To get through my shift, I stuffed hot yeast rolls in my pockets. Sometimes they would burn my legs a bit if there were right out of the oven and then my fingers, too, as I'd pinch off pieces and slyly pop them into my mouth. It helped to pass the time.

The job did teach me to make the best of anything you do. I learned that I enjoyed taking home well-earned money. While a $500 mustard-colored 1970s Volvo sedan might sound kind of cool, it's not so cool when the air conditioning never works and you stick to the leather seats and melt into the interiors while driving to work. I called that car Old Bessie, and when she eventually quit on me the Volvo company sent me a wooden pen in commemoration. Old Bessie was epic.

These soldiers didn't have a rickety old car to get them to the battlefield or hot yeast rolls fresh from the oven to bide the time or even for nourishment in support of their daily march. Rick explained that the troops faced torrential rains and flooding on route to Camden and that they also lacked food and supplies. The army had been eating green apples and unripe peaches.

On August 15, Gates ordered them meat, cornmeal to cook, and molasses as a substitute for rum. Many entered the battle with dysentery from the poor food—and the molasses. Nothing is worse than being sick to your stomach in my opinion. That feeling when your whole body bursts into a sweat and you start to spit as fluids erupt in your mouth, knowing that the stomach acid is coming next. I could only imagine the men and boys just wanting to sit and rest but instead finding themselves stumbling towards British bayonets and hoping not to die. Rick provided background on the soldiers' perspective of the battle.

"At the same time, you have the camaraderie of being a soldier. You all experience this thing together. We like to think life is all about mom, baseball, and apple pie. Well, actually, it's about your fellow soldiers, the sacrifice they made for their friends and companions here on this battlefield. There are several veterans throughout the years that have said that the thing on the battlefield in combat…it's not like Hollywood. You don't hear a soundtrack playing in the background. All you have are your buddies, and that's what you're fighting for."

I didn't hear any music—*Band of Brothers* or otherwise—in my head at Camden Battlefield. In fact, my experience turned out to be one of the most profoundly horrifying visions of a battle—and I've visited a lot of battle sites. I've always been sensitive. Having lost some of the closest people in my life at an early age left me wanting to connect with people that much more. In a way, you appreciate what has been lost more than people lucky enough to have their close relatives and loving families close at hand. I also believe that it makes you more sensitive to other people's situations. So as Rick and I continued our journey through the battlefield, I almost felt dizzy as I passed more longleaf pines and markers and memorials to the men who had fallen on this battlefield in the woods.

Rick again provided his unique perspective: "Do I commune with these guys when I walk around this battlefield? I do, because soldiers have been the same throughout history. The only thing that changes is the tactics and the weapons. So, what took place here? It's very humbling to me when I think about the soldiers and the sacrifices they made."

I glanced over at the white flags again, blowing slightly in the breeze. Patches of small white flowers grew between them. The bodies of these men and boys were found in shallow graves, just six to eight inches beneath the soil. Part of the reason that they were uncovered and excavated was because they were so close to the surface. Researchers and archaeologists have known about the graves for almost twenty-five years and wanted to excavate them to protect them from potential looting and environmental changes. Being so close to the surface, they could be threatened by animals following a scent or people searching for wartime relics. Rick noted that the forensic team took great care to unearth these soldiers.

Since my visit, the white flags have been replaced by granite blocks with bronze plaques memorializing the original graves. The British soldier was reinterred on the battlefield, and the twelve Continentals were buried at the Old Presbyterian Burying Ground, now part of the Quaker Cemetery, located on Meeting Street in Camden, adjacent to Historic Camden Revolutionary War Site's property. Visitors can venture to these locations to pay their respects.

Rick provided additional context on the fighting that took place at Camden, pointing to the location where the militia ran away. They were facing British regulars, the best infantry in the world at the time.

"You can kind of understand, but most of them threw down their weapons and ran without firing a shot. Gates lost two-thirds of his army, and he and the other general officers on this side of the field, which were on the east side, were caught up in that stampede and taken off the battlefield. Unfortunately, he lost command and control at the time," Rick said. "And as we're going along here, some of the things that we can see is the aftermath of the troops [the graves of those killed] that actually delayed the British as they were coming around this way."

At that time, the Maryland Brigade was outnumbered about two to one, and they were pushed back. The only militia unit that didn't flee was a unit under Lieutenant Colonel Hal Dixon. He was a former Continental commander. He had at least one company of North Carolina Continentals with him.

"Those folks stood and fought on the battlefield," Rick said. "And, you know, the amazing thing, Darley, is that when your enemy writes about what you did, that's probably a pretty good thing. Lord Cornwallis and a guy named Sergeant Roger Lamb both wrote about how Dixon's men were fighting because it was remarkable for a militia to do that."

On the battlefield with Rick, I wasn't just learning the history, I was feeling it and so many emotions. There was an energy that seemed more present in the stillness of that day in May. Rick lowered his voice to almost a whisper to describe what he felt when a psychic came to the battlefield in August 2019 and told Rick she was talking with a fallen soldier named Adam.

Rick relayed that everything the psychic said fit the narrative of what took place during the final action on the western side of the battlefield where he stood. Rick said he took it with a grain of salt but did go to the rosters looking for soldiers named Adam. He found three. Two of them showed up on later rosters, but one, Adam Henry, in a regiment that would have been on the western side of the road, had this entry written after his name: "Camden, August 16, 1780......Missing."

He then used Adam Henry as a focal point when he spoke at the annual Battle of Camden Commemoration in August

2021, citing a scenario that led to the young soldier's death at the end of the battle. He recounted the calling of the roll in Hillsborough, North Carolina, later, with Adam Henry's name being called loudly, and, when he failed to answer, being listed as "missing." Because Adam Henry, and about four hundred other soldiers, Patriot and British, remain on the battlefield. After the ceremony, Rick went across the road to the western side of the battlefield where his SUV was parked.

"I went over there," Rick said pointing to area that was used for parking that day, the same area where he and the psychic had stood two years before. "I was putting stuff in my vehicle. Had the doors open…the rear door just shut on its own. No breeze, no nothing, and you can't push that door shut without a significant effort." There was no logical explanation.

Rick laughed nervously.

This was three years before the soldiers were recovered in the fall of 2022. "And so, at the conclusion of the honors ceremonies in April 2023, I came out here the next day and went and just had a moment at each gravesite. I then got back to the area where this guy, Adam, had indicated he wanted that lady to go with him. She said she thought it was to show her where he was buried. But in August, there may be snakes, and she was wearing a dress and sandals, so we didn't go. But as I was walking down the road, I spoke to Adam Henry and said, I hope we honored you guys appropriately. This was for all of you…a cold breeze went up the back of my neck. When I looked over at the grass beside me, it was perfectly still. The leaves were not moving, and it got cold all the way around me on a hot afternoon in South Carolina. And then I was like, okay. Now are their spirits on the battlefield? I don't know. In 2019 I told the lady I had never experienced anything close to what I would call unexplainable on this battlefield or anywhere else. She said I had a strong spirit, that's why nothing approached me."

It appears something got his attention in an inexplicable way. I was not at the reinterment ceremony in April of 2023 where Rick Wise gave the final remarks to a crowd of thousands, but following my time with him on Camden Battlefield, where he spoke candidly and off the cuff with me for my free-flowing-documentary style of interviewing, I wished I had been able to have attended the ceremony to have paid tribute to the fallen soldiers more formally myself.

I was, however, able to hear Rick's remarks from that day in a YouTube video from the comfort of my firm gray couch in my New York City apartment on the Upper West Side of Manhattan, only a block from Central Park. I was working one weekend, as I often do, switching between multiple tasks. I sat with my laptop on my lap, one hand on my calico rescue cat BeBe, stroking her soft, long fur.

The historic event included an outdoor funeral service at Bethesda Presbyterian Church in Camden using eighteenth-century Anglican and Presbyterian liturgies. Horse-drawn caissons with flag-draped coffins and a military honor guard were part of a ceremony that then concluded with a flyover from the US Air Force Seventy-Ninth Fighter Squadron from Shaw Air Force Base in Sumter, South Carolina.

At Camden Battlefield, thousands of people attended the burial ceremony, bringing fold-up lawn chairs trailed behind the more formal chairs for dignitaries, including officers from the US, German, French, and British armies. Many of the participants had flown in to attend the Camden Burials. A small stage was lined with flags, representing the national flags of troops engaged at the battle as well as the state flags of South Carolina, Delaware, Maryland, Virginia, and North Carolina.

Soldiers from the US Army and British Army acted as pall-bearers, marching three on each side of simple light-colored wooden caskets draped with American flags to the sounds of drumming and a band. Soldiers from Second Battalion, Royal Regiment of Scotland carried their one fallen, wearing their green and black kilts and covering the casket with a "King's Colors" flag, which was the Union Flag of Great Britain at the time. While many prominent speakers took the stage to share a tribute, including South Carolina's governor, two stood out to me as having been with me on battlefields in South Carolina: Rick Wise and Doug Bostick. Doug Bostick was an icon in South Carolina and the battlefield and history community. He'd written numerous books and was a staunch advocate of battle-field preservation. Sadly, on October 23, 2023, Doug Bostick passed away. His death was a huge loss.

The audience clapped as Rick took the stage. Rick was dressed in an elegant navy-blue suit with a light blue tie, adorned with various medals from his own service. "Distinguished guests. Ladies and gentlemen. I'll try to be brief, but I want to pay trib-ute to these men." He paused for a few seconds and not another sound was heard from the crowd.

Rick continued, choking up as he spoke, "Please bear with me. They've waited over two hundred forty-two years for this moment."

As I watched Rick's speech, I got emotional, too. I could tell he was having a lot of trouble speaking on that stage. Time had passed, but the importance of this ceremony was clear. It was way past due.

"Today we gather to acknowledge and honor that service and sacrifice with the dignity and faith denied them over two hundred forty-two years ago…for those interred in this hallowed ground, both of our nation and those who fought for king and country, we wish them to know that time has healed these wounds from long ago. America is no longer divided between Patriots and Loyalists but as one great nation."

Rick went on to describe the battle and its aftermath in detail. In the heat of the morning following the battle, those soldiers who had escaped death were tasked with burying the fallen using their bare hands and bayonets to loosen the earth. Some used tin cups. Researchers have since found a tin cup with a missing handle in the grave that held the remains of three teenaged Continental soldiers. Rick explained the significance of a soldier's role in protecting a nation and his fellow soldiers.

"To these soldiers we say: Fate has dictated that you will not be forgotten in an unmarked shallow grave, but you now, in marked graves, are recognizable to all for the role you played… represent the remembrance of all for whom fate has placed in this hallowed ground. God bless their souls, and may you rest in peace."

Rick waited a beat before yelling out a resounding, "Huzzah!"

I felt Rick's emotion. I thought about the parents of the teenaged boys. I wondered how many families had waited and wondered about their son. I imagined the faraway Scottish relatives of the fallen Highlander soldier, hoping to resolve the fate of their son. I wondered how they would feel to know it would finally take place hundreds of years later in a former colony. As meaningful as the 2023 ceremony was, it reminded me of the cruelty of life and of how short it can be. It reminded me that we should all remember each other more each day and listen whenever we can.

The twelve Continental soldiers were later buried in August 2023 near Quaker Cemetery in Camden. Their headstones are just like the ones at Arlington, each marked "UNKNOWN." The Highlander was buried where he was found on the battlefield in April 2024. A granite marker stands at his gravesite. The Loyalist, who was discovered to be Native American, is being managed in collaboration with the Catawba Nation.

I feel fortunate to have been able to hear firsthand about Camden Battlefield from Rick Wise and to document his story of what happened. His recounting of the history creates a more personalized story for us to learn from—so when we walk amid the trees at Camden Battlefield and we think about the soldiers past and present, we can hopefully feel more empathetic and united.

Rick Wise wasn't the only expert I met with at Camden Battlefield. Dr. Tray Dunaway and a group of reenactors were dressed as Continental soldiers wearing blue wool regimental coats and white breeches. They were maneuvering about a hundred yards from a Revolutionary-era three-pounder "grasshopper" cannon. It was positioned along the Great Wagon Road, a wider sandy path that parallels the contemporary Flat Rock Road. Considered the interstate highway of its day, the Great Wagon Road had originally been a Native American trading route. In August of 1780, it was where the two armies would clash in the moonlight.

The three-pounder cannon, or "grasshopper," was supposedly designed for mobility and employed by light infantry units. Though said to be created for flexibility, I had watched from the sidelines as Dr. Dunaway and two other men from his team slowly moved the cannon, which was supported by two wheels through the sandy terrain, its large iron-rimmed wooden wheels sinking into the sand. During the American Revolution, this type of cannon would have ideally been moved using a horse-drawn wagon. I could imagine those horses pulling this down the sandy washes in less-than-ideal conditions. Even today, my feet sank a bit into the sandy footing, and I weigh a lot less than the cannon.

Used at the Battle of Camden and other battles like Saratoga during the American Revolution, the cannon was named because of the way it recoiled—jumping when fired like a grasshopper.

Dr. Dunaway and his team positioned the cannon so that when they fired, it would blast out down the sandy road. Even though we were firing blanks, not actual cannonballs today, it was still deafening. I wondered how drivers passing by, perhaps with their windows down lazily listening to some music, might react to the sound of cannon fire. Maybe the locals knew to roll up their windows when passing the battlefield.

Dr. Dunaway was in the parking lot beside a large white pickup truck fetching a triangular tricorn hat for me to wear, while I learned context on the artillery used in the battle. Dressed as a Continental soldier in a dark blue coat with himself a tricorn hat and his eighteenth-century-style small wire-rimmed glasses, Dr. Dunaway turned to me excitedly as I walked up to meet him. He hastily thrust a large plastic container of bright orange ear plugs towards me with a smile, telling me I would need these.

You know you're in an unusual line of work when your travel bag requires earplugs—not for concerts, but for cannon firing. A few months earlier, I was at Fort Fair Lawn, another South Carolina Revolutionary War battle site where a crew fired a cannon during a reenactment. It was not even close to me as it was fired, but I was so startled by the loud sound that I almost fell to the ground. I felt like I had cotton stuffed inside my ears for the rest of that day.

Given that ear-deafening experience, I gladly took the ear plugs from Dr. Dunaway. In fact, from that day forward, I would bring ear plugs in my travel bag for future occasions like this.

We walked over to meet the rest of the artillery team involved in shooting the cannon. It takes a small village. During the Revolutionary War, a team of six specially trained artillerymen would have operated this type of cannon. Ken Stacey, Ken Seward, and an eleven-year-old boy named Cabe and his mom all participated in the demonstration—dressed as Continental soldiers. We had a smaller team than would have been needed during the Revolution as today we were simply demonstrating and not actually firing any cannonballs. Dr. Dunaway asked Ken Seward to search the piece to make sure no debris was left over from previous firings.

Ken stood to the side of one of the large wooden wheels of the cannon so as not to be in front of the cannon's muzzle as he placed a long wooden rod into the gun. At the end of the rod was an iron corkscrew. Called the wormer, it was placed inside the cannon's gun bore and twisted to extract any debris, like the remains of spent and smoldering powder bags.

"Darley, I'd like you to actually do all the firing," Dr. Dunaway announced.

I nodded with some trepidation, wondering what that meant. Dr. Dunaway relayed that the first thing we'd do was to make sure the cannon was empty of any debris.

"And the command is to search the piece," Dr. Dunaway said.

"Okay," I said.

Ken demonstrated how to use the wormer properly.

"Don't stand directly in front of the muzzle for safety reasons," he said in a quiet voice.

He thrust the wormer in again. I instinctively took a step back, aware of the potential danger.

"You're going to spin it. Keep your hands down, not on top," Ken instructed.

"Okay," I said.

"Because if you put them on top and something happens, you lose your fingers."

"Oh," I said, pursing my lips and looking back at Dr. Dunaway, who was smiling, relishing in my newbie training.

"This is bad," Ken said with his hands hovering just atop of the wooden rod. "This is good, alright? It's called searching the piece."

He rolled the wormer around inside the barrel.

I took the wormer as, again, Dr. Dunaway relayed further instructions.

"And the command is, search the piece!"

"We're going to search the piece," I said with a bit of nervous giddiness. I had seen Ken search the piece twice already, so I knew that there was nothing inside, but nonetheless I felt a bit warm as I thrust the pole into the dark abyss of the bore. Although I'd had some practice, I still didn't have regular experience in searching cannons.

"We've got to advance the charge," Dr. Dunaway called out. "And when I say it, Cade will bring you the gunpowder.

I turned to young Cade and smiled. It was great to see this boy out with these men and so enthusiastic about participating in this educational event. Cade proceeded to hand me the gunpowder, wrapped in aluminum foil. In the past, a silk or cotton bag would have held the charge. I loaded the flat end into the muzzle of the cannon, pushing it in swiftly, but without real force for fear of an explosion. Ken then used a long-handled wooden pole called a rammer to push it in further.

"Ram the charge," Dr. Dunaway yelled.

Ken Stacey jammed it in and then let me try it as well.

"Give it a good whack," Ken Stacey said. "You can't hurt it."

"Now, it's gunpowder, so be careful when you give it a good whack," Dr. Dunaway corrected, with a wink glancing back at Ken. "Just in case."

I laughed nervously, wondering if he was joking or telling the truth. I tapped the end of the flat wooden rammer into the barrel.

"Hard. Hard," Dr. Dunaway commanded, raising his voice another few decibels and yelling. "Hard! Hard! Hard! That's it."

I used the wooden rod to jam it in and heard a thump.

"Hear that sound? The sound changes, you know you have it advanced properly," Dr. Dunaway said.

"Okay," I said, wondering again how I had gotten myself into this somewhat dangerous task.

Dr. Dunaway said that we should go ahead and fire the cannon. I had wanted to interview Dr. Dunaway first to get the background on the cannon and artillery here, but he had already lit a slow match, a smoldering cotton rope that had been soaked in a potassium nitrate solution to keep it burning. I was now holding in my right hand. It all happened so quickly with so many steps that I barely knew how it had arrived in my hand. Dr. Dunaway told me that once lit, it is very hard to put the slow match out, but at the same time, I should blow on it to keep it glowing red hot. It seemed that time was of the essence. Besides, this group seemed to really want me to fire this cannon.

I was instructed to walk behind the cannon and not burn myself on the slow match, which was set aside, well away from any black powder, so I could quickly pick and prime the cannon. The charge was seated inside the cannon's breech. We had to get a spark from the outside to the inside, so touching off the cannon would enter the breech. I was then instructed to put the small pick inside the touchhole and push it straight in and pull it straight out.

I think Dr. Dunaway took delight in yelling instructions at me that day. As I put the long rod into the touchhole he yelled, "Pick and prime! Straight in. You'll get resistance. Pull it straight out."

I then set the brass pick aside, to avoid creating a spark, to prime the cannon. Priming a cannon requires numerous steps, and I won't labor you through any more, but I put what was originally made of duck quills into the touchhole and pushed it in about a quarter inch to prime it. I got ready to ignite the charge and fire, reaching over the wheel and touching it off. Reaching over the wheel was important so as not to get hit by the cannon coming backwards. This was, after all, a grasshopper cannon.

"You don't have to worry today, because we are not using a live round. We're just using a blank," Dr. Dunaway said, nodding reassuringly.

"Okay," I said with a smile, not feeling too sure as to exactly how safe this mock cannon firing was!

I was ready to take the smoldering red slow match and light the cannon.

"Make ready," Dr. Dunaway commanded. "That tells everyone that it's time to put your fingers over your ears, cause it's going to blast."

I was told to sweep it down and sweep it forward to touch the black area. Dr. Dunaway then drew out his sword.

"Why do you have a sword out?" I asked laughing and wondering if his flair for drama had gotten the best of him.

"That's because I'm commanding," Dr. Dunaway said with a boyish smile.

I lifted my arm high into the air as Dr. Dunaway gave his loudest, "Make ready! Fire!"

I swept my arm down in an L-shaped manner and lit the charge and the cannon exploded, firing a blast of smoke into the air. I jumped back with a scream, turning and hopping away from the cannon as the sound echoed in the distance.

"Oh geez," I said, laughing nervously. It was scary. If I had been on that battlefield, I might have run away.

"Darley, I forgot to tell you that if you shoot a cannon and you flinch, you lose style points," Dr. Dunaway joked.

I would have lost more than a few points.

"How fast would they have had to do this?" I asked Dr. Dunaway. "This is a lot of steps."

"Now, a crew could do these four to five times a minute."

"Oh wow," I said, thinking that was fast, given all the steps.

"That's the power of artillery," Dr. Dunaway explained. A good soldier could shoot a musket four times a minute. A trained cannon crew could shoot four to five times a minute launching 200 to 250 projectiles downrange in an instant. Compared to a musket shooting one ball at a time, the cannon was efficient and effective. Going through the many logistics involved and thinking about the six trained men running it, I wondered how accurately one could aim it.

I thought about the current cannon positioned down this desolate road. If it was such a long, multi-step and labor-intensive process, it didn't seem so efficient to me, but then I was potentially thinking about our modern artillery—machine gun fire and things I may have seen in movies like *Die Hard*.

"That's part of the gun captain's job. And he would stand behind the piece, and he would direct the fire. You can change the elevation so you can lift it up or down with the screw, and then you just manually twist it to shoot exactly where you want," Dr. Dunaway explained.

"How much devastation would one cannonball cause potentially?" I asked.

"Well, that's the thing. On the Camden battlefield, they have never recovered a cannonball," Dr. Dunaway said.

"They go collect them and use them again. Recycling," I joked and then asking seriously. "Or because they didn't use cannonballs?"

"They didn't use cannonballs," Dr. Dunaway said. "This is a three-pound cannon, which means it fires a three-pound cannonball, but on a battlefield, you need a big shotgun. This would be used to shoot grapeshot, which is a one-inch iron ball. That's like a big shotgun, or it could be using canister shot, a can packed with musket balls. And again, it amplifies the power of one firing, so this was devastating on the battlefield."

A lot of injuries at Camden were a result of cannon fire, and the smoke would have made it difficult to see what was going on. It would have been disorienting, especially combined with the day's dense fog and heat.

"August, South Carolina, summer day, high humidity with the fire and the smoke that's going on after a couple of rounds," Tray said. "The whole thing, it really defines 'the fog of war.'"

"They would have had another person who would have pointed to where they saw a flash, so that the cannon would aim at that point through the smoke. In the meantime, the other guys would have been moving their cannons around so that they couldn't have been spotted. The same thing happens in warfare today. One side fires a missile. They determine where the missile came from. That's their aim point, and then they move the missile launcher. So, it would have been the same approach, just eighteenth-century style."

Dr. Dunaway is the board chairman of Southern Campaign 1780, an organization that holds the Carolinas Revolutionary War Weekend and Battle Reenactments annually on the second full weekend of November in Kershaw County on Keys Lane, between Kershaw and Camden. Travelers can witness the power of cannons and see what happened on this battlefield through the largest annual force-on-force Revolutionary War reenactment in the nation. Southern Campaign 1780 also operates Liberty Live educational programs year-round, bringing the customized educational programs statewide to schools and other organizations.

I had gotten a taste of what a potential reenactor may experience in learning how to fire a cannon, one of the many types of living history events that happen over the multi-day events in Camden and Kershaw County.

My lesson in firing a cannon gave me a better sense of the power of war, of weapons and their dangers, not only from cannons or iron balls but from the task of firing itself. If I were on the battlefield I might have run, but in my life, I know that it's better to run with a partner, especially if that partner is a horse. My next adventure in Camden would lead me to man's greatest companion, the horse, but one that's rarer in today's world: the Marsh Tacky.

National Steeplechase Museum:
Horses of War and Heritage

I had heard no mention of horses in my time visiting the Battle of Camden, but horses were in fact a big part of that battle as well as the American Revolution at large. They were relied upon to cover the vast distances in the colonies, pull cannons and supplies, and carry men heralding messages and facing the enemy. Famous figures like Paul Revere and George Washington are often pictured on their horses. Horses were also used to carry the wounded. The animals themselves were some of the casualties at battles like the Battle of Camden. Part of this story in the South is shrouded in myth and legend with many oral histories swirling around a lesser known, rare horse breed that still survives today, with its roots in colonial times and, prior to that, with the Spanish Conquistadors.

In Camden today, horses are big business. Camden is home to the Carolina Cup, where tens of thousands of fans descend for an annual steeplechase horse race. I was heading to the National Steeplechase Museum to learn about the horses that were involved in the Revolution, along with Camden's love affair with horses that goes back much further than the first steeplechase in the 1930s.

Museum curator Wesley Faulkenberry met me on the grounds of historic Springdale Race Course in Camden at the National Steeplechase Museum. Outside, a statue of the famous steeplechase horse Lonesome Glory greets visitors. Wesley greeted me in casual jeans and a beige button-down. We were twinning, apart from my favorite bright yellow cardigan. He invited me into large white clapboard building, which looks like a large Southern home.

I walked along the red brick sidewalk and past the two figures of jockeys outside and into the museum. To the left was an alcove with wooden interiors filled with large trophies, colorful pink, blue, orange, green, and white jerseys, and engraved silver platters and trays set inside glass cases against green walls. In front of me, a large, white-walled room opened up with the feel of an event space. I walked across the shiny wooden floors and looked up to the rounded, domed wooden ceiling and over to the walls, where paintings and printed information shared the story of the Marsh Tacky horses.

After Wesley provided a brief introduction to this museum, the only museum dedicated to the history of steeplechase racing in America, he launched into the topic I'd come to learn about. He started in about the importance of the Carolina Marsh Tacky in the lowlands of South Carolina. They were descended from Spanish colonial horses that were thought to have come from St. Augustine and stayed on the coast.

"They were weirdly kept in feral packs, and whenever they needed horses, people would just kind of round them up. Every so often you would have a family that would take in a horse and would keep it, but the horses tended to otherwise remain in the herds," Wesley said. "It was these horses that Frances Marion and his forces would use to great effect against the British, who tended to be mounted on more hot-blooded Arabian-descended breeds."

European horses weren't as good at navigating the swamps and marshes of the lowlands of South Carolina. The Marsh Tacky, however, thrived. It was their home turf, and they were adapted to the terrain, the heat and muggy conditions, and the mud.

"They were seen as being a poor man's horse," said Wesley. "Anyone could use them. But they were very smart. They were very gentle as well."

"How did they get their name?" I asked.

Wesley explained that their name is not as flattering as it might seem. They took on the name "Tacky," meaning common, because they were the most common breed of horse. They were on the small side and often used for everyday tasks by families. They transported kids to school and were used as vehicles by families because they were so reliable and had great stamina.

"Having that stamina would have been essential to moving around during the American Revolution, going to these different battle sites and having to get away from your enemy and move supplies," I suggested.

"If you have a horse that's starting to get stuck in mud, starting to get tangled up, a lot of horses will panic and that will only make the situation worse. The Marsh Tacky horses never panic in those kinds of situations," Wesley explained. "They just lay down and slowly work themselves out until they get their legs and hooves freed and then pick back up and keep on going."

Having myself spent the last two decades riding horses around the world, I knew a lot about panicky horses. Often, it was their owners' nervousness that rubbed off on them, but some breeds were naturally known to be more nervous or hot-blooded and jittery.

Wesley went on to note that the Marsh Tacky are also easy keepers, eating plants like marsh grasses. This means that owners don't have to buy or grow a lot of forage or keep so many supplies stocked. Their coarse coat also helps them move through areas of more shrubbery, including places where burrs, vines, and thorns may be prevalent.

South Carolina's swamp warriors, I thought. Inside the Steeplechase Museum, I examined a glass display case that held spurs, harnesses, buckles, and other artifacts from horses and cavalry recovered from the Camden Battlefield in the 1970s and 1980s. Cavalry horses and horses pulling baggage were involved in the battle, and there are accounts that as the Americans realized that the battle could not be won, some cut their horses free from their harnesses so they could escape. Wesley tells me that they are not sure if Marsh Tacky horses were present at the Battle of Camden, though some may have been ridden with Colonel Pinckney, whose leg was shattered by a musket ball during the battle.

Horses were a commodity during the American Revolution for many practical reasons, but they also served to boost morale. Having been around a lot of horses and ridden through diverse and oftentimes challenging terrain, I could see why. Horses can often navigate places quickly that would take a person much longer to trudge through. They pick their way through uneven lands and tight spaces, sometimes super confidently. If you're thinking of John Wayne and his trusty horse Dollor right now, you are right on!

"Because of the logistical issues of transporting horses across the Atlantic in the 1770s, most of the horses were bred in America," Wesley explained. "The British army lost some five hundred horses off New York during a hurricane while they were trying to transport them to America for the war. Many times, when the army passed through an area, they would confiscate any horses they came across, which is just a nice way of saying that they stole them. If you were lucky, you would be paid in gold for your horse, but often you would just get an IOU saying: *Hey, we took your horses.*"

The Springdale Races date back to 1928, and the Carolina Cup has been run every year since 1930, except during the Second World War and the COVID epidemic. Every year, the winner gets his silks put in a trophy case inside the museum. They hang over a trophy that looks to be about the size of my upper body.

"Back in the day, the winning owner was able to take it home for a year. But now they just get to hold it up and take some pictures before we bring it back up here. But we do engrave the names of the winner every year," Wesley said.

It was overcast as I headed outside and back into my car to drive to a spot on the grounds of the National Steeplechase Museum, where I could ride a Marsh Tacky horse. These horses are not easy to find. There are only about six hundred of the breed left today. They are endangered.

For this next learning experience, I enlisted the help of Wylie Bell and members of the Carolina Marsh Tacky Association. Their organization is working to increase the numbers of this special breed, South Carolina's state heritage horse, and help safeguard its survival.

We drove down a series of dirt roads to an area of the steeple-chase grounds where a few trees shaded two large trailers carrying Marsh Tacky horses. We would be riding the grounds and hopefully dodging into the forest to understand what made this breed stand out during colonial times and the war. I took off the yellow sweater layer, so I was just wearing a light cotton button-down, and popped on my firm straw cowboy hat before exiting the SUV to meet Wylie.

Wylie was brushing the long tail of the horse I'd be riding—a fourteen-year-old grulla-colored Marsh Tacky named Breeze. On Breeze's back sat a Western saddle, which meant my cowboy boots and legs would hang longer in my stirrups, and I'd mostly sit during each stride. I ride both Western and English style. If you think about England and hunting, you can imagine the

English style, where a rider wears paddock boots or high boots with chaps and rises up and down in the saddle in line with the horse's strides. If you think about the American West and cowboys moving cattle out on the range, you're likely imaging Western style.

Wylie was wearing a light blue button-down western-style blouse. Covering her shortish brown hair tied messily in a ponytail, she donned a darker brown, well-worn straw cowboy hat, along with jeans, paddock boots, and chaps. I went over to say hello to her horse, CMTO Southern Cross, whose barn name or nickname is Faith. I let the sweet, dun-colored horse smell my flat, outstretched hand and gave Faith a pet on her withers. At fifteen hands high, Wylie's horses were a bit larger than the typical Marsh Tacky. She joked that she wasn't sure what she fed them to get them to this size.

"Faith had a baby for me this past year, and she's twelve years old," Wylie said as she brushed Faith's hindquarters. I noticed the darker stripe along her back, what's called a dorsal stripe and is typical for a dun horse. "And that's Sweet Home Alabama, a.k.a. Bama."

"Yeah," I nodded, thinking fondly of Alabama, another state I've traveled extensively through.

Bama was a beautiful clay-baked dun Marsh Tacky. All the horses looked exceedingly well groomed and cared for. In addition to Wylie and me riding Faith and Breeze today, Colin Drew and Travis McKnight, president and vice president of the Marsh Tacky Association, were out riding with us.

Wylie shared more about the lineage of these Marsh Tacky horses, who descended from the early Spanish settlers or conquistadors who brought horses with them to the Americas and built settlements along the East Coast trade routes. Over time, some of those settlements were either destroyed or abandoned, with the horses being left to fend for themselves. These Marsh Tacky horses are descendants of those original Spanish colonial horses. They are proven survivors.

During colonial times, these horses were used to plow fields and carry people. Basically, they were used to do anything that you can think of where today we'd use cars or trucks. During the Revolution, Francis Marion and the Patriot troops who rode with him are thought to have used these hardy descendants of Spanish horses to navigate the South Carolina backcountry. Wylie explained that the reasons these Marsh Tacky horses were so desired in South Carolina is why she and others are trying to save them today.

"My personal experience is hog hunting," Wylie said in her high-pitched Southern voice. "When you get into those swamps, it gets pretty rough. There's a lot of mud, a lot of briars, under-brush. These horses are very surefooted. They're very agile. As you see, they're on the smaller side, so that makes them able to navigate some of the tighter areas of the swamps."

Wylie seemed confident, leading me to believe that we'd have a good ride on these non-temperamental and thoughtful Marsh Tacky horses today.

We saddled up and began riding down a dirt trail which had lush green paddocks lined with dark wooden fences on the left and more dense forest on the right. I was riding side by side with Wylie. Colin and Travis rode behind us.

"We do have one document that puts the Marsh Tacky in Marion's militia," Wylie said as we rode. I could hear my saddle squeaking a bit under my seat as I turned to listen more closely. "Marion's men were just common folk. They would have brought their own horses. We like the folklore of thinking that he was riding these little agile ponies that we are now riding today."

"It's interesting to think that these horses were so prevalent during colonial times and today they're endangered," I said.

"Marsh Tacky horses will remain on the critically endangered list until we reach one thousand," Wylie replied.

That is still a long way to go. In recent years, the total number of foals born in one year may be nineteen, which the association considers good. In my mind, I just hoped for more, because already I was falling in love with these horses. Breeze was a smooth ride and super calm. Then again, I was feeling very relaxed as my mind wandered back in time envisioning these horses through the ages as family members, warriors, helpers, and Patriot heroes.

"They also have a story with the Civil War," Wylie said.

Colin explained that when plantation owners were evacuating during Sherman's March to the Sea, his destructive path in 1864 across Georgia and then South Carolina, a lot of horses were sent to the barrier islands, where they were taken care of by the Gullah community that already had settlements there. They were used by the Gullah in farming and daily tasks and proved useful. That's why today the Marsh Tacky horses also have a lot of history with the Gullah community.

We decided to ride off the trails into the woods to a deeper spot where there weren't any more trails but there was a slight clearing.

"We're doing an off-road adventure here," I exclaimed as Wylie turned to lead us into a more densely forested area on horseback.

"To really appreciate the horses is to get in the woods and experience that kind of riding, just to see exactly what they can do," Wylie said as I used my hand to shield by face from a lower branch. I gingerly moved to my right and let the branch swing back to my left as we trudged through the leaves and brambles underfoot.

"This is the type of more difficult riding that the horses would have had to go through during the American Revolution," I wondered aloud, thinking it would have been much more difficult, especially under the threat of enemy forces lurking about.

I was starting to imagine it all more clearly, with Francis Marion and the rag-tag Patriots engaging in guerrilla warfare in the swamps of South Carolina's backcountry, mounting one of these hardy steeds to maneuver around British soldiers while carrying a message to another farm or camp.

"Okay," I exclaimed, as Breeze navigated boldly around some thin trees. I helped to guide her through vines hanging from branches all the way to the ground. I was impressed, thinking about how on these horses, I was faring better than I would alone in the woods.

"Sometimes you can probably just drop the reins and let them do the work." Wylie said.

I thought that Breeze would do better without me interfering, so I loosened my reins. She took the opportunity to lower her head further to almost sniff her way along, taking bigger strides.

"You said that those Marsh Tacky horses can go through anything. I'm believing this is proof,"

I called out to Wylie, smiling as we rode through the challenging terrain.

"We're really proud of the part that the Marsh Tacky played in South Carolina," Wylie said, giving Faith a pat on her withers as we went through a clearing leading back out to the main road and out of the woods.

I was delighted to know more about these horses and extremely proud of people like Wylie, Colin, and Travis who were helping to keep the breed alive and sharing their history and modern prowess with people like me.

"The protection of the Country greatly depends upon…a superior cavalry," Nathanael Greene said in February of 1782. I was experiencing firsthand how true Greene's words were.

During the Southern Campaign, it wasn't an elite group of polished soldiers or horses that helped lead the Patriots' charge or helped Continental soldiers and their families survive. It was a common "tacky" horse. Being from Myrtle Beach, where the word *tacky* is often used by outsiders to describe aspects of the Grand Strand, and it can be an affront, I felt a kindred spirit with these horses. In fact, I was learning they were polished, confident, and capable. They definitely weren't common at all.

Historic Camden: Life Under Redcoats and Resilience

I admit that I do love visiting with a good costumed interpreter, but it was even better to meet one who came with chickens. Stacey Ferguson met me at Historic Camden, a 104-acre Revolutionary War living history park located a few blocks from downtown and a fifteen-minute drive from the Camden Battlefield.

With an effervescent smile, Stacey was dressed in a long brown colonial-style working woman's dress with a red-and-white-striped sash around her top and a white bonnet atop her reddish hair, which was neatly pulled back. She was telling me about the four Dominique chickens running through the grass and across the red brick sidewalk around her feet. A heritage breed that has been around since the early settlers, Dominique chickens were popular for their versatility on farms.

The chickens, with their striking black-and-white-striped feathers and their red combs (the crests on their heads), ran close to the small white wooden home that serves as the visitor's center for Historic Camden. Stacey scooped one up so I could touch its super soft coat. It felt like wet silk.

She casually plopped it back onto the grass. It clucked and ran in a circle before skirting over to the blacksmith shop. In the distance, I spotted a blacksmith banging on a red-hot iron rod that he would be making into a large kitchen spoon. He worked away in a dark wooden workshop beside another covered area housing two eighteenth-century cannons that had been used by the British at the Battle of Camden and abandoned by them when they left Camden in 1781.

Interpreters like Stacey work to translate to visitors what life was like in Camden during the eighteenth century when the British were occupying the town. Tight on the details and passionate about history, she served twenty-four years in the Air Force and has a master of science in military arts. Anyone who sources and makes their own historically correct clothing already has me impressed, but Stacey was also impressive in that she takes the time to really learn and internalize the past for visitors. These interpreters often serve as guides or docents and are usually volunteers with whom you can interact at various historic sites across the nation.

I looked over from Stacey to the near distance to see the pillory and stocks. The pillory consisted of wooden boards nailed to poles with holes in the middle to accommodate head and hands. They were used as a punishment for crimes during colonial times, like cheating, where public shame and humiliation seemed fit. If you were lucky, you would be able to hunch over your hands and feet in the wooden board, staying for a day or less. More intense punishment was met with the stocks, where your legs would be restrained and you could be left for days or even weeks, allowing all who passed by to torture you. Sometimes they would nail your ear to the post in the middle.

Stacey walked over to an old water pump and began to fill a wooden bucket. This common work was a task normally performed by women, children, and servants, including enslaved people. Hand-driven pumps were popular in the late eighteenth century, but Stacey told me that we are not sure how prevalent they were in Camden before the early nineteenth century. It's just one of those things that no one wrote down, nor has an old pump been found in town. Wells were prevalent—the kind where you drop a bucket down to fill up. Some residents would have had their own wells on their property, and some would use communal wells, having to walk back and forth to fill their buckets.

Stacey picked up the thick wooden handle and motioned for me to take ahold of it. I grabbed the handle with both hands and bent my knees to lift it up, struggling to raise it even a few inches. It felt like lead. The middle of the old town was about a block north of where the pump is today. I thought about how strong people, including children, must have been, carrying these buckets a couple of blocks each day.

"Camden would have been bursting at the seams with all these visiting troops. Not to mention, underneath it all there was this animosity between the Loyalist families and the Patriot families that never went away," Stacey said as we walked towards one of the many original buildings on site that was moved here from another part of Camden to populate this historic park.

Historic Camden was created so that visitors could get a better a sense of life in colonial times in the backcountry of South Carolina, both when the British occupied Camden and afterwards. I like to visit places like this where I can immerse myself in action-oriented learning, as I feel it makes for a more in-depth, experiential understanding.

We walked over to the white wooden McCaa's Tavern, whose sign dated to 1794. It was painted with a colorful Macaw bird on the front. At one time the home and office of Dr. John McCaa, Historic Camden has turned it into a recreated eighteenth-century tavern. Taverns were central to life in colonial times in Camden. It had around twenty taverns by the early nineteenth century. Inside McCaa's you can walk the pine floors through two long side halls used for dining and dancing. You can also belly up to the cage bar in the taproom.

Cage bars had a gate that could be closed to protect the alcohol when the proprietor wanted to shut down the bar for the evening. As taverns were the place to get news, entertainment, or gossip, and where travelers could get a room for the night, they were often busy places. Sometimes, travelers would also need to share that room or even a bed with other travelers. As a frequent traveler myself, I can see how one might want to get into that cage bar late in the evening if one's roommate was perhaps snoring. I won't name any of the travelers or friends who have given me this experience of a bad's night sleep. But I will say wine or a beer can help!

Camden is the oldest inland town in South Carolina, originally founded by Irish Quakers. Later, Camden would be developed by Joseph Kershaw, who came to town from England, and opened a mercantile, a brewery, and a sawmill. Colonel Joseph Kershaw is called the "father of Camden" for his work in helping develop the town. Today, Camden is located in Kershaw County, named after the colonel.

In 1776, South Carolina joined the other twelve North American colonies and declared independence from Great Britain. Following the siege of Charleston in 1780, General Cornwallis marched with British soldiers to Camden to establish their main supply headquarters and a garrison. Camden was a center for trade and was chosen for its location along a main route between Charleston and Philadelphia, adjacent to the Wateree River and Big Pine Tree Creek with their booming milling operations. The town was situated within a network of British fortifications and posts in South Carolina in an area that could be well defended. Before the British arrived, word had spread about their imminent arrival, and residents destroyed gunpowder and munitions that had been stored in the powder magazine, a building used to warehouse gunpowder.

General Cornwallis and Lieutenant Colonel Rawdon, his second-in-command, had started off for Camden from Charleston on May 18, 1780, with 2,500 men in tow. Arriving in town, the British pillaged the local supplies, food, and forage and took over the home of Colonel Joseph Kershaw. Captured at the Battle of Camden, the British sent Kershaw to a prison in Bermuda. He would eventually return to South Carolina. His gravesite is at the old Episcopal cemetery off Bull Street between Broad and Church Street and his reconstructed home at Historic Camden.

The British completed making Camden an important garrison on June 1, 1780, just two months before the Battle of Camden. More action would happen in the town during the war. A second battle on April 25, 1781, the Battle of Hobkirk's Hill, was another British Victory. The army led by Major General Nathanael Greene was outmatched by Lieutenant Colonel

Francis Rawdon. Soon afterward, however, the British abandoned Camden, destroying what they could as they departed.

Stacey and I were standing by the cage bar in the tavern as she shared more about how the British took over Camden.

"After the fall of Charleston, the British started making their way towards Camden, and the citizens of Camden asked the British for protection, which is another way of saying, if you can't beat them, join them," Stacey said. "So, they basically asked the British to come in, and they let them take it over, as opposed to being utterly destroyed by the British. They were going to take it either way. Unfortunately, a lot of the fighting-aged men of Camden were on parole because they were in Charleston when that fell. So, by the terms of surrender for Charleston, they were not allowed to pick up a weapon and fight and therefore couldn't come here to defend their town. So, we invited in the British in 1780."

We know about life here from the impeccable records that the British kept. There was a lot of sickness, including malaria and dysentery. The British weren't used to the hot, humid South Carolina inland climate. When Cornwallis first arrived at Camden, as many as eight hundred soldiers were ill. Times were tense, as the British worked to keep a stronghold on this rugged area, which was also occupied by Patriots.

We walked outside across a wooden bridge to an area where there's a reconstructed British redoubt. Redoubts, or forts, like this one would have been positioned all around town. It was an outpost where the British soldiers would be stationed to guard the town, living in the block house in the middle of the fort.

"The population of soldiers here during the war, they really grew outside of their resources," Stacey said as we walked across the grass towards the redoubt. "If you think about how much food they need to feed that many soldiers, and then about a third of them at one point were sick with malaria and yellow fever and dysentery and all those kinds of wonderful things. So that would have completely taken over this town. And I think normal life, for the most part, was no longer normal. Not to mention underneath it all there was this animosity between the Loyalist families and the Patriot families that never went away. When the British moved in here, it emboldened those loyalists and they tried to kind of take the upper hand for a lot of local politics, if you will, which would have ramifications well after the war."

"They were surrounded by these redoubts and British and a lot of disease," I said. "They really needed to get a drink at that pub!"

Stacey explained that Camden would have been bursting with the troops and all the resources needed to feed, clothe, and house the many men, camp followers, and animals in tow. After the British left, many Loyalist families lost their property and ended up leaving the town.

Tumultuous times in Camden would change the dynamics of the population and the appearance of the landscape. The British destroyed much of the town's infrastructure when they left, burning what they could and leaving it to the Patriots to rebuild. They eventually would. Camden would rise again from the ashes to become a destination for visitors and horse lovers.

The Southern Campaign was a civil war with neighbors, families, and friends often having to choose sides. From my time in Camden with Rick Wise, riding Marsh Tacky horses with Wiley, and exploring everyday life in the backcountry with Stacey, I could see that while every location I visited on my travels was different, the throughlines of determination, ingenuity, and perseverance rang through. Camden's story reminded me of the story of so many Americans I meet on my travels today, who work hard and persevere despite challenges.

Steps away and across the parking lot from Historic Camden, travelers can stop for more historical context at the Revolutionary War Visitor Center, where interactive exhibitions reveal area history from the early days of the Cherokee through the Southern Campaign. Camden also has a lovely downtown that's great for antiquing and a colorful county farmer's market. For those exploring, keep a lookout for the Boykin Spaniel, both alive and immortalized. A series of statues of Boykin Spaniel puppies are sprinkled around the city, including outside of the Revolutionary War Visitor Center. The Boykin Spaniel is South Carolina's official state dog, and people in Camden love these chocolate-brown family pets, originally bred for hunting in South Carolina.

CHAPTER V

Delaware—Small State, Great Resolve

New Castle: Open-Air Museum of Colonial Curiosities

Walk around New Castle, Delaware, and you'll find yourself in an open-air museum of colonial curiosities. Except this is not a museum collection. Instead, it's a living and working collection of more than five hundred well-preserved buildings dating from the seventeenth to nineteenth centuries. Part of the New Castle Historic District, these were not recreated into a colonial theme park. They are, in fact, treasured and authentic historic spaces that make up a picture-perfect city overflowing with centuries-old stories of its past inhabitants. I had traveled to New Castle twice over the years and was always captivated by its outwardly regal appearance and meticulously preserved buildings. My most recent exploration of the city would shed a light on the more clandestine and rebellious side of New Castle's fascinating history.

New Castle is located just south of Wilmington along the Delaware River. First settled by the Dutch who established a fort in 1651, New Castle would be fought over by the Netherlands, Sweden, and England in its early years. Each group of Europeans built their own forts and vied for control, but in 1664, it was England who would claim the land. In 1682, William Penn would land in New Castle before making his way to Philadelphia.

Today, there are a myriad of architectural styles spanning the centuries, including Colonial, Victorian, Victorian Revival, and Craftsman. Michael Connolly, executive director of the New Castle Historical Society, met with me on two visits to provide a historical overview of this interesting city. Having lived in New Castle for more than thirty years and with a special focus on historic preservation, he was the perfect guide. Wearing a tweed jacket and light blue button-down, along with thicker-rimmed glasses, he looked all the part of a New Castle gentleman on my most recent visit.

It was a gorgeous spring day with not a cloud in the sky and the local flowers in full bloom, as we walked outside of the New Castle Court House Museum, just three blocks from the mighty Delaware River. The Court House dates to 1732, and it is the very site where the state of Delaware was born.

At the time, the Court House hosted all levels of Delaware's legal system and from its beginnings in 1732, it would be the site of many conversations that shaped the future of Delaware. From 1682 to 1776, New Castle and Delaware were part of the Pennsylvania colony. On June 15, 1776, inside the Court House, the Delaware Assembly decided to separate from Great Britain and Pennsylvania and form its own independent state.

Part of Delaware's First State National Historic Park, the New Castle Court House is one of the oldest surviving courthouses in the United States and a registered National Historic Landmark. Inside are portraits of the state's past leaders like George Read, artifacts, and exhibits related to Delaware's rich history, including its Native American history, the colonization of the land, and Delaware's role in the Underground Railroad.

Michael and I walked along New Castle's brick sidewalks looking up at the red brick Georgian-style building, accented with windows framed by blue metal shutters. The Court House's wood-shingle gable roof is topped with an eight-sided frame cupola detailed with a dome. Michael pointed out the balcony where on July 24, 1776, the Declaration of Independence was read for the first time to the citizens of New Castle.

The Court House is also significant for being an Underground Railroad Network to Freedom site. In 1848, Thomas Garrett and fellow abolitionist John Hunn were accused by Charles Glanding and Elizabeth Turner of violating the Fugitive Slave Acts. Garrett and Hunn were active in helping enslaved people escape to freedom as part of the Underground Railroad. Garrett covertly served as stationmaster from his house in Wilmington, Delaware.

A judge ruled that Garrett and Hunn were guilty of the charges, and they were sentenced to pay huge fines. Despite their convictions, both would continue their work to help others escape to freedom. Garrett frequently met with Harriet Tubman in Wilmington and helped an estimated 2,700 enslaved individuals in their journey to freedom before his death in 1871.

Michael and I walked along brick sidewalks past the town center's Green, originally laid out by a Dutch governor in 1655. Today a park, the Green has been a meeting place for more than two hundred years. We crossed the street to visit the colonial-era Van Dyke House. Outside, a marker for the Washington-Rochambeau National Historic Trail informed us that the Van

Dyke House was an important stop on the over six-hundred-mile trail that the French and Colonial troops traveled on with French General Rochambeau from Newport, Rhode Island, to Yorktown, Virginia, during the American Revolution. The French troops fought alongside Patriots to help the Colonialists defeat the British. The classic, red-brick Federal-style house is accented with white shutters and a poppy-red door, dating back to 1820. It was visited by the Marquis de Lafayette on his farewell tour of the colonies in 1824. While in Delaware, Lafayette attended the wedding of Dorcas Van Dyke to Charles I. DuPont in this house on October 6, 1824. Lafayette was recorded as the official witness to the marriage ceremony.

Like many who stop here to read the historic placard and photograph the house, I wondered what it would have been like for the residents of the Van Dyke house to care for and maintain such a grand home. It looked so well kept. I later investigated this topic further and found that the owners do say you can't own a house like this without truly loving it. I also learned that the home had a history with Hollywood. *Dead Poets Society* director Peter Weir rented the house and its furnishings during the movie's filming. He lived there with his wife and two children, and the house was frequently visited by actor and comedian Robin Williams and the production team. In the film, New Castle serves as the fictional backdrop for many scenes, along with St. Andrew's School in Middletown, Delaware, representing Welton Academy in Vermont.

Steps away, we passed an ornate wooden sign for Bridgewater Jewelers, a Delaware small business since 1883. It's amazing when businesses like this stand the test of time! It started in Wilmington and moved to New Castle in 1885.

As I looked around at the historical placards and architecture, it seemed that every dwelling and building was significant. Michael and I turned onto Fourth Street towards the elegant Amstel House, whose name reminded me of beer. Named after New Castle's seventeenth-century Dutch name, New Amstel, the Georgian-style red brick house was built in 1738 by Irish immigrant Dr. John Finney, who at the time was New Castle's largest landowner. Nicholas Van Dyke Sr. would rent the house to Dr. Finney's children following Finney's passing and would reside there during the American Revolution. Van Dyke lived in the house from 1776 until 1785 and he was a member of the Second Continental Congress, a signatory to the Articles of Confederation, and governor of Delaware from 1783 to 1786.

The blue-green door creaked as Michael and I opened it. I could smell the remnants of a wood-burning fire. Michael shared that they demonstrate hearth cooking here, as part of their public education programs. Hearth cooking was common in colonial times, but not without its mishaps. Imagine cooking in a large, open fireplace using long-handled pots and utensils, and you might feel your hand start to burn just from your thoughts.

From the main entranceway, we turned to the room on the right, the parlor, where a grandfather clock stood in one corner and a grayed-blue trimmed the doorway, windows, and wood paneling and decoratively split the white walls on one side. A large fireplace was set amid a wall lined completely with blue paneling and built-in cabinetry displaying a set of china amid a vibrant orange colored-backdrop.

Michael told me that an important wedding took place here on April 30, 1784, when Anne Van Dyke married Kensey Johns. On his way back to Mount Vernon from Philadelphia,

George Washington traveled through New Castle and attended the wedding.

"He crashed the wedding," Michael said. "My thing is, a lot of these houses have signs that say, George Washington slept here. I say we should put a sign that says George Washington partied here."

"He seemed to find those parties all over the place," I said, thinking that I'd heard a similar story that took place at the Old Exchange and Provost Dungeon in Charleston, South Carolina. In fact, in many places I'd visited, there were stories of George Washington stopping by, staying, or even "partying."

Following his American Revolution victory, George Washington was an extremely popular public figure. Michael pointed out that the chairs in this room were used at Dorcas Van Dyke's wedding to Charles I. DuPont.

"And one chair in particular has been tracked by the family," Michael said, pointing to a dark wooden dining chair. "They have a little plaque on the back. It says that Lafayette sat in this chair, so that's a very special chair to us here."

I examined the chair for the plaque, and it did indeed! Now, Michael and I just needed a good colonial wedding to crash. Colonial weddings were often held in the bride's family home. Sometimes multi-day parties, they involved food, dancing, and games. I could imagine guests eating oysters and dancing, perhaps in this very parlor.

We ventured across the hall to another parlor that also served as an office. On the wooden desk, papers were spread across the table. In 1777, British warships on their way to Philadelphia were anchored in the river right off New Castle. At the time, Nicholas Van Dyke Sr. may have contemplated what to do in this very office.

"One of the British officers made a comment that most of the principal houses in New Castle are vacant because of their inhabitants' participation in the rebellion," Michael relayed.

It seemed to be a theme in New Castle—people speaking their minds and acting according to what they believed as they took risks to vie for independence. But not in the back of the house, where the enslaved people would have been stoking a grand fire in the large English hearth fireplace. They may have overheard conversations about breaking free from Great Britain. Imagine what they must have thought as these conversations and celebrations went on in their midst?

"One of the things we have to recognize about the Revolution is that there is this paradox," Michael said, as we stand alongside the giant fireplace. "You have people like Nicholas Van Dyke who are clamoring for liberty and yelling cries of freedom while at the same time, people are enslaved in their households."

Standing in what had been a kitchen where the enslaved would be toiling over a hot fire, making food and perhaps washing laundry, it didn't make sense to me.

Some people of the time period did recognize the hypocrisy, like Abigail Adams, who wrote in a September 22, 1774 letter to her husband, John, "It always appeared a most iniquitous scheme to me—to fight ourselves for what we are daily robbing and plundering from those who have as good a right to freedom as we have." The 1776 United States Declaration of Independence would go on to state "that all men are created equal, that they are endowed by their Creator with certain unalienable Rights, that among these are Life, Liberty and the pursuit of Happiness," yet this actual right to African Americans wouldn't be granted for almost another hundred years, in 1865, with the Thirteenth Amendment to the US Constitution.

We left the Amstel House and strolled over to the Northeast end of the Green to explore the cemetery at the historic Immanuel Episcopal Church, located on Harmony Street. Founded in 1689, this is one of the oldest Episcopal parishes in the United States. George Read, who signed the Declaration of Independence on behalf of Delaware and who helped draft the Constitution, is buried here along with other leaders from the American Revolution. The church still has an active congregation.

We were treated to a symphony as we entered through the iron gate into the churchyard cemetery. I listened to the melodic mix of birds chirping and the church bells ringing. I followed Michael past gravestones that dated to the early 1700s and was struck by a marker for Ann Blount, who passed away in 1885. Her cemetery plot was blanketed with blooming purple iris. How wonderful, I thought, that Ann's grave was alight with fresh flowers all these years later. I wondered who tended to Ann Blount's gravesite and if she had family still in New Castle. Some people living in New Castle today do have roots in the Revolution. I noticed another large, upright gravestone etched with the name Gertrude, my grandmother's name, and felt a twinge of sad remembrance. It reminded me of how much I loved my grandmother. Being in a cemetery can be a fascinating walk through history, but it can also be a little sad.

I examined the church with its gray stucco walls, tall white steeple, and clock tower. Originally constructed in 1703, in the 1980s the church suffered a massive fire and had to be reconstructed. What was created is what we see today—simple and elegant. I walked inside the cool interiors. The walls were a cream color with bright white wooden pews and an elegant gold chandelier hanging high above the alter. The space filled with music. I looked up to see an organist was beginning to practice in the organ loft.

Not far from this Episcopal church was a Presbyterian church. Michael shared that the Presbyterians were known to be feisty, with a large population hailing from Scotland who were interested in separating from the King. Unlike those Presbyterians, not everyone in Delaware was comfortable standing up to Great Britain.

I asked Michael more about the character of the Delaware people and why from the early days of our nation, they were so independent, despite the perils of being so.

"A lot of it comes from the fact that we're a really small state, so we are maybe a little feisty, because we busted away from Pennsylvania and we're out on our own now. We all know each other. Also, we say there's six degrees of separation between people in Delaware, so we all have a sort of camaraderie as Delawareans. We're very close knit. We're proud of the communities in Delaware and proud of the state in general," Michael said.

It sounded like a small family with an independent spirit that had sprung out of a melting pot of peoples, beginning with Delaware's Native American Lenape tribes and continuing with the Swedish, Dutch, Finnish, Irish, Scottish, and English settlers.

I had heard that there was another historical building that would be a good place to grab a bite for lunch. Back in colonial times, an "ordinary" would have been a gathering place for travelers to stop on their travels to eat, drink, and stay the night for a set price. These ordinaries often began in people's homes and evolved into the first bed-and-breakfasts or inns.

I left Michael to dine at Jessop's Tavern, which has been recreated to depict a colonial ordinary with cozy wood paneling lining the ceiling. It is housed in a historic building, dating to 1674, when a craftsman cooper named Abraham Jessop lived there. Although the restaurant itself is a recreation, I truly felt like I was stepping back to colonial times on my visit. Beer was a top drink during that time, as water was often potentially dangerous to consume. Today, Jessop's Tavern has a vast beer offering, with more than three hundred bottles of Belgian beer, which pairs well with the Tavern's delicious shepherd's pie.

It was served in a big silver bowl, and the thick, dark gravy made it look like a whole chocolate cake. My server was dressed in colonial serving attire. She brought the human-head-sized plate of shepherd's pie to my table. It jiggled like a rigid Jello. I used a fork to sink into the layers of mashed potatoes, vegetables, and meat, each one pushing the next down just a little before curving up along the bifurcated end. I knew that once I ate this and drank some of this Belgian beer, I'd soon be suffering from a food coma. I chased down each bite of the savory pie with sips from a glass of Brasserie d'Achouffe beer which has a fantastic mix of savory, sweet, and hoppy spice.

Leaving Jessop's Tavern, I could have used a walk or run, but I figured some fresh air would be just as helpful. I strolled around the corner to the Read House & Gardens, a National Historic Landmark that one shouldn't miss when visiting New Castle. This house has been called the best example of a Philadelphia Federal-style house still in existence. It was the vision of George Read II, whose father was an important Delaware statesman, having served as the state's governor, US senator, and signatory to both the Declaration of Independence and Constitution. The Read House was built in the late eighteenth century and was at the time the largest home in Delaware—a title it held for a century. The interiors are exquisite and thought provoking, displaying artwork that shares and interprets the rich history of New Castle.

The back gardens are a good place to sit and contemplate the history of the space, but I was lucky enough to have a docent provide me access to the roof, where the views of the Delaware River and the Delaware Memorial Bridge mix sights of historic New Castle with more modern homes and buildings. It made me think of how wild it would be to see a timelapse of New Castle over time from above, as European ships arrived with settlers to meet Native Americans, armies marched through the city during Revolutionary times, and Underground Railroad travelers ran through the night prior to and during the Civil War. Equally as stellar was that this historic American city is so well preserved and lived-in today with residents maintaining its beguiling past.

Hale–Byrnes House: Under the Sycamore with Washington

It's not every day you get welcomed by a soldier from the First Delaware Regiment at a house where George Washington presided over a council of war during the American Revolution. Historian Josh Loper was standing at the ready by the entrance to the Hale-Byrnes House, dressed as a member of the distinguished regimental unit known as the "Delaware Blues," with a blue regimental coat with red facings. It was the kind of reception I could look forward to in Delaware, a small state where only one American Revolution battle took place, but one that stood at the crossroads of Revolutionary activity during the founding of our nation.

I would discover on my travels throughout Delaware that the residents had a zeal for history and preservation. Josh Loper was my introduction to this time over 250 years ago, as he stood outside of red brick Georgian house located today along Stanton Christiana Road in Newark, Delaware. The home is not far from the site of the Battle of Cooch's Bridge, that one Revolutionary War battle fought in Delaware, and less than a fifteen-minute drive from the cities of Wilmington and New Castle, Delaware.

An American flag waved in the wind from the second floor of the Hale-Byrnes House. Just below it, a white sign memorialized that the house was first constructed in 1750. Next to the front door, a wooden and canvas piece of art depicted a colonial flag, with thirteen red and white stripes and thirteen stars arranged in a circle. I examined Josh's black tricorn hat lined with bright yellow trim and blue coat with red cuffs lined with buttons and red facings. He carried a rifle, the butt of which hung alongside his white breeches. The First Delaware Regiment was organized in January of 1776 and was known for its members' dependability in battles. As I entered the historic home I smiled at Josh, who attempted to remain at guard and not glance at me, though he did slightly wrinkle his mustache.

It was here that all the military leaders of the Patriots of the American Revolution—Generals Washington, Lafayette, Wayne, Maxwell, Sullivan, and Greene—held a council of war on September 6, 1777. They were strategizing on how to best defend Wilmington from the British Army. The Battle of Cooch's Bridge had occurred just three days earlier, when the British Army—led by General Sir William Howe—was on its way to capture Philadelphia. At Cooch's Bridge, British soldiers defeated General Washington's Corps of Light Infantry, led by General William Maxwell. I visited this location in Delaware, too, considered hallowed ground today.

Following the battle, General Washington needed to regroup in this house and, on my visit, apparently so did Josh Loper. As I walked inside, he whizzed past me, almost in the blink of an eye. He was heading for an outfit change. He called to me from the other room informing me that he'd meet me in the kitchen. I tilted my head and made a funny face, thinking of how some of these reenactors can be quite eccentric.

I was in the main entranceway of the Hale-Byrnes House. The walls were painted a colonial teal with brown wood period furnishings. Paintings or reproductions from colonial times, including, of course, of George Washington, lined the walls. Built in 1750 by Samuel Hale and owned in 1776 by Daniel Byrnes, a miller and preacher, the Hale-Byrnes House was restored by the Delaware Society for the Preservation of Antiquities and donated to the State of Delaware in 1971.

Open each month for tours and for special events, signs outside share its brief story, describing details about its location on the Washington-Rochambeau National Historic Trail.

I walked over to look out the back door through a wood-framed window. The backyard view was of a small patch of grass and the peaceful White Clay Creek. At the time of the American Revolution, waterways like this would have been highways—the most efficient way for people and goods to travel thought the colonies. The Delaware River and its many tributaries were of great strategic importance during the American Revolution. Delaware's lower counties of New Castle, Kent, and Sussex were part of the Province of Pennsylvania beginning in 1682 and up to June 15, 1776, when the Delaware legislature voted to break all ties with Great Britain, creating the independent State of Delaware. In September of that year, the name "The Delaware State" was coined.

I heard someone shuffling around in the next room and walked through the open doorway to meet Josh in what was set up as the kitchen, a cozy room with a grand brick walk-in fireplace appointed with various kettles and pans for hearth cooking. Josh had changed clothes and was now dressed in shades of brown, red, and blue, wearing something that a mill hand might wear. He was depicting someone who might have worked for Daniel Byrnes, one of the home's namesakes. Josh had switched his black tricorn hat to a lighter brown with darker trim and the red-and-blue jacket to one of all navy. I wondered what his closet at home looked like!

"This is truly one of Delaware's little hidden gems," Josh said, as I went to take a seat with him at the wooden table in front of the hearth. "Most people don't even realize we are here when they drive by us on the highway, not a stone's throw away."

The house was built in 1750, but like many homes, it expanded over time in several stages. We had entered the original 1750 portion and were now in the 1775 addition with its servant's wing and walk-in kitchen and charming English-style hearth.

The house is located near the confluence of Red Clay and White Clay Creeks and the Christiana River—a great location near the highways of colonial times. Mr. Byrnes was a Quaker lay minister and wanted to stay out of the war but, like so many people, couldn't ignore the turmoil. He found himself square in the middle of the British Army's northern advance from Maryland and Washington's Continental Army's southern advance from Philadelphia.

Early in the morning, there had been a knock on the door. Several of Washington's scouts told Daniel that at 5:00 p.m., George Washington would be holding a council of war at his house. We do not know if Daniel's wife and children were there that evening or had escaped upstream to Daniel's brother Caleb Byrnes's mill on the Red Clay Creek.

The following day, the Americans took forty wheels of cheese from the spring house for their troops to eat and headed towards Chadds Ford where they participated in the Battle of Brandywine on September 11.

"A very bad day indeed," I agreed, thinking not at the very least about all that cheese. Mrs. Byrnes must have been truly downtrodden to lose it.

I think we all might be able to relate to what Mr. and Mrs. Byrnes went through to some degree: Their entire lives, everything they had worked, saved, and strived for, was very suddenly and completely upended. They must have wondered if the sacrifices they'd made were all for naught. I'm sure they also thought about how they would recover.

Perhaps Mr. Byrnes thought that if the British proved victorious, the Continental Army's promissory note would likely be worthless. He may not have even had the time to think that much, because the council-of-war meeting happened so quickly on September 6. It included the Marquis de Lafayette, General Washington and his staff, and Generals Knox, Sullivan, and Greene. It was a meeting involving some of the great military minds of the day.

A few days later, on September 11, 1777, the Battle of Brandywine would be the largest battle of the American Revolution, and the Continental Army would lose. The British would go on to take Philadelphia.

I asked Josh about the American sycamore tree out front, standing between the home and the road. It struck me as unusual when I entered. I'd also noticed it was featured in a painting on the western wall by reenactor Bryant White depicting George Washington and the other generals outside with their horses under and around a huge, more verdant tree.

It was April when I visited and there were just a few leaves on the spindly branches of the old tree, whose trunk was so hollowed out on one side that you could walk inside. The other had a tall, thinner open cavity, just large enough that I could almost squeeze in. An oblong opening hollowed out above looked like a fun place to try to throw a basketball, almost like a hoop.

The inner wood decays as sycamore trees age, so this hollowing-out is not unusual, but it did remind me that this tree had seen a lot over time. Sycamores were fashionable in the mid-eighteenth century, and this tree, known as a Witness Tree, is known to have been full-grown when the council of war was held here, and it raised the awe factor at this historic site.

"I tell people, put your hand on this tree," Josh said. "And I do. And I get the amazing chance to tell them this was alive when General Washington was here. The horses were probably picketed underneath it."

Having had a child act shocked when they hear my age (somewhere in the forties realm), I imagine they'd be wonderstruck by a tree that's well over two hundred years old. I know that even in my older years, these trees were truly special to me. The fact that this one stood in front of this significant historical home and building was even more extraordinary.

I felt something moving behind me and looked down to see an orange cat stretching his front legs by the door in the sun, the afternoon light streaming in. Josh introduced the cat as Kenny, the historic home's resident cat. He called Kenny his assistant docent.

"He is convinced that this house is here specifically for him. And he is convinced that we all come to see him specifically and pay him homage," Josh laughed.

Being a cat lady myself and coming from generations of devout cat owners, I clearly understood that Kenny knew he ruled the place. I wondered if he ever climbed the witness tree outside and what energy he'd felt there if so.

Outside of the Hale-Byrnes home, cars passed by every minute or so. I walked out and put my hand on the witness tree, seeing what wisdom it might deliver. This tree had seen so much, from famous generals to great turmoil, and for sure one of the lesser known, but interesting, events that affected the founding of our nation. If only trees could speak! I was glad that Josh Loper could, so I could step back in time for even a few minutes to better understand the significance of what had happened here—how every little piece of history contributes to the future and how when we enable people to visit sites like these, they can better understand our past.

First State Heritage Park in Dover: Capitol of Conviction

Many people might skip Delaware in favor of places with more well-known Revolutionary War sites, like Philadelphia or Williamsburg, Virginia, but this small state, where only one battle was fought, is well worth the diversion. In the middle of Britain's thirteen colonies, Delaware's many waterways served as a trading hub during the colonial period. Places like New Castle, Wilmington, Newark, Cooch's Bridge, Odessa, and Dover all carry interesting stories.

About a forty-five-minute drive south from the Hale-Byrnes House and I was in Dover, Delaware's capital city. Also home to Delaware State University, this fetching capital city—with its Victorian homes and Georgian-style historic buildings—brings travelers back in time. A prime location to learn about Delaware's historic significance is at Dover's Green, which for hundreds of years has been a central hub in the city. Today, this small park is part of the First State National Historical Park and First State Heritage Park. It hosts the occasional festival and is surrounded by historic buildings.

Dover has roots in 1683, when it was founded as a town by William Penn, who is better known for founding the Province of Pennsylvania. Towns in Delaware were developed along its waterways. The site for Dover was chosen because of its high ground along the Saint Jones River, which flows to the Delaware Bay, and because it was already bisected by an active travel route known as the King's Highway. William Penn named the city after its namesake port city in England. The land had been taken over by English colonizers and acquired by Penn. Prior to that, the lands were the home of the Lenape and Nanticoke.

The Green was first laid out in 1717, and it became a central place for the people of Dover to live and work, as well as for the trading and sale of goods. During the American Revolution, it was also a place for markets, gatherings, and troop reviews. While it is lush and emerald colored with grass and trees today, then it was mostly dirt and a bit messy, without the manicured lawn and planned park we see today.

On my visit, it was a gorgeous April day with bright blue skies, and I walked up to the Old State House. The Georgian-style Delaware State House rests alongside the Green. A stately two-story building, it was completed in 1791 and served as

Delaware's capitol during the early years of our nation. With the courtroom in session and the way the roads were during colonial times, the Green would have been a noisy and sometimes chaotic place. Prior to the construction of the current building, which has been painstakingly restored over the years, a small brick building stood at this site, dating to 1722. It was here that on July 29, 1776, the Declaration of Independence was read from its porch.

I was meeting Vertie Lee, the curator of education for Delaware's Division of Historical and Cultural Affairs, who had attended the University of Delaware. She was wearing a dark, long-sleeved and high-necked flower-print dress and high boots, which clicked as she walked over to shake my hand. She had long, reddish hair, pale skin, and blue-rimmed glasses and spoke quickly as she introduced me to the capitol building. She first described the layout of the building. On the first floor, there's an eighteenth-century-style courtroom, while on the second floor decisions would be made by the state legislature. It's here that we'd also find notable art.

As we walked through the first-floor courthouse, I looked over to the two freestanding geometrical staircases, the banisters of which were painted a shade of robin's-egg blue. At the time they were constructed, the staircases were an architectural nod to Great Britain and one that would have been rare to see in America. The courtroom was designed as an English courtroom with jury boxes and witness boxes. The building was restored in the 1970s as part of Delaware's bicentennial commemorations of the signing of the Declaration of Independence. The restoration ensured that it looked as it would have in the eighteenth century, including the paint colors.

Four columns inside the courtroom today framed the stunning floating staircases. I made a fist and knocked on the column by me, which turned out to be hollow, while the one closest to Vertie was solid. She knocked on it to prove it. Three of the four columns are original and solid. The hollow column was added during the renovations.

"They looked at the plaster, and they were able to find the balusters embedded in the wall, the imprint of them. They were able to figure out the whole scale and angle and then even what the balusters used to look like," Vertie said excitedly.

We were geeking out about this historical architecture.

"These architects and designers, they were like investigators here," I said.

"Yes. Yes. And that's a fun thing about history, right?"

The courtroom would be the setting for many historical events, including the trial and conviction of Samuel D. Burris, a free Black Underground Railroad conductor, who in 1847 was arrested for helping enslaved people escape to freedom. He spent time in jail and was eventually moved to California, where he rallied for freedom for the enslaved. It wouldn't be until 2015 that he was recognized through a pardon by Delaware Governor Jack Markell in the very courtroom where Vertie and I were standing.

In this building, we also saw evidence of Delaware's complicated history with enslavement. On the second floor in the General Assembly, the legislature unsuccessfully voted on three occasions to abolish slavery, but it remained legal in Delaware long after other states and up until December 1865, when the Thirteenth Amendment was ratified and slavery was finally abolished in all states and territories. Delaware, however, did not itself ratify the Thirteenth Amendment until February 1901, more than thirty-five years after the end of the Civil War.

We walked up the floating staircase to investigate the second floor, where Vertie told me I might have a George Washington sighting. George Washington seemed to have been everywhere during the American Revolution. Once you see him in artwork at various historic sites across the east coast or hear his name repeated by many docents on your visits, you'll think, like I did, that he must have been the rockstar of the American Revolution.

We entered the Senate Chamber—a beautiful, neat, echoey room with walls painted Prussian blue on top and lower moldings painted white. To the right of a row of desks set with quill ink pens, there was a large fireplace. I was sure that it would have been quite drafty in these cavernous, regal spaces in cooler months. Immediately in front of us stood a large seven-foot-high oil painting of General George Washington, so large that it almost didn't fit between the two windows.

"Last time they took the painting for conservation, he had to go out of the second-floor window," Vertie laughed—the *he* referring to George Washington.

Painted by French artist Denis Alexander Volozan after George Wahington's death in 1799 at the age of sixty-seven, it was commissioned by the Delaware General Assembly.

"But the people who commissioned it did not like the way he looked," Vertie said. "They thought his face was a little too old for it to have been what he looked like during the American Revolution."

"He does look strange in this case," I said, looking at a rather wrinkled George Washington.

"Yeah, a little aged for the Revolution. So, 1802 and 1803, there were still people who knew Washington, and they didn't like it. The rumor is the painting ended up in one of the closets or put away, so that we didn't get a chance to see him," Vertie said with a chuckle.

Whether it was an accurate portrayal or not, the painting today lines the walls of the Senate Chamber. Ironic that it was George Washington who is believed to have felt awkward about his appearance. Here we have a French artist getting flack for painting a George Wahington that others didn't like at all.

Across the hall is the House of Representatives, where seven members from each of the three counties, twenty-one representatives in total, would congregate. The walls were an eighteenth-century green shade that I could have seen in a cool, swanky New York City upscale hotel bar or Park Avenue home today. There were also paintings by Thomas Sully of two Delaware heroes from the War of 1812, Jacob Jones and Thomas Macdonough. Vertie told me that big things were voted upon in this very room, like compensation for emancipation.

As I looked around at the meticulously preserved room, I thought about how much time had been spent restoring, preserving, and maintaining this building. The care taken showed me as a traveler that events of importance had happened here. It made me want to learn more about Delaware's history and how this small state had an effect not only on the American Revolution, but also on subsequent history.

From my various visits to Delaware, I knew the people I had met knew quite a bit about the state's history. My next stop on the Green would take me to a historic workshop and tavern complex outbuilding, where I discovered that even young people appeared to have a passion for history in Delaware. Just across from the Old State House is the small John Bell House, a tiny gem teeming with history. It is worth a stop inside to speak to a costumed interpreter docent. If you're on a guided walking tour of the Dover Green, many of these tours start here.

The John Bell House is the oldest wood-framed structure in Dover and one of the oldest wooden structures in the state of Delaware. Its exact date of construction is unknown, but what is known is that the building stood here in 1760. In the attic, workers found the date 1743 punched with an awl in a stud, so the building may in fact be older than that. The tiny building has a basement and small loft space. Its exterior is plain, tan colored with brown shutters, unassuming. Rather like the history it holds. The John Bell House is shadowed on the Green by grander brick buildings, which makes it stand out. I looked at it and thought that it could be one of our nation's first tiny houses!

I walked up the brick sidewalk and inside to meet Jane Pilato, a historical interpreter dressed the part of an upper middle-class woman of the eighteenth century. She was seated at a table with a willow basket filled with materials for what we might today call a craft project, but which would have been a necessity in colonial times. She was spinning raw wool into yarn to eventually be woven into fabric like that of her shift—a light undergarment worn by women of the time. She was wearing clothing that she had sewn by hand, including a white cap with a blue ribbon, a white apron, and petticoats.

I couldn't see her stays—which were also handmade. If you think about corsets, then you'll have a good picture of stays. These boned undergarments had practical uses, providing back and breast support, helping create an upright posture and holding up the heavy garments that were then in fashion. While stays worn by working women were more for practicality, stays worn by upper-class women served, more like corsets, to bring in the waist and provide women with more of an hourglass figure.

She had purchased only one part of her outfit: her necklace. I asked her how long it took her to make her clothing, and she told me over one hundred hours. Her time spent making garments proved her dedication to her job. It was not the fast fashion we can easily acquire today.

Jane told me that one of the beautiful things about the clothing from the Revolutionary period is that it was highly adjustable. Still in her early twenties, Jane said this was her first recorded interview, though she was prolific in filming her own videos for TikTok. She was giddy with excitement as we spoke.

"You'll notice I have my pins here and my apron is tied on. My petticoats are tied on. You can gain or lose about forty pounds, and all your clothes will still fit. We all have that favorite pair of jeans. But if we gain forty pounds, we're not going to fit into them," Jane said with a smile. "That's just because women are known to have bodily fluctuations in weight, especially with pregnancy."

These garments, which took a long time to make, were created to last a very long time, through many stages of life. With Colonial women having larger families than we may have today, sometimes seven to ten children, these long-lasting, adjustable garments were practical. I asked Jane for more details about the John Bell House.

"This building is remarkable for how unremarkable it is. Most buildings from the eighteenth century survive because they're made of stone or brick or because they had important people living or working there. This building has none of that," said Jane. "The people of Dover knew it was historic. They just didn't know its significance. It's one of the best testaments to what a wood-frame structure would have looked like in the eighteenth century."

The John Bell House is across the Green from a historical marker for the Golden Fleece Tavern. It was at this very tavern that thirty delegates from Delaware met to formally ratify the United States Constitution, honoring Delaware as "The First State" on December 7, 1787. Elizabeth Battell was the proprietor of the Golden Fleece Tavern at the time. Called the "Godmother of the First State," she ran it with her husband, French Battell, a quartermaster in the local militia. Many people called it Battell's Tavern, and like all taverns, it was a gathering place that provided some of the community's only opportunity for social interaction. During the American Revolution, it was a key site for much wartime communication and exchange. Elizabeth ran the tavern from 1777 to 1792, continuing as manager even after her husband's death in 1781.

A church bell rang in the distance, and I thought about how the small John Bell House remained through it all. It served as the working space for John Bell, who owned a tavern beside it, which he ran with his wife, Margaret. Their son, also named John Bell, would run it through the Revolution. His son, John Bell III, would open a hat shop and use the space as his workshop and storage space. Later it would become a print shop, post office, lawyers' offices, and had other uses until it became part of the First State Heritage Park.

Inside there was a small bed on one side of the room atop which rested various hats. Dried meats, corn husks, and onions hung from the ceiling along white plaster walls which were accented with exposed wood timber frames. On the other side of the room was a small white fireplace with a small fire burning. Jane continued to work, pulling and picking out fluffy pieces of wool and twisting them onto her drop spindle.

"There was very devastating fire in 1863 that would burn down the hotel that's next door. And the people of Dover knew that this building was historic and so they rushed to preserve it," Jane said. "If not for their actions that night, this building would have also gone up in flames."

The Tavern of the Golden Fleece had two large assembly rooms that could accommodate the legislature's meetings. It was the best place of the times for this type of gathering.

"You had French and Elizabeth Battell. They were known as the best host and hostesses this side of Philadelphia," Jane said excitedly. "They boasted seventeen beds, and they had a stable for carriages. It was advertised in Philadelphia newspapers as the best tavern on this side of that city—and was very genteel because the proprietors could afford linen curtains. So, there were a lot of well-to-do people coming to the Tavern of the Golden Fleece."

"I love the name 'the Golden Fleece,'" I said. "It sounds so regal."

I asked Jane how she got involved in becoming a historical interpreter. She explained that growing up in Bound Brook, New Jersey, near Somerville, an area rich in American Revolution history, she had an early interest in the subject. Ten years ago, her mother had asked if she might want to help volunteer as a docent at a local Revolutionary War historic site. Jane got the gig and loved it. She went on to study history in college and landed a job where she could combine her love of history with sewing at the John Bell House. Not only have fellow historians been helpful to her but she has also followed intricate YouTube how-to videos to improve her sewing skills.

As we sat together at the table, she showed me how to use a drop spindle. It was quite the scene, with Jane in her eighteenth-century, authentically reproduced clothing and me in my peach

J.Crew sweater, navy palazzo pants, and sneakers. Jane explained that in colonial times women didn't have leisure time, but they would have used something like this to spin, or something to sew when they did have time to sit.

It was mesmerizing to watch her spin. I appreciated her desire to learn and intimately get to know Dover's history and then take the time and effort to share it with visitors. Even though Jane wasn't originally from Delaware, I think she fit right in with the Delaware community as I was discovering it. So many in the small First State are lovers of history, preservation, and enjoy diving into a good story. If she didn't know most of the state now, it sounded like she soon would.

Many travelers include the Green and First State National Historical Park as part of their trip through Delaware. A good time to visit, though a busy one, is during Dover Days, an annual spring festival that has taken place since the 1930s, with maypole dancing, colonial demonstrations, and a nod to the history ever present in Dover.

John Dickinson Plantation: A Patriot's Pen and a People's Past

Not a household name of the American Revolution, but nonetheless important, the John Dickinson Plantation reveals much about the complexities of our Founding Fathers and life for those who were enslaved on plantations. Less than ten miles from the Old State House, the Plantation was the childhood home of John Dickinson, who is known as the "Penman of the Revolution." The Plantation is now a place where new discoveries are being made, with a big one as recently as 2021.

John Dickinson was a lawyer, farmer, politician, and Founding Father. He wrote *Letters from a Farmer in Pennsylvania*, which was widely read throughout the colonies and believed to help unite the colonists in the lead-up to the American Revolution. A member of the Continental Congress, he also authored many political documents. Travelers can tour this home and the grounds, starting at the visitors' center. I met the site's lead interpreter, Anne Fenimore, to explore the mansion house and hear about the variety of people who lived on this plantation.

The plantation house was originally built in the 1730s by Samuel Dickinson, John's father and a third-generation tobacco farmer and merchant. The Dickinson family included Samuel and his wife, Mary Cadwalader, and their two sons, John and Philemon, and they moved into the home in 1740. With them came a number of enslaved individuals. John would be educated by a tutor and then sailed to England to study law. Samuel would live in the home with Mary until his death in 1760. Mary would continue to live there until at least 1764. John would keep the farm and rent it to tenant farmers, who would run it relying on enslaved people for labor. Throughout the Revolution and later, the plantation would be a place from which multiple enslaved people would seek freedom.

I've traveled to a few plantations over the years. Many people think about plantations as being from the Civil War period, but there are others that date back to colonial times, too. Many of these plantations are making a conscious effort to tell a more complete story of the founding of the United States. Part of this effort involves research, as there is much that is unknown about what occurred during this time. Often, it wasn't recorded.

Anne Fenimore and I walked up the brick sidewalk towards the front of the original red brick Georgian-style home, which was first known as the Poplar Hall with its green door and yellow shutters on the windows. We had just passed several wooden outbuildings, created in recent decades to provide more context about life on a working farm. It is believed that more than sixty men, women, and children were enslaved on John Dickinson's plantation. John Dickinson was one of the larger slave owners in Delaware—if not the largest.

"One man named Clem in 1790 sought his freedom from here," Anne said. "We only know because there is one document about him, a newspaper ad offering a six-dollar reward for his return. We don't believe that that money was ever claimed. Not from anything we can find, so we believe that he made it to freedom and stayed free."

In 1781, there was a raid on the mansion by Tories: colonists who were loyal to Britain during the Revolution. Books, plates, wine, salted meat, clothing, and other items necessary to daily life were taken.

"They took everything that was valuable out of the mansion—as much as they could carry, with one exception: a cask of cherry rum," Anne said. I wondered why they didn't take the cherry rum! Perhaps it was too heavy.

Anne continued to explain that the Tories took what they had stolen out to their small boat and sailed back to the Delaware Bay where they were able to escape. In the chaos, an enslaved individual named Isaac took the opportunity to flee and seek his freedom.

"Isaac fled, and we're not sure what happened to him next?" I asked, intrigued at his timing and risk taking.

"Unfortunately, that's the case for a lot of free, enslaved, and indentured black individuals in history. We just don't have a lot of documentation about their lives," Anne said.

We opened the green squeaky hinged door and stepped onto the wooden floor in the main entranceway of the home, which led to a stairwell. A longer hall opened to the left. In the back of the home was another door. Opening it would have allowed for a cross breeze to cool the interior spaces. The walls in the interior were painted a muted yellow. Directly to the right, we peeked into the formal parlor, set up much as it might have been if John Dickinson were still living here. A portrait of John hung on the wall over the fireplace and on one of the tables was a copy of *Letters from a Farmer in Pennsylvania*.

Dickinson published *Letters from a Farmer in Pennsylvania* under the pseudonym "a farmer," with twelve letters taking the voice of a farmer and arguing that the British didn't have the right to tax the colonists for things like glass, paint, paper, lead, and tea. These goods were taxed under the Townshend Acts by laws passed by the British Parliament in 1767. His letters would be published and circulated widely, creating a buzz amid the colonists.

John Dickinson was a member of the First and Second Continental Congress. At the Second Continental Congress, from 1775–1776, he refused to sign the Declaration of Independence, believing that the colonists had legitimate grievances but should not separate from Great Britain. It's one of the decisions that greatly affected the rest of his life and career. Dickinson would later fight as a Patriot in the American Revolution and then serve as president of the states of Delaware and Pennsylvania, but his refusal to sign the Declaration of Independence would always tarnish his reputation.

We walked further back into the home, seeing the paint colors change from room to room. Original period furniture mixed with other artifacts that have been sourced with authenticity in mind. The house was expanded multiple times, having suffered a fire and been rebuilt. As we walked to an older section of the home, I could see that the brickwork had changed, likely from the fire.

It smelled like herbs and spices as we walked further into the home. In the back dining room, they were prepping to teach students how to make fragrant sachets. Often, interpreters at historic homes and plantations like this one invite students and the public to visit for creative events and provide opportunities to learn about history firsthand. Anne shared more about what they'd discovered through their research, including information about an enslaved woman named Violet. In the recreated dining room, they also had a mannequin figure of Violet, seated across from where we were standing. Violet had obtained her freedom in 1781 and continued to work as a paid employee for John's daughter Sally.

"Then later in life, Sally took Violet's recollections where Violet talked about her early life on the plantation, including some information that has helped us find the African burial ground," Anne said.

The African burial ground was discovered in 2021. It was found on farmland about a half mile from the main house.

"Violet's recollection was that her father, Pompey, passed away and had a funeral that went past this mansion and then out to what they called 'the interment for the colored people.' We figured what would be a reasonable walking distance from the front of the mansion. Then we started delving into other records, including aerial photography." Anne shared.

These details recorded by Violet ultimately helped them pinpoint a location. There were so many mysteries. They did an initial search but did not uncover any human remains. I wondered who was buried at the site and what their stories could reveal. Ultimately, John Dickinson freed the enslaved individuals he owned in 1786.

I left Anne and walked down the brick sidewalk outside and onto a stretch of fields where Gloria Henry was waiting for me in the distance. It was windy and bright as we walked out into the open grass where Gloria explained that they had made a determined effort to look for the burial grounds. They hired archaeologists and researchers who poured through documents and records and even actively looked near where Samuel Dickinson was buried. They found nothing. They expanded the search using a National Park report that referenced a burial ground on the property. Using aerial photography from decades ago, the team dug trenches in an area where they were finally able to locate the tops of burial shafts.

"Based on that, we know that there are several people buried here. Oral history says four hundred. We don't know that for sure, but we also noticed that some of the burial grounds are adjacent to each other. Some were almost on top of each other," Gloria said. "So, we believe that there are adult people and children buried here. We have records of some of the enslaved people...so people like Violet, and also Nanny, who was purchased by the Dickinson family."

Gloria continued to explain that a short time later, Nanny and her youngest child, Daniel, died. She believes Nanny and Daniel may have been buried in the burial ground. The remaining children were separated.

It is amazing that the burial grounds lay all these years undiscovered. Today, I could only see tall grass swaying in the breeze and the ends of two fences. Gloria and others involved in the project have formed a descendant community engagement group to help make decisions about what to do with the burial ground.

"They will help us make the sometimes emotional and painful decisions on what to do with the African burial ground. How do we memorialize it? What do we want? How do we move forward?" Gloria said.

Gloria told me that they do have the last names of some of the enslaved people who lived here, including Violet Brown. Other names include Nathan and Abigail Phillips, and Toby Stout.

"We consider this sacred space, and we understand that the people who lived here need to be remembered and honored," Gloria said.

I looked at Gloria, her face earnest in seeking the truth. She worked here every day. She had spent a lot of time uncovering this story but still longed for more. I hoped for her that more could be discovered. In the meantime, like so many places where history bubbles to the surface with only clues, there still are a lot of unanswered questions.

CHAPTER VI

North Carolina— Whispers of Freedom

Guilford Courthouse National Military Park: Preservation and Black Patriots

A battlefield and national park amid a suburban neighborhood? In my travels, I've found it's more common than you'd think. Guilford Courthouse National Military Park is one of the most fascinating battlefields I've visited, but one in which the depth of its stories isn't always readily revealed. Many people are working to change that. A visit to this battlefield, whose preservation story as the first Revolutionary War battleground to be protected by the federal government, reveals layers of history. Stories of the role of women, Black soldiers, and what monuments tell us about history combine for a textured look at a turning point in the Revolutionary War. This park provides intriguing insights about human nature, military strategy, and when people care and come together, how obstacles can be overcome. It's a similar sentiment I'd encountered at many of the historic places I'd visited in North Carolina, where individuals have helped communities unite to share from their past.

When many people think about national parks, they imagine grand, natural open spaces of Yellowstone, Yosemite, and Grand Teton, but many national park sites are in more settled and sometimes urban locations. Many of these sites were preserved after areas around them had already been developed. Other preserved park sites that were once in more rural areas have witnessed development spring up around them, altering the original landscape. Knowing this, I wasn't totally surprised to see that Guilford Courthouse National Military Park was in a suburban neighborhood.

I was standing with Park Ranger Jason Baum at this national park in Greensboro, North Carolina, a city located in the north central part of the state. While the battlefield and parkland were green and serene, in the near distance I could see modern brick apartments.

We were walking on an American Revolution farmstead owned at that time by Joseph and Hannah Hoskins. Under the dappled shade of trees, we strolled along a rustic wood fence. Before us was a large rock monument with a plaque by the Guilford Battleground Company commemorating the men and women who fought here on March 15, 1781. Just twenty yards behind the monument was a street and neighborhood with two-story apartments. It was strange and yet it wasn't, this mix of historic significance and modern normality.

My first major American Revolution stop in North Carolina would reveal more surprising finds and new discoveries related to ongoing research about the roles of women and Black Patriots in the war.

Given the significant development in the United States since Revolutionary times, many key sites from the American Revolution have been paved over or rebuilt with new construction. Guilford Courthouse National Military Park's preservation story starts with vision of one man: David Schenck. You might call him one of the original battlefield recreation preservationists. He has also been called the father of Guilford Courthouse National Military Park.

A lawyer and former judge, David Schenck moved his family to Greensboro in the 1880s. He had a keen interest in history and often stopped to look at the land where the Battle of Guilford Courthouse was fought. It was land that had been neglected, overgrown with brambles and weeds—perhaps not befitting of its considerable past.

Schenck, who had immersed himself in studying the region's history, wanted to change that. In 1886, the same day he wrote in his diary that he would "redeem the battlefield from oblivion," he purchased thirty acres of the unkempt land. The next year, he would purchase more property and convince others in the community to help with his efforts, forming an organization called the Guilford Battleground Company. Though Schenck passed away in 1902, the organization he founded would donate the land to the Interior Department in 1917. It would eventually be organized as the Guilford Courthouse National Military Park. Other examples of National Military Parks include Gettysburg, Antietam, and Vicksburg.

The Guilford Battleground Company would dissolve shortly following this success, but when Guilford Courthouse National Military Park came under the pressures of encroaching development in the 1980s, citizens reinvigorated the Guilford Battleground Company and its mission of preservation. Still today, the group, along with others like the American Battlefield Trust, work to preserve and protect the battleground and park, which is open to visitors.

I examined the historical marker inscribed with Guilford Battleground Company's name. Scanning down, I would have needed glasses to read all the names of the companies, organizations and patrons who have donated and assisted with the preservation of this important historical site over many years. The list went on and on. Like so many preserved places I'd visited, this was yet another example of a community uniting around a common cause.

Ranger Jason Baum was wearing his National Park Service uniform—a short-sleeved button-down with a National Park Service patch on his left shoulder and that signature Stratton straw campaign uniform hat. As he reached up to scratch his nose, I noticed his arms were laced in red flower tattoo art. He had a magnetic smile, accented by a graying mustache, goatee, and transparent, yet bold eyeglasses with a retro, 1950s browline-style frame.

We continued to walk in the location where the battle began, as Jason relayed information about this pivotal Southern battle fought on a cold March day. Major General Nathanael Greene commanded the American forces, and General Charles Cornwallis led the British, two powerful generals of the time. There were some 4,400 American troops and over 1,900 British troops. Greene used a military strategy like that which had been successfully deployed by Greene's subordinate officer General Daniel Morgan at the Battle of Cowpens, an earlier battle on January 17, 1781, in South Carolina. Greene separated his troops in three lines, with his third line being Continentals, the full-time professional soldiers who were the most skilled of his men.

The first line would consist of North Carolina militia, whose members were citizen soldiers. By this late stage in the war, as manpower was of critical importance, some were conscripted to serve, but participation was also seen as a citizen's duty. These part-time soldiers had not received the training that the British troops had, and the British forces also included large numbers of professionally trained Hessian solders. Despite their inexperience, Greene's first two lines would inflict heavy casualties on the British forces.

"They're kind of like the forerunner of the modern-day National Guard," Ranger Jason said, referring to the militia. "This was new for a lot of them; in fact, for many of them this might have been the worst day of their lives, because it was their first time in battle and they had to fight a seasoned, professional, well-trained British army."

The Battle of Guilford Courthouse would be a turning point in the Southern Campaign of the American Revolution. Though it was considered a British win with the Americans forced off the battlefield, Cornwallis would lose around a quarter of his men. Losses were disproportionately incurred by the British. The victory was called a "pyrrhic victory," meaning a triumph that's not really a win because there are so many costs. Cornwallis's forces were weakened, and he would decide to change his course of strategy. After abandoning his pursuit of Greene by retreating to Wilmington for rest and resupplies, Cornwallis focused on Virginia, where he found himself besieged at Yorktown and forced to surrender to the Continental Army led by George Washington with the support of the Marquis de Lafayette and French Army troops.

We were standing on what had been the 150-acre farm of the Hoskins family and only a short drive to the park's visitor center.

Today there's an old farmhouse, log cabin kitchen, double pen barn, and blacksmith shop, reconstructed to look as they would have during the time. The log house is authentic. It was built by Joseph and Hannah Hoskins's son Ellis after the Revolution in the 1810s.

Many people tried to avoid being part of the armed conflict during the Revolution, but all too often it was simply unavoidable. This was the unfortunate case for the Hoskins family, whose homestead became a battleground. The family had left Valley Forge, Pennsylvania, in May of 1778 to escape the war's conflict. They moved to what was a quiet farming backcountry of North Carolina to avoid the bloodshed that would tragically land right on their very own farm just a few years later in March 1781. Joseph and his wife Hannah would flee, and their farm would be severely damaged. Homes and farms were often commandeered for use by troops for provisions or, in the Hoskinses' case, a battle.

As Ranger Jason and I spoke, I noticed someone emerge from across the street and enter the park grounds for a walk. Ranger Jason said that many locals use the battlefield park daily or weekly for recreation. It was, in a sense, their gym. They'd run, bike, or walk the trails. While it is considered hallowed ground today, it's also open space.

I spotted interpretive signage and historical markers in my immediate vicinity and guessed that these markers were placed throughout the park, where the topography is typical of the hilly Piedmont of North Carolina. I wondered how many people stop to read the signs. I have often stopped running to photograph a marker. It breaks up my workout, but I love to know an area's history, and these historical markers and signs are often a great starting point. Photographing them is like keeping a journal that's fun to read later for context and memories.

I left the Hoskins Farm and Ranger Jason. I drove along roads winding through the forested park, passing oak and chestnut trees. Just a few minutes east, I arrived in the parking lot of the area that had been about halfway between the first and second American defensive lines during the battle. There is a self-guided driving route through this park and miles of trails to explore on foot.

I was meeting park superintendent Aaron LaRocca where the actual county courthouse stood in 1781. Today, it was an open field where large monuments stand a distance from a parking lot.

Aaron LaRocca had chosen this area of the park for us to chat because it was his favorite. A longtime veteran of the National Park Service, LaRocca hails from Arlington, Virginia, and studied history in college, gaining an interest in the subject from childhood trips to the many museums around Washington, DC. His time volunteering at national parks got him interested in pursuing the National Park Service as a career.

LaRocca also wore a National Park Service uniform, and if I were looking for a poster person for our national parks, I might pick him. Charismatic and brimming with frequent smiles, LaRocca is in his early forties and is definitely made for the camera. Well over six feet tall, he has a thicker, dark beard and kind, blue eyes. He obviously takes joy in sharing with others a place that he helps to safeguard.

We walked on the sidewalk from the parking lot through a shaded area towards a clearing. Up a few stairs, we hit the verdant, manicured grasses leading to a gigantic statue in the distance. Trees surrounded the grassy area, and the woods in the distance framed the large equestrian monument.

"You're walking through the woods and then, all of a sudden, the largest monument in Guilford Courthouse National Military Park is unveiled right in front of you. That's the Greene Monument that was placed here in 1915 before this place was even a national park," Ranger Aaron said.

"Larger than life, for sure," I said.

As we reached the Greene Monument, I was forced to crane my neck to look up at Greene on his stallion, which stands over twenty-seven feet tall. It rests on a granite base that is on top of a brick platform. In front of the Greene statue is an allegorical sculpture of a Greek Goddess. She stands with a shield in her left hand and laurels in her right, signifying military triumph and protection. I read the dedication plaque that said much about what was on the minds of the preservationists of the Guilford Battleground Company, who placed the monument in 1915, before the battlegrounds were even a national military park.

Joseph Morehead, the second president of the Guilford Battleground Company, aided in getting federal funding for the Greene Monument. The statue was sculpted by noted artist Francis Herman Packer.

I examined the inscription on the Greene Monument further, understanding that the people of the Guilford Battleground Company must have believed that this battle was *the* turning point of the American Revolution.

The inscription by Professor C. Alphonso Smith reads; "The Battle of Guilford Courthouse is second to no battle fought on American soil. Over the brave men who fell here their comrades marched to ultimate victory at Yorktown, and the cause of constitutional self-government to assured triumph at Philadelphia. To officer and private, to Continental soldier and volunteer militiaman, honor and award are alike due. They need neither defense nor eulogy but only just recognition."

Near the Greene Monument stands the Signers' Monument, recognizing North Carolina's three signers of the Declaration of Independence: William Hooper, John Penn, and Joseph Hewes. It was dedicated in 1897. The remains of Hooper and Penn were reinterred at the monument.

I looked up at the grand bronze figure of a colonial man, framed by the bright green leaves of trees and clear blue sky. The statue portrays a man raising his right hand in the air with the Declaration of Independence in his left hand. An interpretive sign near their monument conveys the Guilford Courthouse Company's sentiment that winning independence "required courage, determination and sacrifice."

I was drawn back to reexamine the larger monument to Greene. A quote attributed to Cornwallis appears at the monument's base: "Greene is as dangerous as Washington. I never feel secure when encamped in his neighborhood." It was chilling.

Ranger Aaron continued. "Everyone thinks of General Washington during the Revolutionary War, and they're not necessarily familiar with General Nathanael Greene and this idea of the Southern campaign. It puts them together. Cornwallis is the mutual villain, if you will. And so, I like that quote, too, because it connects those two iconic American heroes. That was one of the discussions about this monument when it was being constructed: Was it to be dedicated to one person, understanding that Greene wasn't an army of one? How do we recognize all the people that participated in the Revolutionary War battle that happened here? A lot of the inscriptions speak to that—it's more than just Greene, even though he's the guy on the horse in bronze."

Ranger Jason had underscored the militiamen and their lack of training compared to the British Army, and I wondered more about those who had fought here.

Ranger Aaron told me that the makeup of the Continentals was diverse, including Black soldiers. The American Revolution would force many people to choose sides. Many Black Americans sided with the British and fought with the Loyalists. In November of 1775, Virginia Royal Governor Lord Dunmore offered freedom to enslaved people who joined the British. Others were forced to fight by their enslavers. The American Revolution became an enslaved rebellion, with Black soldiers fighting on both sides for their freedom. The estimates on the number of freedom seekers vary widely, including at the Battle of Guilford Courthouse. Researchers, including civilian volunteers, are working to uncover more information on this topic.

What is currently known according to park volunteers and researchers is that at least forty-four Black Patriots participated in the Battle of Guilford Courthouse. Andrew Pebbles, for example, served in "Light Horse" Harry Lee's Legion and also fought and was wounded at the September 1781 Battle of Eutaw Springs in South Carolina. His pension affidavit from a courthouse in Richmond, Virginia on June 14, 1819, stated that he couldn't recollect the year he enlisted because he was "a poor unlearned Mulatto." In it, he also stated that he fought at the Battle of Brandywine. Andrew Pebbles received a pension, and following his death, his heirs received a land bounty for his service.

Others were not compensated or even recognized. A freed Black man named Primes Record, also called Record Primus, was eighty-six years old when he applied for a pension. He said that he enlisted in 1777 and fought in many southern battles, including Camden, Kings Mountain, Cowpens, Guilford Courthouse,

Eutaw Springs, and the siege of Yorktown. He was not granted a pension. We are not sure why this was the case.

Ranger Aaron told me that Guilford Courthouse National Military Park is part of the National Archives' ongoing Citizen Archivist program. This project uses volunteers to transcribe pension records to find out more about the people involved in the battle. They are especially searching for new stories related to underrepresented groups, including women, Native Americans, and African Americans. It sounded like a fascinating project to me. These pension records often included deeper and unexpected stories, which help weave together a richer tapestry of what occurred during the American Revolution.

Of the twenty-nine monuments in the park, two are dedicated to lesser-known heroines of the American Revolution. The monument to Martha McFarlane McGee Bell is set near the American First Line. It recognizes her contributions after the battle. A nurse and midwife, she was forced to open her and her husband's gristmill to the British Army and General Cornwallis while her husband was fighting with the Patriots. Bell made Cornwallis promise that he wouldn't damage her property or the mill. In exchange, he and his troops would camp there for two days. Bell tended to and nursed wounded troops. American General "Light Horse" Harry Lee arrived at Bell's mill and farm shortly after Cornwallis had departed. Bell shared details about Cornwallis's next location, provisions, and supplies, acting as a Patriot spy.

Guilford Courthouse National Military Park was open and easily accessible. Many people who frequent this park are from the neighborhood and can walk or drive a short distance to the trails. The park is only fifteen minutes from downtown Greensboro, where you can learn about the city's evolution from a railroad and transportation hub to a textile manufacturing giant as well as more about Greensboro's Revolutionary and Civil Rights history at downtown museums. Greensboro is, after all, named after Revolutionary War hero Nathanael Greene.

As I left the park and drove through the neighborhoods of the city of Greensboro, I tried to imagine what David Schenck might think today if he was able to see his vision of the park go from neglected to a verdant and valued national battlefield park, preserved and open for all to visit. I think he would be proud.

Greensboro History Museum: Attic and Archival Treasures

Local history is at the forefront of the Greensboro History Museum. Founded in 1924, the museum has been telling the story of the city and its people for more than a century. Located in downtown Greensboro in a red brick complex consisting of the former Romanesque Revival-style First Presbyterian Church of Greensboro and Smith Memorial Building on Summit Avenue, the museum is located downtown. On the mid-September day that I visited, the North Carolina Folk Festival was in full swing, so parking was scarce and live music blared from a nearby stage. I was heading to the quiet interior of this Smithsonian Affiliate Museum to meet with Museum Director Carol Ghiorsi Hart and see a rare artifact related to the Battle of Guilford Courthouse, among other historic finds.

Carol has been the museum director since 2012 and is passionate about both history and community connections. She studied cultural anthropology at Indiana University Bloomington and taught the subject at Farmingdale State University of New York, where she served as adjunct instructor of anthropology. I met a few of the museum staff at the entrance of the museum, along with Carol. She was dressed in a black tweed blazer with a black V-neck shirt and long flared pants. Her long dark hair had touches of salt and pepper and draped a good part of the way down her back. Her skin had a pinkish tint, and she wore light peachy-pink lipstick without much makeup.

Natural and comfortable, Carol spoke with a hint of a New York accent and with lots of expression, moving her thin eyebrows up and down and nodding her head as she conveyed what we could discover while at the museum.

Like any museum, there was a lot to unpack here. Sections of the museum dove into the history of Greensboro's indigenous peoples, including the Saura and Keyauwee. There was an exhibition on early Greensboro, Greensboro's transformation into "the Gate City" as a railroad center, its role in the Underground Railroad, and its title as a denim capital, giving the city its nickname of "Jeansboro." I asked that Carol stick to the city's role in the Revolution because, as usual, I was running on limited time and wanted especially to link what I learned here with my earlier visit to the battleground. I would breeze through the entire museum, however, and realize that I'd simply have to make my way back to Greensboro to discover more.

Dolley Madison, First Lady and the wife of the fourth president of the United States, James Madison, was born in Guilford County. She is locally beloved, even though she only lived in the area for a few months. An exhibit showcasing objects owned by and associated with Dolley and her family was on view at the museum at the time of my visit. It was something that we both agreed I had to see. After perusing the exhibition, Carol told me that the museum had in its vault what was believed to be Dolley's prized red velvet dress, which is thought to be made from White

House drapes. We ventured into the vaults to see the dress, in addition to other Revolutionary-era finds.

Around 1960, the museum received a treasure—a trunk containing clothing, dresses, shoes, letters, daguerreotypes, old photos, artifacts, and paintings belonging to Dolley Madison. Carol shared some interesting facts about Dolley Madison as we examined the thick velvet of the dress, laid out gingerly on a table in a cool white storage room. It's not always on display, because of its fragile nature.

The color of the dress was a rich scarlet. It was utterly plush and luxurious, and I could imagine Dolley Madison walking into a grand affair wearing it. Carol said that she believed that it might have been made from White House drapery that Dolley Madison saved before the British burned the building in 1814, along with a Gilbert Stuart full-length portrait of George Washington. Whether or not it was truly made from the White House drapes, a tale that I agree is enticing, the dress itself is a treasure, and seeing this artifact provided me with a special connection to Dolley Madison.

Carol then shared a tidbit that I didn't know about Dolley Madison. Apparently, she was known to use snuff, a finely ground tobacco. In fact, many women of all social classes used snuff in the eighteenth and nineteenth centuries. Dolley was raised Quaker. Thus, playing cards, using snuff, and dancing would have been forbidden. Dolley did all of these things, all the while donning the latest fashions. Known to be a gregarious, she was a charismatic rule-breaker.

The story behind the trunk was also quite amusing. It was found in an attic in a home in Allentown, Pennsylvania, in 1956. The trunk had been passed on through Dolley's sister's family, who obviously hadn't paid attention to what they had.

Eventually, Eleanor Fox Pearson, the president of the Dolley Madison Memorial Association, became aware of the trunk and rallied a group of women in Greensboro to raise the funds to purchase it.

"They threw chicken dinners to bring it back so we could honor Dolley in this way," Carol said. "So that trunk alone tells a lot. This is the culmination of a community effort to bring the past to life."

Such artifacts draw in school children and other local visitors to the museum, who take pride in North Carolina's role as the birthplace of Dolley Madison, the only First Lady in history to hail from the state. While not all the museum's artifacts, like the coveted red velvet gown, are now on display, Carol told me that anyone who calls and makes an appointment, especially individuals doing research, can take a behind-the-scenes tour to see these fragile, rare items. There are tens of thousands of objects housed in the museum that aren't on display because there simply isn't room, so the objects are showcased by rotation. Some are also fragile, needing low light and special temperatures to best survive over time.

We moved to another vault to examine an item that tied directly to the Battle of Guilford Courthouse. The previous vault had mostly contained cabinets and boxes, but this vault had open shelving, so we could get a better peek at some rare pieces held in storage here at the museum. There were rows and rows of paintings of various sizes, many of them in opulent gold frames. I spotted what looked like a chandelier made from cutlery and a clothing rack of antique army bomber jackets and uniforms. There were rows of colorful pottery, vases, and statues. It was a feast for the eyes and the imagination. I could have probably spent days just perusing the items stored in the back vaults.

As a curator rolled out a table to the front of the vault, it rumbled and clattered across the smooth surface. Wearing a sleeveless navy dress covered in white flowers and donning protective gloves, the curator gingerly placed silver riding spurs on a black velvet swatch of fabric on the table. She then set down a box with what looked to be a tattered winter hat inside. The hat looked like it was made of a wool blend and woven with thick stripes of various browns. Had I not known better, I'd say this beanie could still be worn and sold today by the likes of Eddie Bauer or L.L.Bean. I mentioned this to Carol, and she agreed.

"Often very utilitarian objects keep the same design through the ages because they work well," Carol said. "They're not typically saved because they're everyday objects. A beanie is not a fancy uniform item. It's just something to keep you warm, but it's very special because of the story that it can continue to tell."

Called a "liberty cap," this warm, finely knit cap was worn by Captain Arthur Forbis during the Battle at Guilford Courthouse, where he was wounded. Forbis was a farmer and part of the North Carolina militia, one of the many in the first line of defense at Guilford Courthouse during the battle. He was transported home following the battle and died a few days after his arrival.

Hats like these were often made at home, woven from a woman's silk stocking and embroidered with knitted wool. Forbis may have worn it beneath his hat for warmth. They were widely used in the 1700 and 1800s, yet few of them survive. Called a watch cap, liberty cap, or knit cap, these utilitarian caps were usually striped.

Descendents of Arthur Forbis saved the cap and passed it through the generations without knowing the historical significance of what they had in their possession. The cap was kept in a sock drawer and then on a top shelf of the family's bedroom closet, not the same care it was now receiving in a special vault in the Greensboro History Museum! Yet it survived. When the family realized just how special it was, they donated it to the museum in 1926. It was one of the museum's earliest objects.

"There was a stain on it…John's blood was on it," Carol said. "About eight years ago, we contacted a local crime lab to do blood analysis to see if they could get DNA. They couldn't at that time, but by being very careful, preserving it, maybe at some future time we'll be able to get more information about the man who wore this cap."

It was another mystery from a time long ago that is difficult to investigate. Locals do like to say that it was Forbis who fired the very first shot at the Battle of Guilford Courthouse.

A mystery was easily solved with our next item, a pair of George Washington's horse-riding spurs. I asked Carol how they acquired the spurs and how they knew they were from George Washington.

"It's because of the history that we do have of where it came from that we're pretty confident that yes, these did belong to George Washington," Carol said. "And it makes it special. Another thing that connects to a person that's larger than life. But he had spurs!"

These pieces of history reveal much more than a physical object like a simple hat or a pair of spurs can convey. They provide tangibility and context to a story by connecting notable past events to something real. Seeing these objects—things that we have today or may even still use today—helps us see these people and makes past events more real. George Washington's initials are on the inside of both spurs.

The cap at the Greensboro History Museum also connected to Guilford Courthouse National Military Park, where one of the park's oldest monuments is a tribute to Captain Forbis. The monument is set where local lore says he was wounded.

Among other Revolutionary objects on display at the museum's *Voices of a City* collection are a sword thought to have been used by Captain Forbis in the battle, a camp cup made for General Nathanael Greene by a Boston silversmith, and a spur and belt buckle recovered from the battle. Just like at Guilford Courthouse National Military Park, there's a greater story of preservation and community, of sharing and safeguarding, and of opening up for all to see.

Halifax State Historic Site: Rolling Dice with History

At Halifax State Historic Site, just ten miles from the Virgina border in northeastern North Carolina, I found myself sitting at a table in an old tavern and gambling with two costumed historical interpreters. Granted, we were only using play money, but I was learning the colonial-era dice game of Hazard. Commonly played in taverns and homes, Hazard was a sort of a precursor to the now-common casino game of craps. The rules were quite complicated from what I could initially surmise as a novice. I'd already lost quite a few dollars of my funny money.

During the American Revolution, Halifax was a town that adamantly supported colonial independence. Today, it's a veritable American Revolution time machine. Travelers can immerse themselves in living history and the touch, feel, smell, and taste of the past. While not as well-known as living-history-site meccas like Colonial Williamsburg, those seeking a more intimate, personalized experience and tour should add Halifax to their list.

I rolled the dice and looked down at the paper bills in my hands. During colonial times, bills such as this would have been endorsed right here in Halifax by the authority of the Fourth Provincial Congress. The Congress was meeting to create what we would later call the Halifax Resolves. I examined the money closely, as one might have done during the American Revolution, when counterfeiting was common. Black script across the middle of the note proclaimed that the note was issued by "Authority of Congress at Halifax, April 2nd, 1776." This was money that I might have encountered if I had been here during Revolutionary times.

The Fourth Provincial Congress consisted of eighty-three delegates led by President Samuel Johnston of Edenton. They met on April 4, 1776 to discuss grievances and make changes. The members concurred that Great Britain had committed "violations" against America. On April 12, they took the stage by formally submitting the Halifax Resolves. It was the first official provincial action for independence from Great Britain in the colonies.

I was in Halifax to understand more about this landmark event and to step back in time. At Halifax State Historic Site today, costumed interpreters are spread throughout eight historic buildings that date from the late eighteenth to early nineteenth centuries. These authentically interpreted, carefully restored buildings include the early nineteenth-century Sally Billy House and the Burgess Law Office, the 1838 Halifax County Jail, the 1760s Tap Room, the Owens House, the 1790s Eagle Tavern, and a clerk's office dating to 1832. Inside, you'll find exhibitions and recreated colonial interiors complete with furniture both original and reproduction.

At my Hazard game in the Tap Room, interpreter and site manager Frank McMahon was explaining how to play. He was seated on my right and dressed as a member of the eighteenth-century militia in North Carolina. Frank has a passion for making history approachable. That's why he suggested we start our visit in the Tap Room. What's more approachable than a gambling game, pretend beer included?

Though the pewter cup in front of me and the deep red, hand-thrown ceramic pitcher in the middle of the table were empty, I could imagine the foaming liquid and at one point even went to lift the cup. Across from me, a rosy-cheeked interpreter, Kristal Chapman, sat with her deep red hair tied up in a white cap under a straw bonnet with a six-inch brim. She was dressed in a long yellow linen gown accented by a blue apron atop and under which she wore a petticoat and stays. I must admit, it was pretty fun to be playing Hazard with these two characters, who were truly acting their historical parts.

The furnishings inside the historic reconstructed Tap Room, which itself was a maroon, wooden-sided building dating from 1760, cleverly portrayed a historic tavern. Interior details included a sign lining a cupboard calling for recruits to fight for the Patriots. The Tap Room's architectural design included a gambrel roof, a popular Dutch colonial architectural feature of the eighteenth century, as it allowed for more attic and storage space.

Frank wore a cream-colored hunting shirt, an unbleached linen shirt with long, loose sleeves. Hunting shirts were worn by professional hunters on the frontier of Virginia and became part of the culture of hunting in Western Virginia, Western

Pennsylvania, and parts of North Carolina. The style and shirt were adopted by the Continental Army during the Revolution, and the shirts were used by the militia in North Carolina. While Europeans favored wearing wool clothes, there was a shortage of wool in America, as the British had closed off access to colonial ports after the conflict started. Linen, which was easier and cheaper to import, became one of the colonists' materials of choice. Sporting a wool felt hat on his head, Frank's curly, slightly bushy brown hair stuck out on the sides, and his thicker eyebrows drew my attention towards his blue eyes and away from the red bandana wrapped around his neck.

Back in the eighteenth century, we might have played Hazard in a tavern like this: a place to get a drink, a meal, and sleep. Patrons used taverns, also called ordinaries, as meeting spaces and places for entertainment. If you were lucky, you might be able to play a game of billiards, table bowling, or Hazard. It's always nice to converse while playing a game or drinking coffee.

Halifax is located along the Roanoke River about an hour and a half northeast from North Carolina's capital city of Raleigh. Halifax's location along the river was one reason why Halifax developed into a commercial and political hub during the American Revolution. The state's historic sites roster concluded that Halifax would grow to have nearly sixty houses and public buildings, including many taverns.

North Carolina had moved onto the colonial stage early with changes in leadership and mounting tension. In the summer of 1775, North Carolina lost its Royal Governor Josiah Martin, who fled to the coast for the safety and protection of a British warship. Martin's stubborn loyalty to the Crown was unsettling to locals, and Martin felt an insurrection was on the horizon. Fearing for his family's safety, he moved them to New York and, in May of 1775, fled his palace in New Bern, making it to North Carolina's coast and boarding the HMS Cruizer in July. It was stories like this that spoke to the spirit of the people early on, with a healthy population, especially in Halifax, who boldly stepped out for independence.

Frank and I were in the first of our locations and a fitting place to start, as one of the dozen pubs or taverns that would have been abuzz here during colonial times. After I'd gotten a feel for gambling during colonial times, and sorely lost, Frank and I departed the Tap Room. We crossed the quiet, two-lane King Street to explore the Eagle Tavern, which wasn't originally in this location. Like many of the buildings here, it was relocated to Historic Halifax. Built in the 1790s, the Marquis de Lafayette would hold a banquet at the Eagle Tavern in 1825.

Today, Historic Halifax is easily walkable. The historic buildings are spaced just well enough across open grasslands dotted with trees so that visitors don't feel claustrophobic. I asked Frank what Halifax might have looked like during the eighteenth century. He said that back then, it was a trade center, situated on one of North Carolina's few main roads. The courthouse also drew in visitors, as did a nearby ferry landing on the Roanoke River. It was located as far as you could bring an oceangoing ship up the Roanoke River, so traders would stop in Halifax to unload their cargo to one of the many warehouses located here.

The yellow, two-story Eagle Tavern, with windows lined with black trim, contained an exhibition detailing various aspects of tavern life in Halifax during the colonial period. We peeked inside before walking across the lawn towards a simple two-story brick building. It dated back to 1838 and was used as a jail. Prior to the historic building we see today, an earlier jail constructed of wood served as a prisoner-of-war camp during the Revolutionary War. It held British and Loyalist prisoners from the Battle of Moores Creek Bridge, a Patriot victory against Loyalist militia troops outside of the coastal city of Wilmington on February 21, 1776.

"At the same time that members of the Fourth Provincial Congress were here deciding to empower their delegates to vote for independence from Great Britain, there was a prisoner-of-war camp filled with prisoners…right across the street," Frank said. "They needed not look any farther than across the street to see that they were in the middle of a war."

There are no sidewalks along north King Street, so Frank and I walked further across the grassy lawns, where only a few trees dotted the landscape, to another red brick building: the print shop. While the print shop was interesting, Frank had brought me here to discuss something that is no longer here today. From the print shop, up on a rise in the land, was the location of the original T-shaped courthouse during colonial times. Small blue flags mounted on metal rods and surveying stakes stuck out of the ground, outlining where the courthouse was originally located.

A few years ago, archaeologists used ground-penetrating radar to pinpoint its original location. It was here that the Halifax Resolves were signed. Frank informed me that other significant events occurred at the courthouse. On August 1, 1776, the first official public reading of the Declaration of Independence in North Carolina was held here, and during the winter of 1776, North Carolina's first state constitution was created here.

"Darley, would you like to have a copy of the Halifax Resolves?" Frank dramatically offered.

"Sure," I said with a smile, continuing to play along.

"Come on down to our printing press," Frank replied, turning towards the red brick building with black shutters, where a man dressed as an eighteenth-century merchant was standing in the doorway.

Merchants and printers had shops in Halifax, including Abraham Hodge, who was elected as the state printer of North Carolina in 1785. Inside the print shop, a man wearing a tricorn hat and burgundy jacket was rolling out ink onto a table and demonstrating how the printing press worked by printing a copy of the Halifax Resolves. As a gathering place for trade and politics, Halifax citizens would have consumed the latest news and talked about it in various area taverns.

On our way to another complex of historic homes in Halifax, we passed another marker with information about the Underground Railroad. Travelers visiting today can walk the quarter-mile Underground Railroad Trail that features outdoor exhibits providing information on the freedom seekers from the local area. Long before the Underground Railroad existed, free and enslaved Black men with ties to Halifax joined in the Colonies' fight for freedom during the Revolutionary War. Frank has been researching some of these men through pension records. These records provide long-forgotten details of the lives of men like Charles Roe, Joel Taburn, John Womble, Asa Spelmore, and Arthur Toney.

Frank and I left King Street to visit the Bradford-Denton House. While it's not part of the State Historic Site, it is another example of the community's preservation efforts, and one that started with a single individual, Jeff Dickens. The house was first owned by Colonel John Bradford, a delegate to the Fourth Provincial Congress. He was also treasurer and sheriff.

In front of the carefully restored, circa-1760s house of an early middle-class Halifax County family, I met Jeff Dickens of the Historical Halifax Restoration Association. A tall, older gentleman, he was dressed as Colonel John Bradford, wearing a black felt tricorn hat, a yellow waistcoat, a black jacket with gold buttons, and cream-colored breeches.

Jeff discovered and was the catalyst for saving the 1760s home of Colonel Bradford. In his thick, soft Southern accent, he told the story of how he was farming in Enfield about ten miles away, when he spotted what was then an old, dilapidated farmhouse. He crawled under it and surmised that it was indeed very old. The house was in utter disrepair with plants and vines all but taking over the exterior. The porch was rotting and broken and the plaster walls inside were crumbling, but Jeff saw a glimmer of the future. He thought the home might be worth saving. Jeff approached the Historical Halifax Restoration Association to see if the organization wanted to take on the restoration, and Jeff soon became project manager and its chief fundraiser.

With the help from the Bradford descendants and the local tourism association, the house was dismantled, preserved, and moved to its present location, just steps away from the State Historic Site. The group was also able to reconstruct outbuildings, using some period materials, to give visitors the experience of life in the eighteenth century.

One of the outbuildings is a timber-framed kitchen, a replica of the type of kitchen that would have been found in Halifax during the 1780s. Inside, Tara Fowler was dressed as a working woman of the time and cooking over a hearth. Her table was filled with replica dishes from the period that must have taken her a very long time to make. Cooking near an open fire with extremely high heat was often a dangerous endeavor. Kitchens were typically located in outbuildings for a few reasons, one of which was that these wooden buildings sometimes met their demise through accidental cooking fires. Tara was preparing a meal of green beans, pork, rolls, and meat pies to be served inside the small wooden brick-floored building.

I passed a well house with white clapboards to explore more of the outbuildings, including the smokehouse, where faux hams were drying from the ceiling. Past the blacksmith shop in the brickyard, I met two young boys who were taking clay from a pit and using their hands to fill wooden brick molds. Apparently, reenacting could be a family affair! Tara's two boys, ten-year-old Breton and eight-year-old Lachlan, were making the bricks.

The brothers wore long-sleeved linen shirts and broad-brimmed straw hats as they labored with messy clay. Breton shared the process in his high-pitched Southern drawl. He would first wet the wooden brick mold and then sprinkle sand inside the mold so the clay wouldn't stick. After placing the mold on a flat wooden surface, he'd throw small, wet pieces of clay inside it, pushing the clay into the corners and pressing it flat. Once the clay was packed into the mold, he'd take a wooden board, angle it, and then pull it across the top to form an even brick. Impressive, I thought, as I looked at seven bricks drying in the sun. I jokingly asked these young reenactors if they might build me a house, but they solemnly replied that they didn't have enough bricks.

All the reenactors at the Bradford-Denton House are volunteers, who enjoy sharing what daily life was like 250 years ago. Sometimes they share a love of theatrics, too.

During the annual Halifax Resolves Days, reenactors come together for even more living-history demonstrations. Visitors can get involved, too, with hearth cooking, blacksmithing, guided tours and ceremonies. The date that the Halifax Resolves were adopted is also commemorated through North Carolina's state flag, where April 12, 1775, is listed, along with May 20,

1775, the controversial date of the much-disputed Mecklenburg Declaration of Independence.

In this document, Mecklenburg County, whose county seat today is the city of Charlotte and was then known as Charlottetown, declared its independence from Great Britain. This, if it is true, would mean that this declaration preceded the United States Declaration of Independence. Historians and Founding Fathers including Jefferson and Adams have gone back and forth over time about the authenticity of this document, and more recent scholars have as well. As there is no original copy that's surfaced, it hasn't been totally disproven. Nonetheless, the early government of North Carolina did believe it was authentic and thus, the date is still today on the North Carolina flag.

What most stood out about a visit to charming Halifax was the lesser-known history that took place here when North Carolinians took a bold stand against the British before other colonies stuck their necks out. I was also touched by the care that the people here have for restoring and preserving this small locale. There are fewer than three hundred people living here in the county seat. It's a more rural, less frequently visited location that is working to share its history. I'd seen a smaller, but significant part of the American story in this area that was just a bit off the beaten path.

CHAPTER VII

Pennsylvania—York, Brandywine, and Gettysburg Colonial Toasts and Triumphs

York: Street Art and Street Foods in A Historic US Capital

Sometimes you must take to the streets with a local to truly discover the intricacies of a place's history. In York, a city in South Central Pennsylvania, I'd find that history and charming diversions were at every turn with the right local guide to steer my footsteps.

York is a pedestrian-friendly place to explore, and in downtown York around the Central Market, I'd recommend a walking tour to take in the sights. It's the best way to stumble upon not only colonial architecture but also a tapestry of Victorian and Greek Revival architectural styles. York is a gem for architecture and history lovers, which is why I was keen to explore the city with my guide, Blake Gifford.

Blake was supposed to meet me at the Central Market House, a historic Romanesque Revival public market that dates to 1888. Specialty vendors sprawl over an indoor city block and offer everything from candles to croissants inside. I had some time to explore before our meeting and found myself eating a delicious cannoli and staring at the ceiling, which resembles the hull of a ship. The Central Market was built by ship builders. It started out as a farmers' market and is a total foodie spot today with cuisines from around the world. I was delighted to find Korean bulgogi mixed with a medieval soup purveyor and a sourdough bakery with divine chocolate chip cookies.

Blake found me along one of the many aisles filled with culinary temptations. He was wearing woven shoes and jeans with a gray wool cardigan over a red-and-black-checkered flannel shirt and black nylon bomber jacket. A reddish-brown beard, blue eyes, and pale skin made his thick-rimmed glasses and black hat embroidered with his brand, York Architecture Illustrated, stand out. When I asked him about his style, he told me he was sort of a hipster in that millennial age that you just can't move past. We both chuckled.

Blake is active with community preservation and leads travelers on walking tours with an architectural focus. A talented architect and artist, I got lost in Blake's social-media feed prior to meeting him in York. One of his passion projects is drawing pencil-and-ink portraits of York's historic buildings.

We exited the large brick Central Market, and I asked Blake how he'd ended up in York. Blake said he is originally from the Houston suburbs and came to York, where he's been for the last seven years, for love. As a hopeless romantic myself, it warmed my heart to hear him say that. He had met his future wife at Penn State University. She hails from York, and Blake followed her back home. He then also fell in love with York. The city's mix of being economical and centrally located in proximity to cities like Baltimore, Lancaster, Harrisburg, and Philadelphia, were selling points, too.

We walked around the corner to Beaver Street, and I immediately thought, *How cute*—right out of a Hallmark movie where Victorian charm meets the hip city. Flower-potted plants were neatly placed outside the two- and three-story brick facades. The sky was nearly cloudless and blue and the fall air crisp as we walked by bubbles magically strewn into the breeze from the locally owned handmade soap shop. *Clever*, I thought.

Next, we passed a vintage clothing store, which had a rack of funky women's clothes on the sidewalk in front of the shop. I couldn't help myself taking a quick look at the ten-dollar rack. Blake said that Beaver Street was easily one of the most well-trafficked streets in York, his favorite, and historically the busiest intersection in downtown. Gorgeous preserved and restored buildings from various time periods were mixed with colorful modern murals. One mural adorned with violins, cheese, and a large glass of red wine—all things to make you more creative— was dedicated to "York's art, makers, doers, and dreamers."

We continued down Beaver Street closer to the corner of West Market Street and the National House hotel. The hotel was built in 1828 in a Spanish Colonial and French Colonial-influenced architectural style and the four-story brick building includes three stories of long verandas overlooking Beaver Street. Originally the White Hall Hotel, it was changed to National House during the Civil War. It hosted President Martin Van Buren and author Charles Dickens while he was on tour for his book *Oliver Twist*. It now houses apartments and a taproom.

Just across the street are several Revolutionary War-era buildings, including the former recruitment headquarters for "Mad Anthony" Wayne, a well-known Continental general during the Revolutionary War. Currently a bank, the red brick Federal- and Colonial-style complex was originally built as a shop for George Irwin but was soon commandeered to be used for the war effort. A historical marker on the sidewalk on West Market Street stated that from February to May of 1781, this site was General Wayne's hub for recruitment while he was in York awaiting orders to join Lafayette in Yorktown.

Known for his feisty personality and forceful military tactics, Mad Anthony and his recruits would fight and be defeated at the Battle of Brandywine in Pennsylvania. Later his troops would be part of the initial advance at the longest and hottest battle of the Revolution, the Battle of Monmouth in New Jersey. The recruitment headquarters would have been primarily located in the front portion of the building on the corner. Looking at the building, I imagined the men who would have come here, their lives changed forever by the decisions they would make to enlist.

Blake explained that the building would later become the Indian Queen Hotel and would transition through many other stages of renovations and reconstructions after it was taken over by a local bank in the mid-1800s. I took a closer look at the red brick buildings with their white shutters, which looked like three big brick buildings of different heights affixed together. A plaque on the brick facade stated that it served as General Anthony Wayne's spring 1781 headquarters for the Pennsylvania Line and that his recruitment for the campaign would end in the surrender of Lord Cornwallis to Geroge Washington on October 19, 1781, in Yorktown. The plaque was dated 1912 and it was yet another historical marker instituted by the Daughters of the American Revolution, this time the Yorktown Chapter.

I asked Blake more about what York was like during the American Revolution. He shared that it wasn't nearly as built up as it is today.

"We were the first town west of the Susquehanna River," Blake said. "We weren't colonized until about the 1740s, so basically our claim to fame is that we were a safe place for the Founding Fathers to hide after the British invaded Philadelphia. They fled the entire Continental Congress, first to Lancaster, then to York, and they hid out here because it was then a frontier outpost in the middle of nowhere."

One of York's major Revolutionary claims to fame, and one that brought me to York in the first place, was that it served as the makeshift capital of the colonies from September 30, 1777, to June 27, 1778, when the Continental Congress held sessions at the York County Court House. The Congress adopted the Articles of Confederation right here in York and proclaimed the first national Thanksgiving Day here. The Congress also ratified the French Treaty of Alliance here, adding to the list of American "firsts" that occurred here. This is the type of history that I was keen to see and experience while in York, and thanks to the community's and preservationists' efforts, I could.

As Blake and I continued our stroll down West Market Street towards the Golden Plough Tavern, every building I glanced at appeared to have a historical story to tell. I'd read a plaque or sign posted outside and then turn to my trusty architectural guide for further fodder and color commentary. That's the fun part of touring a place with an expert like Blake—since they live and breathe the subject, you're sure to learn more than you could on your own.

Across from Mad Anthony's former headquarters is the early 1900s white porcelain Bon-Ton department store building. A marker points out what stood here before, the house of American Revolution officer Major John Clark, known for the spy network he operated out of Philadelphia for George Washington. It was also the site of the first printing press west of the Susquehanna River, where some $10 million in Continental currency was printed by Hall & Sellers Press during the Continental Congress's stay in York.

Facing Market Street, the old headquarters is today joined with a larger 1950s brick building in the colonial revival style, a replica of the Old State House that stood in the center of what is today called Continental Square next to the Court House, where Congress held their sessions during the American Revolution. Back then, it was called Centre Square but was renamed in 1925 to honor the city's past related to the Continental Congress. Both the Court House and the Old State House were torn down and later reconstructed. The reconstructed York County Colonial Court House was one of our next stops further down Market Street.

We were walking towards the historic Golden Plough Tavern and General Horatio Gates's house. Walking past the Victorian mansions along Market Street, Blake spoke about how many colonial buildings didn't survive through waves of construction booms and changes from the Industrial Age to the present. Some were turned into department stores or other retail ventures and are now office spaces. Blake noted that many of the buildings still have their Revolutionary-era basements. During the teardown and construction of new spaces, they often left the basements intact. I wondered more about what had been found in these old basements and perhaps what still might remain to be discovered.

I noticed how close everything was as we continued our walk. Blake said that York was designed ergonomically in the 1740s. It was deliberate, so people walking or on horseback could easily wander from place to place. We passed another mural depicting York's Revolutionary history on the red brick wall of a five-story building overlooking a parking lot. I was impressed by the street art in York. Blake told me that later, he'd be taking me to the ultimate street art location.

We hit the corner of North Pershing Avenue and West Market Street, and the sidewalk changed from cement to red brick at the Colonial Complex, which stretches from Market Street all the way down the block along Pershing Avenue towards the History Center Museum. The Colonial Complex consists of a few buildings that really stand out amid the many Victorian and Colonial red brick structures in York.

There's the General Horatio Gates House, where Gates stayed during a winter in York in 1778. Beside it is the Golden Plough Tavern, which was constructed in 1741: the same year York was settled. Across Pershing Street is the reconstructed Colonial Court House. In addition to my tour with Blake, there are other guided tours of these buildings in the Colonial Complex.

The gray stone building that served as the residence for General Horatio Gates abuts the Golden Plough Tavern. In front of these two historic houses is a statue of Lafayette, who first visited York to attend a dinner at Gate's house. On his second visit, returning as a war hero, he would spend time at the Globe Inn in what was Centre Square.

Blake described the Golden Plough Tavern as an example of German colonial architecture, a style that originated from the Black Forest area of Germany. That's where Martin Eichelberger, who built this cabin as a family home, originated. The Golden

Plough Tavern is located along what was first a Native American trading path and then the thoroughfare through York in the 1700s, which gave it some traffic and made it apt for Martin Eichelberger to open his doors to travelers and passersby.

A short, bright red door and red-framed windows are juxtaposed with exposed logs and half timbers in the older bottom half of the building. The complete structure was restored to be authentically colonial-style. Blake pointed out the Roman numerals carved on the front of the timbers. I noticed the *X*'s and *V*'s, which he said were originally used as assembly instructions. It was sort of like what you get today from Ikea, except back then they had no YouTube videos to watch or TaskRabbits to call for further assistance.

Across the street at the corner of Pershing Avenue and Market Street is the York County Colonial Court House, a reconstruction of the courthouse which stood in Centre Square and where the Articles of Confederation were adopted on November 15, 1777. A simple brown-brick, Georgian-style, two-story building with a white, centrally placed door and symmetrical white pane windows accented by white shutters and a cupola sits on a small grassy lawn. Atop the cupola, which still has a working bell, sits a figure of a soldier. I noticed the pillory and stocks outside, crafted in wood and painted deep red—a true colonial touch.

We stood along the brick sidewalk, admiring this reconstructed building and the vibrant orange leaves of the trees outside, which had started to turn colors for fall. There were a few leaves scattered across the grass in front of the Court House. Several plaques and markers provided an overview of the history of this building, which was reconstructed by the Bicentennial Commission in 1976. It was erected in 1754 in Centre Square, now Continental Square, just a few blocks away from where we were today. The original Court House was later demolished in the nineteenth century. I read a sign about the reconstructed building, which was designed by architect C. William Dize, known for designing many of York's notable historic buildings.

An architect as well as a U.S. Veteran, Dize was at Pearl Harbor when the Japanese attacked the islands in 1941. He then fought in World War II including serving in the Battle of the Bulge, where he received the Purple Heart, Bronze Star and Infantry Badge. More of Dize's projects live on just steps away from each other in downtown, including the Barnett Bobb Log House, the Gates House, the Golden Plough Tavern, and Quaker Meetinghouse.

A marker outside of the Court House in the shadow of an American flag, waving in the light breeze, pays tribute to Revolutionary War Patriots. It was yet another marker from the Yorktown Chapter of the Daughters of the American Revolution.

"Very faithful recreation of our courthouse," Blake said. "In order to build this building faithfully, they dug up the asphalt of Continental Square, measured the foundations of the original courthouse, which are still dug underneath the reconstructed courthouse. They used that information to rebuild this with the exact size and materials. They utilized colonial construction meeting minutes and inventories to determine what materials they needed. And basically, everything that they used was done to authentically recreate this original Revolutionary War–era building where Continental Congress held session."

I asked Blake more about what it was like for the Continental Congress here in York during that time. From what he described it was quite tense. It was the same winter that General George Washington and the Continental Army were at Valley Forge: a desperate situation. Members of the Continental Congress traveled to Valley Forge to meet the army encamped there.

I was both excited and surprised to be here in York, Pennsylvania, having also been at Nassau Hall at Princeton University, which held sessions for the Continental Congress and was also briefly a capitol. I was hitting all the historic capitals and also uncovering little known details along the way.

The fact that local people had wanted to take the time and money to reconstruct this Colonial Court House, complete with period-accurate materials down to the shingles on the roof, told me a lot about how they felt about the value of preserving history and sharing it here in York.

The interiors of the Court House can be toured. They've been restored to look as they would have in colonial times with handmade materials. It was a walk through time.

We next moved along North Pershing Avenue to see the backyard of the Golden Plough Tavern and Horatio Gates House. The small backyard includes a colonial garden with herbs and vegetables and is lined with a deep-red wooden fence. Beyond the yard is the Barnett Bobb Log House. This two-story house looked like its nickname, the Old Log House, with exposed logs, dovetailed corners, two red front doors, and red-trimmed windows.

Just beyond the Colonial Complex on North Pershing Avenue is the York County History Center, which houses the original Articles of Confederation inside. The first constitution of the United States, this rare document was on display during my visit. It must be taken in and out of display rotation, because it is delicate and light sensitive. I was excited for the opportunity to see this treasure firsthand, along with other artifacts related to the history of York and our nation's founding.

Dr. Valerie Long, manager of school programs, would be taking me on a tour. She led me inside this new museum, which was constructed in 2024. Another young York historian, Dr. Long has a cherubic face with long brown wavy hair. She wore jeans and a navy-blue sweatshirt with a handmade green-and-yellow yarn necktie.

As an undergraduate, Dr. Long majored in history at Albright College and pursued classical studies and archaeology at Hunter College in New York City. Because she so often catered programs for kids, I knew she would make for a great guide.

This modern history museum is located in a repurposed steam plant from the 1890s. The entranceway is open, bright, and expansive. The interior is further illuminated by the twelve-foot-tall stick figure alight with 256 lightbulbs—Reddy Kilowatt. This retro 1920s-era advertising sign was affixed to the grand window in the back of the main hallway. It gave a nod to York County's contributions to industry.

We entered the main exhibition area. The Articles of Confederation were in a glass case on the far wall past an old Conestoga wagon and a towering display of LED touchscreens featuring impactful people throughout history.

Printed by Hall & Sellers printing press in Lancaster in 1777—before there was a printing press in York—the Articles were created at a time when things started to take a turn for the better in the war. The British had surrendered at Saratoga in October of 1777, and by December 18, 1777, Congress had proclaimed a National Day of Thanksgiving. George Washington declared it should be "for solemn Thanksgiving and praise."

Also in the glass case were other artifacts from the time, including four-pence, forty-dollar, and five-dollar Continental currency, all printed by Hall & Sellers in 1777 and 1778. A chair that was used when Lafayette came to town on his tour in February of 1822 was shown along with a deep red and gold copper luster pitcher with Lafayette's portrait inked in black on the front. Commemorative ribbons were created as a type of merchandise, too. Lafayette had been in York in 1778 in Horatio Gates's home, toasting Geoge Washington as a sign of his loyalty when things were dire in the war. In 1825, he returned to York a hero.

I laughed at the thought of Lafayette merchandise akin to concert-style T-shirts and buttons, but these items did indeed feature Lafayette's image, and they were more than tastefully done. It was a testament to how important Lafayette and the French were to the founding of our nation. He was like a rock star of the Revolution.

Today, where Lafayette once stayed in Centre Square is now called Continental Square and is located at the intersection of Market and George Streets. The Globe Inn was on the square's southwest corner. The Victorian Romanesque Rupp Building stands in its place today, home to a café and a historical marker to Lafayette. Hearing Dr. Long talk about Lafayette's visit to York, I considered that I may need to sit in this café in Continental Square later and raise a glass and offer a toast to Lafayette.

I asked Dr. Long about why the Continental Congress had chosen York as their hideaway after leaving Philadelphia, thus making York one of a few early capitals of the United States. Prior capitals had included Philadelphia—before British occupation in 1777. The Continental Congress then moved to Lancaster, where they would make the city their capital for just one day on September 27, 1777, before skipping over to York, which would serve as the capital for nine months.

"York was chosen for strategic reasons. Lancaster was the location of the Pennsylvania state government at the time, and it was too close to Philadelphia," Dr. Long explained. "So, they continued over to York because we have this mile-wide river between Lancaster and York. Additionally, there are other kinds of routes north and south so that if the British decided that they wanted to pursue Continental Congress, they had ways to escape this area and flee to other parts of the country into safety."

That river, the Susquehanna, was a significant physical barrier to cross. With the colonial government occupying Lancaster, there wasn't room in Lancaster to accommodate all the delegates, so they crossed the Susquehanna to York where a courthouse welcomed hosting their meetings and the residents opened their homes, taverns and provided resources.

I found it amazing that these old, fragile documents were still housed here and had survived all this time. Sometimes documents and artifacts like these are part of people's collections that are donated to museums. Dr. Long said that the Articles of Confederation have been kept in the York County History Center's archives.

"They are extremely significant because, first, they are our first constitution," Dr. Long said. "We did not have a way of governing ourselves before we declared independence, so they were crucial for that. But additionally, we were trying to seek outside help from France, and why would they support us? We had nothing. We couldn't even show that we are able to unify, so this document is one of those things that helped us get France's help. It showed that we could unify and come together as a country."

I looked closely at the parchment paper. This document served as our first Constitution. The first article gave our nation the title of the United States of America. The Articles gave our Congress a way of voting and governing ourselves. These articles were later revamped to create the Constitution that we have today.

Around the corner from the history museum at 135 West Philadelphia Street is another significant Revolutionary War-era building, the Quaker Friends Meetinghouse, dating to 1766. It's one of the oldest continuously active houses of worship in York County. The one-story, red brick building with a sunny yellow door and windows lined with yellow shutters sits up on a little hill. An interpretive sign by the street calls out that the eastern part of the building is the oldest, dating to 1766, while the newer 1783 portion is on the western side. A gold plaque at the front of the building notes that the meeting house has been continuously in use since 1764. Many of York's early English Quaker families are buried on the grounds here.

Following my time with Dr. Long, Blake Gifford was helping me end my history dive in York with a mix of modern street art painted with reflections on history over at the Royal Square District, about a ten-minute walk from the museum. It's bordered by King, Queen, Princess, and Duke Streets. I've seen a lot of street art in my time, but I would truly call this area a street art lover's dream. An area of parking lots and old Victorian-era mansions and industrial complexes became giant canvases for artists. Blake said the project managers even added in shipping containers, for more usable canvas space.

I twirled around the outdoor art gallery, delighted at the thirty murals on display for residents and those who decided to park here to enjoy the view. A light pink cinder-block wall was painted like a giant can of wild-caught sardines in olive oil, the kind conveniently packed in little cans that fit in your palm with pull tops. I looked at the rainbow of bright blue, white, yellow, red, and pink colors. I didn't notice until Blake pointed it out that there was a date on the mural: 1741. It was the date that York was founded. Blake called it a fun little Easter egg to discover.

Two children raced each other across the parking lot: a little girl in a shirt and tights moving quickly on a scooter, outpacing her older brother on a small bicycle. They whizzed by a yellow and orange mural painted with a heron of various shades of blue holding what looked like a lollypop in its beak. The murals had likely made this area a more friendly place to play.

York's mix of street art, architectural marvels, history and food had made me want to seek out more interesting places. I was glad Blake and Dr. Long had agreed to be my guides. While many travelers head to places like Philadelphia or Washington, DC, to learn about our nation's early history, my visit to York made me happy that I continue to be able to find hidden gems like this colorful, historic city to learn something new.

Dills Tavern and Distillery: Toasting George Washington on the Pennsylvania Frontier

Drinking cherry bounce with a group of reenactors by a roaring fire inside an old tavern would be my next immersive history lesson in Dillsburg, Pennsylvania. Managed by the Northern York County Historical and Preservation Society, Dills Tavern and the surrounding outbuildings transport visitors into eighteenth- and nineteenth-century life in this part of Central Pennsylvania on what was Dills Plantation.

Located just over a thirty-minute drive northwest of York, Dills Tavern was a gathering place on the old Pennsylvania frontier, including for militia during the American Revolution. The tavern was located on a plantation, which grew over time in several stages, running as a farm and tavern and expanding to a large-capacity distillery that shipped whiskey down to the port of Baltimore, Maryland.

I parked streetside and read the interpretive signs outside of the old stone Dills Tavern. In addition to all the rich colonial history, the site also has ties to the Civil War. Two signs out by the sidewalk share the Confederate invasion of Dillsburg, when General Jeb Stuart's southern cavalry of six thousand men rolled through town on Baltimore Street and vandalized Dillsburg in July of 1863 before joining General Lee's army at Gettysburg. They stopped at Dills Tavern to water their horses.

I walked along the brick sidewalk inside the complex past Dills Tavern and a large white barn towards Eichelberger Distillery, so named after the Eichelbergers, who distilled spirits for three generations in the area. I had an appointment for a tour and tasting.

In addition to Dills Tavern, there are several buildings where you can experience living history, including the nineteenth-century wheelwright building and 1798 log barn, both transported to this location in pieces and reconstructed on the property.

When the Eichelbergers moved to Dills Planation, they set up additional trades like barrel-making and wagon and wheel repair onsite. Wagons were the cars and moving trucks of the day, and wheelwrights were the auto mechanics of the day.

Eichelberger Distillery at Dills Tavern was not original to the property. It was built as a replica of an eighteenth-century distillery, much like what had been here in colonial times when Central Pennsylvania was producing a lot of spirits. Most of the population during colonial times were of German, Scots-Irish, and Quaker descent. Matthew Dill, the original owner of the plantation and tavern, was Scots-Irish. He settled in Dillsburg in 1742, garnering five hundred acres of patent land.

Dill's original log cabin was built near a spring not far from where Dills Tavern sits today. Matthew would eventually plant crops on his plantation and start a tavern. Dillsburg is named after this enterprising new American.

I stepped inside the recreated Eichelberger Distillery, greeted by reenactors standing by a copper still. I surveyed the room to see a large wooden barrel topped with a flat woven basket. Behind it was a big copper pot, resting on a floor made of muted colored bricks.

A few men were dressed as workers and distillers in late-seventeenth-century clothing, including Murray Small, my guide for the tasting and tour. He wore a checkered button-down shirt, a leather apron, trousers, and hat, dressed practically, as a work-man would have dressed in the late 1600s. Murray shared that their archivist had pulled out libation recipes from the tavern's historic ledger to find out what was served here, which included whiskey and cherry bounce, among other drinks.

He showed me a document with more of the libations that were made here, including peach brandy, eggnog, hot toddies, mint toddies, whiskey grog, stewed whiskey, and sillabub. Some of these were not familiar to me, like sillabub, so I had to look it up. It was a frothy dessert or drink made from apple cider, lemon juice, heavy cream or milk, and sugar. Because of the abundance of grain in this part of Pennsylvania, they made a lot of whiskey. They also used the orchards in the area to fuel cordials like the popular cherry bounce.

Murray's recipe came from Martha Washington and was named so "to make an excellent bounce." I wondered if I'd be bouncing or sleeping following a few sips of the cherry liquid.

"Generally poor people made it from whiskey. People with a little bit more wealth made it from brandy. I follow Martha Washington's recipe, which calls for brandy," Murray said.

The cherries came from a local farm—Peters Orchards—and the recipe isn't too difficult to prepare. Montmorency or morello cherries are pressed and then brandy is added to the mushy sour mix along with sugar, cinnamon, cloves, and nutmeg. It sounded like a holiday drink to me!

Murray led me from the main distillery into a second room, set with a long slender wooden table in the center. The room was sparse but cozy. On one wall, a large hearth accented by a red wood mantle was set with candles and a miniature copper-pot still, complete with a line arm and onion head. Below the mantle a fire was ablaze flanked with various tools for stoking the fire. Fire would have been used to directly heat copper stills during the distilling process in colonial times.

The other side of the room had windows and at one end, a red wooden wall and staircase, where various old, framed images of the distilling process were featured alongside the distillery's official designation as an American Distilling Institute member. Under it was a black-and-white image of a rowdy scene inside a colonial tavern. One man had likely had so much cherry bounce, he'd fallen out of his chair. I hoped my time with Murray wouldn't be that wild.

Murray set two bottles and two tapered-rim whiskey tasting glasses on the table. Next, he opened a bottle of cherry bounce. I looked at the label whose front had an image of Colonel George Spangler, who hailed from York County, filling a barrel with cherry bounce in 1806. Our bottle of cherry bounce was one that Murray had made himself right here at this very distillery.

I asked him how often people would have historically imbibed cherry bounce.

Murray told me George Washington used to take cherry bounce in his canteen on trips. In fact, many sources cite it as a favorite of his. People around Dillsburg enjoy cherry bounce frequently, though Murray said that the best way to drink it is on a cold day in front of a warm fire, perhaps for an aperitif or after-dinner drink. That sounded nice to me. It wasn't dinnertime, but the fire was on inside Eichelberger Distillery. Why not taste some cherry bounce!

Matt Dill, the original tavern and plantation owner, would have a son, James, who would go on to expand the tavern business. James's son John would then develop and expand the tavern and plantation further. This meant more people were needed to work at Dills Tavern including indentured servants and enslaved people.

John would eventually sell the tavern in 1800 to Leonard Eichelberger, a German immigrant and wagon maker who had been living in Hanover, Pennsylvania. He kept the tavern open and renamed it Eichelberger's Tavern. Leonard expanded the business even more, transporting the whiskey he distilled to Baltimore and bringing back goods to Dillsburg, generating a boost in the local economy. Eichelberger and his crew were making about ten thousand barrels of distilled spirits by 1814, making Eichelberger's one of the biggest distillers in the United States. He would add on to the tavern and pass on the business to his sons.

It was wonderful to think that the story of this historic distillery was being shared again today through Eichelberger's Distillery at Dills Tavern and the work of people like Murray, who had obviously researched so many details to help to bring visitors back in time.

I asked Murray how he got into distilling. "When I came here first, I was doing whiskey tastings, and while I got a lot of engagement from the guys, I noticed that their wives were standing in the background, kind of checking their watches. And I started to look for other libations to serve," Murray recounted.

He found an old tavern log and had an archivist comb through it. They discovered thirty-three different recipes for drinks. The cherry bounce caught his eye. At first, they made it in small jars, and now they produce it in thirty-gallon vats.

This tavern log also shared information about the daily life of the tavern's guests, including how some patrons would exchange work for whiskey, bartering their skills such as shoe-making, chopping wood, or farming for booze.

I smiled when Murray poured me some cherry bounce, the deep red liquid filling the thick bottom of my small glass. He offered to grate a little fresh nutmeg on top, and I obliged. Murray used a small, antique-looking handmade grater that fit between his index finger and thumb. Nutmeg was a common spice added to many drinks of the time like eggnog and punches. Before the cherry bounce, Murray decided to first have a little of the Old Monaghan Whiskey he'd distilled.

Finally, it was time for the cherry bounce! We both took sips, and I closed my eyes—the brandy and sugar balanced each other out, and the mix of sweet spice flavors complemented the alcohol. I was instantly being transported to a cozy wingback chair beside a Christmas tree and roaring fire after a big holiday meal. When I opened my eyes, I looked over at Murray, dressed as a colonial distiller and was reminded that I was in a colonial tavern in Dillsburg. It was definitely not a normal day of travels!

Murray told me there's an annual Cherry Bounce Festival where participants show off and compete for the best homemade cherry bounce. Murray, who competed himself in the festival, shared a secret.

"The key is to try to get the brandy balance just right and then not overwhelm it with too much cinnamon," Murray said. "Some of the folks get it a little bit too much like cough syrup."

He'd been working on fine-tuning his cherry bounce for about a decade, but surprisingly shared that he'd only won the cherry bounce contest at the annual festival once. He said that's because of the way it's judged. One of the criteria is complexity, and he is a purist, sticking to Martha Washington's recipe to a tee. Even as a cherry bounce newbie, I could tell that he was doing something right.

It was remarkable, too, that it was made right here on the site of this old plantation, following the same environment, techniques, and procedures that would have been used in the 1700s.

Murray shared more about the process of fermenting whiskey in wooden barrels, which are cleaned only with boiling water. They keep the process pure, not using extra enzymes, and instead using only the enzymes found naturally in the grains. They distill on two stills; the larger stripping still is named Mary Dill. The smaller still is named after Catherine Eichelberger. The mashing process takes about a half a day. The fermentation process takes three to five days, and the stripping is another part of a day. Finally, the whiskey rests in the smaller still for about four hours. About twenty-five pounds of grain will yield about 1.75 gallons of whiskey. It's a time-intensive process.

During colonial times, distilling was a popular endeavor in Central Pennsylvania and there were lots of taverns for travelers to choose from. People traveled by water, and if they were traveling by land, they either walked or rode on a horse and wagons. They needed regular places to stop along their journeys to refuel, both for themselves and their horses. These taverns were there to feed and water the humans, and thus distilling became an essential business. Taverns were like convenience stores, hotels, and gas stations all rolled into one.

In 1783 in York County alone, tax records and a census list 220 stills operating under license. A more agricultural area, by 1840 it's thought that almost one fifth of all farms would have had a still. York County was one of the largest distilling counties in what was the number one distilling state at the time.

"There weren't a lot of medicines here and the workdays were long," Murray said. "And after a ten-hour workday, guys would go to the tavern and, you know, ease their pain a little bit with a couple of whiskeys. It was a very profitable way to deal with large volumes of grain because it's easier to transport a couple of barrels of whiskey than tons of grain. The Scots-Irish and the German heritage of this region, it was almost genetic that people were good distillers."

Murray was a good distiller. He made me want to bounce again! Back in the distillery, he showed me the brown mushy fermenting grain inside one of the barrels, which looked like porridge. This would eventually be transformed into whiskey.

Over at the original 1794 Dills Tavern site, I made a stop inside the kitchen, where meals for the tavern would have been made on the big hearth over an open fire. There was also a tap-room with another large fireplace and a big table set with candles and pewter dining utensils and plates where guests would have eaten and socialized. At the table's center were remnants of oyster shells, a popular staple of the time. Upstairs were the sleeping quarters.

Interpreter Mindy Bower was dressed in what a working woman of the latter half of the eighteenth century would have worn—a jacket, petticoat, apron, white linen cap, and handkerchief around her neck. At a time when people didn't have the luxury to bathe or wash their clothing every day, caps would help to protect her hair from the elements and an apron would shield her clothing, keeping it cleaner, especially when working over an open fire. She stoked the flames and mentioned she sometimes led cooking demonstrations here in Dills Tavern.

It was remarkable that we were standing inside this tavern dating back centuries that still today reveals so many fascinating details that travelers can taste, smell, and see firsthand on a living history tasting and tour.

Gettysburg's Dobbin House: A Colonial Cocktail and Tavern Stop

Civil War history is the focus of most travelers' visit to Gettysburg with its famous battlefield and National Military Park. For history lovers or anyone seeking a superb and classical colonial meal, the Dobbin House's potent colonial cocktails, delicious dishes, and authentically reproduced ambience is a must. Less than an hour drive from Dillsburg, I met with the entrepreneurial owner who lives and breathes this 1776 building's history, making it quite the step back in time.

It was a crisp fall evening when I arrived at the Dobbin House following a day touring the battlefield. With its white shutters, well-lit exterior, and fall display of hay bales and pumpkins, the old stone building beckoned me to the warmth promised inside. A few other guests scurried out, and I got a glimpse of the packed interior hostess stand and entranceway. I could tell it was a busy night at the Dobbin House, but then again, I had heard that almost every weekend night was busy.

I stopped outside to photograph the various historical plaques. Normally, when I visit a historic property, including those on the National Register of Historic Places, there are one or two plaques or markers outside. The Dobbin House had five! There was one referencing it being a Civil War building; a bronze National Register of Historic Places plaque; one for being an American Presbyterian and Reformed Historical Site from the Presbyterian Historical Society; one honoring its 1776 roots from Adams County; and another from the National Society of Colonial Dames commemorating it as the First Classical School West of the Susquehanna River. It might have been a historical-plaque record.

Jackie White, a history lover through and through with an effervescent personality, met me at the entrance. She was ready to show me around this buzzing historic tavern, restaurant, and bed and breakfast that she's owned and run for fifty years. She was wearing a three-quarter-zip navy pullover and white turtleneck. The pocket area of her navy layer was embroidered with the Historic Dobbin House Tavern and an image of the stone façade. Her red, wavy hair was parted on the side and pulled back in a low ponytail. She wore small earrings and a big smile—her understated confidence and zest for life showing through. The kind of person I love to meet on my travels, Jackie was passionate about her small business and eager to share it with curious travelers like me.

By the host stand in the entrance was a large fireplace whose red wooden mantle was lined with pewter cups. A taxidermy upside-down turkey hung over a vase of sunflowers, further setting the scene for this colonial-style experience. Jackie corralled me past the crowd waiting to get tables and down a set of stairs to the Springhouse Tavern. I stopped along the way to read a sign about the original spring. The Dobbin family had first built the home over a spring for easy access to water—and to ensure that they would have access to water during a potential Indian raid or attack. The spring area was cooler, so it was also a good place to store perishable goods at a time of no electric refrigeration.

The Springhouse Tavern evoked a true colonial tavern feel with its wood beamed ceilings, gray stone walls, large bar, and various long wooden tables alit with candles, where families and groups enjoyed the charming setting for dinner. A server dressed in traditional period clothing passed me carrying a steaming tray of spit-roasted chicken and New York strip steaks.

While I had taken only a few moments to read the sign about the spring, Jackie had already made new friends. She introduced me to some locals before ushering me upstairs by a roped-off side stairway to a small area that was once a secret hideaway for enslaved people. The Dobbin House was a station on the Underground Railroad and thought to be the first stop north of the Mason-Dixon Line.

Three mannequin figures inside the sparse wooden area were positioned with their legs stretched out and backs to the walls. They would have had to crawl inside on their hands and knees to fit inside the cramped space between two floors whose ceiling was the base of the second floor above. Concealed but claustrophobic, I could only imagine the stifling fear of an enslaved person hiding here while someone searched the home.

We emerged from the staircase into a small dining room, where artifacts in a glass case from the 1820s, including a skeleton key, pieces of porcelain china, and other framed items, told the story of the Dobbin House over time. I noticed a larger poster with black-and-white photos of the Dobbin House during its more recent restoration. A young Jackie was pictured in a turtleneck and jeans, happily driving a bulldozer. Other photographs showed the inside of the tavern and inn during the renovations.

I asked Jackie how old she had been when she brought this place. She said just twenty-five years old. I did the math and was astonished that she was now seventy-five years old. What ingenuity and gumption it took to take on a major project like this when she was so young! I asked her how she decided to take the leap.

"Well, there was this thing called a husband," Jackie said with a smile. "He said, no, it will be fun. And then I said, if you own your own business, you work seven days a week, it never ends. You're never off. He didn't like that, so…"

Jackie gave a laugh. It was just her and the cat now. Whatever the impetus to get started, I could tell from the photo of her during the restoration and from the fact that she'd now run the restaurant and inn for fifty-some years that she liked it and was doing something right. Plus, she was here on a Friday night entertaining me. Running a small business is difficult. Restoring a historic property is difficult. Combining the two is a super-sized challenge.

I walked up a few stairs into what Jackie called "the Spinning Room," which indeed had an antique spinning wheel in the corner. Period clothes hung alongside other colonial knickknacks and curiosities. A mantle was lined with raw wool, cotton, and flax: staple materials used in the frontier colonist's clothing. Hanging beside these were carders and hackles, combs and hand tools, used to clean the natural materials of dirt so they could be ready for the spinning wheel.

I walked through this cozy candlelit room to a series of larger "Alexander Dobbin" dining rooms, each decorated differently. Tables were lit only by candles in the fine dining area. There were a few unusual tables situated under fabric canopies. Covered canopy beds were popular in colonial times for sleeping, helping those in bed to keep in the heat in drafty rooms often heated only by a fireplace. Guests dining in these canopy-covered dining tables had an experience like sleeping in a colonial bed.

Our quick tour combined with a long day on the battlefield had my head spinning and my stomach rumbling. I put both hands on my abdomen to hide the sound and wondered if Jackie heard it. She must have, because she began to tell me about their homemade breads and motioned for me to take a seat back in the Spinning Room, also a snug dining room. A basket of cornbread and yeast rolls arrived at the table and Jackie told me that we had to enjoy a colonial cocktail. She knew just the one, she said with a wink.

Jackie put in an order for the Rum Bellies Vengeance, their most popular drink.

"People love them, and they are really, really good. They taste a little too good," she smiled. "So, we have to put a limit on them of two per customer."

Our loquacious server appeared quickly with two iced red punch drinks, topped with a twist of lemon and a cherry. Their color reminded me of the Hurricane cocktail from New Orleans, so from that experience and Jackie's comments I figured they would be strong. The Rum Bellies Vengeance was made with light and dark rums, various liqueurs, and fruit juices: a concoction sure to get us talking.

Dating to 1776, the Dobbin House is the same age as the United States, Jackie proudly shared. It was built by Reverend

Alexander Dobbin. Dobbin had been recruited to America from Scotland to preach. He was a Covenanter, an early form of Presbyterian, which at the time was persecuted in Scotland. This may have made Dobbin more interested in relocating to the New World. Either way, he took a leap of faith and eventually landed in Pennsylvania. He purchased land around what is today Gettysburg and built the foundation of what today is the Dobbin House.

In America, Reverend Dobbin had his hands full with his work and his children. With his first wife, he had ten children, and following her death, he remarried a widow who already had nine children. His home must have been quite busy, and inside he also housed a classical school, the first of its kind west of the Susquehanna River. A well-respected school, students learned Latin, Hebrew, and Greek. Dobbin would go on to help found the first presbytery of the Reformed Presbyterian Church in America, and later, the Associate Reformed Presbyterian Church.

Knowing so much about Gettysburg's Civil War past, before this visit I had failed to even consider what the Gettysburg area looked like in colonial times. I asked Jackie more about the area during the American Revolution.

Jackie shared that it wasn't a battleground at the time of the Revolution but was comprised of a healthy population of Scots-Irish immigrants, including Reverend Dobbin. Dobbin supported the Patriots, and he and others provided horses and food to the Continental Army in Valley Forge during the winters of 1777 and 1778. Jackie explained that there were many here who supported colonial independence because the area was comprised of mostly Scots-Irish people, who weren't too fond of the English.

In the 1730s and '40s, prior to Reverend Dobbin's family moving in, other settlers had come to the region. It was a wooded area, and enterprising Scots-Irish and German settlers cleared the land and set up farms. Before Dobbin arrived in 1761, Samuel Gettys founded a tavern. His son James, with the help of Reverend Dobbin, would lay out the streets of what became the town of Gettysburg. Gettysburg was named the county seat of Adams County in 1800 and incorporated as a borough in 1806. Thus, Dobbin had quite a few influences on the Pennsylvania frontier area of Gettysburg. He would pass away in 1809 and is buried in Gettysburg's Lower Marsh Creek Presbyterian Cemetery.

As I gingerly sipped my Rum Bellies Vengeance, for sure knowing that I wouldn't order a second, I looked around at the interior and wondered how much was from the period. Jackie said that it had been reconstructed to look like a colonial tavern, but that the building has a lot of the original elements that it would have had in its early days. The woodwork, walls, and the plaster are pretty much original to 1776. Jackie said it was fortunate that over time, the property was rented to various people, who, because they were renting, didn't want to put a lot of money into refurbishments. Thus, much of the original structure remained intact.

It was amazing that it had survived from the American Revolution and through the tumultuous Civil War battle in Gettysburg, when it was used as a hospital.

When our meals arrived, I was presented with the drunken scallops, perhaps made within whiffing-distance of the Rum Bellies punch, and the famous King's Onion soup served in blue and white colonial patterned bowls. Savory broth with beef chunks, the soup had a heaping helping of cheese melted on top, almost like a charred, thick lid. I was presented scissors by Jackie.

The cheese was so thick that the Dobbin House provides scissors so you can cut through it. I attempted to finagle a spoonful of broth and cheese, slowly stretching the cheese to about a six-inch cheese pull before slurping a bit into my mouth. It was delicious and an impressive presentation.

Jackie ordered the Adams County roast duck. Adams County is the largest apple producer in the state of Pennsylvania, and in this dish the duck is roasted in a hearth oven with apples and hard cider, forming a tangy apple sauce. My drunken scallops entree, sauteed in bacon, spices, and Chablis, looked swimmingly good.

As I ate the delicious meal with Jackie, I thought about how brilliant it was that this little colonial treasure was preserved and restored so that all who venture to Gettysburg can take a trip further into the past, tasting history with every sip and bite.

"The best thing about the Dobbin House is the wonderful guests who come here to Gettysburg. They come because they want to learn a little bit of American history," Jackie said. "I always tell our staff that they could be on a beach sipping a mai tai, but they want to come and learn about the sacrifices that the soldiers who struggled and fought here made for the freedoms that we have today."

I do love a good mai tai on a beach, but I also just discovered that a good Rum Bellies Vengeance in a colonial tavern does a mind pretty good, too. And isn't that a trip?

Battle of Brandywine: A Farm Stand Battle Site

From Gettysburg, it's about an hour-and-forty-minute drive to the Brandywine Valley, where the Battle of Brandywine took place on September 11, 1777, on farmland just twenty-five miles southwest of Philadelphia. Most travelers to Brandywine

Battlefield will stop by the Pennsylvania State Park sites in Chadds Ford. Not everyone decides to make a stop at Thornbury Farm in West Chester or Birmingham Hill, both on my list for area hidden gems.

The Battle of Brandywine was one of the deadliest battles of the American Revolution. Around thirty thousand soldiers traversed forests, hills, farms, and meadows over ten square miles, the largest land area on which any Revolutionary War battle was fought. It ended with a British victory and, shortly after, on September 26, the British were finally able to capture Philadelphia.

Those who stop in Chadds Ford can explore the visitors' center with a small exhibit gallery and gift shop and the two historic homes on the park grounds. The Benjamin Ring House was a Quaker farmhouse that was used as George Washington's headquarters before the battle. Now a house museum, visitors can step inside, where recreated interiors and furniture share what it would have looked like when Washington was there. There's also the neighboring home of Gideon Gilpin, used as a headquarters by British General Howe post battle.

I decided to adventure further afield to Thornbury Farm to meet Randell Spackman, who exuberantly bounced over to greet me outside of his red wooden one-story farm store along a paved country road in West Chester, Pennsylvania. He was dressed in a bright red British regimental coat. The owner of Thornbury Farm, one of the locations where the Battle of Brandywine took place, and a reenactor, Randell is passionate about history, preservation, and restoration, and his passion is one of the reasons he works to keep the farm open and preserved. Thornbury Farm was the site of some of the final conflicts of the Battle of Brandywine.

Randell's grandfather brought the farm in the 1930s and today it's still in his family. Randell runs the farm store and a small business, and he lives there with his four daughters and little boy. It's a family farm that's also a community gathering place.

Under the cover in the outdoor pavilion on the farm, which the night before had played host to a wedding, Randell laid out items on a large wooden dining table to complete his look as a British soldier. At over 6'2" tall with grayish brown thick curly hair, Randell appeared all the part in his white breeches and wool red coat, whose facings were lined with buttons emblazoned with Royal Provencal. He placed a black tricorn hat on his head and adjusted the thick, stiff collar, called a neck stock. Its purpose was to protect a soldier's neck from sabers or other sharp objects. Attached to the front chest of his coat was a pick and whisk used to clean his musket.

These uniforms would have been worn year-round through winters and summers. "So, you were either way too hot or way too cold," Randell laughed. I could only imagine how often they were laundered. Not a lot.

Randell mentioned other items a soldier might carry, since they had to have on their person almost everything that they needed to survive. He began to layer on a leather cartridge box with extra flints, which resembled a small messenger bag or purse. He snatched from the table a canvas bag, called a haversack, used to carry food or other necessary items, along with a flask, bowl, and cup. He had items for his daily food and nourishment, along with protection. He armed his musket with a bayonet, pulling the short sword out of a leather case to let me examine it.

"This was one of the fighting tools that they used that got outlawed later," Randell said. "The British Army was actually very good with the bayonet. Here at Brandywine, when they ran out of materials, the American soldiers came out of the woods with their bayonets and used the end of their musket for defense, because they had run out of supplies."

The soldiers had just come from Chadds Ford to an area called Sandy Hollow by Thornbury Farm. Randell said that's when the American spirit really emerged as soldiers bravely went into hand-to-hand combat with the elite British troops. This bold and perilous move would give Washington time to retreat.

Once Randell's outfit was all set, he gave a nod, and we walked back to the entrance of the small farm store. Inside, displays of honey, baked goods, jellies, jams, apples, handmade soaps, coffee, and relishes were mixed with crafts. A whiteboard by the register gave news about upcoming events on the farm. We walked out front, where a display of orange, white, and green pumpkins of various sizes and seasonal fall red, yellow, white, and orange mums were alongside a large Tow Mater car, a replica of the character from the Disney Pixar film *Cars*. Randell has kids, but also a bit of a childlike spirit himself. He'd shared that he built the Tow Mater one cold winter for his daughter out of three old trucks and puts it out for the holidays.

We crossed the quiet country road to survey more of Thornbury Farm, part of the historic Thornbury Township, where a few farms still exist amid encroaching development from nearby Philadelphia. Travelers can learn about the Battle of Brandywine if they stop by Randell's farm market to pick up products. Randell's many special events are mostly open to the public and include historical ghost walks, history talks, a Christmas market, weddings, and battle reenactments. He also regularly hosts school tours. Randell keeps the farm busy and welcomes the entire community to visit to learn about the history.

Thornbury Farm dates to 1709, and there are multiple historic buildings on the farm today. The main house was the first quarried home in Pennsylvania and the stones used to construct it were mined on the property. During the battle, this old stone house was used as a hospital. The property also includes a barn constructed in the 1740s that held prisoners after the Battle of Brandywine.

During the eighteenth century, the farm was owned by a Quaker family, who grew buckwheat, wheat, corn, and potatoes and stored dairy products and root crops in the spring house. Today, it's still producing crops and is home to numerous farm animals, including rescue horses, pigs, and goats. Randell and his family live in the "new" house on the property, dating to 1812. It was once a stop on the Underground Railroad. History abounds on Thornbury Farm.

A historical sign by a wooden fence across the road in front of the farm store provides details about General Stephen's Stand on September 11, 1777, when General Stephen's division utilized a high point on Thornbury Farm to hold off attacks by Hessian and British soldiers. Stephen's forces eventually retreated and General Howe was able to win the day, but their retreat was not met without initial bravery.

After reading the sign, I looked out across the field of grass and down the cascading country lane to the eighteenth-century stone house, the oldest on the property. The morning sun streamed through the trees and there were just a few stratus clouds amid the bright blue sky. The birds were singing, and, in the distance, horses grazed on patchwork land. The whole scene reminded me of one of the pretty villages I'd visited in Northern England. The setting was bucolic and surprising at the same time since we were so close to a major city like Philadelphia.

Randell mentioned that British soldiers had written that this area reminded them of home. In fact, the name Thornbury came from the village of the same name in Gloucestershire, England, and had ties to Her Majesty's Rose Gardens at Thornbury Castle in England. It was so named by the original owner who built the stone house here in 1709.

Inside the wooden paddock fence below the historical marker was an open field of soft grass, just turning brown in the crisp October air. A chestnut-colored mini horse was grazing in the distance. Randell said that was his rescue mini named Roo. Curious about the new visitor, Roo sauntered over to greet me. I reached my flat palm down between post and rail fence boards towards Roo's muzzle, so she could sniff me. At the same time, out of the tall grass in the distance a large black pig and goat emerged.

I was delighted. Being a horse and animal lover, I couldn't wait to meet these rescues. Randell said that the pig is named Clover, because he got her on St. Patrick's Day. Clover has a loyal following of locals who regularly pet her belly. She must have foreseen belly rubs, because the big hairy pig quickly came over to greet us.

Clover put her soft, wet snout close to the wooden fence. Randell gave her belly scratches. Willow, the pygmy goat, was a bit shyer, but she slowly came over to join the party. Willow had a thick black coat with a blotch of white and black on her sides and face.

It was heartwarming to see these animals living out their days on this special farm and being part of the Thornbury Farm experience for visitors. The farm reminded me of a different, long-forgotten sort of life that is in stark contrast with our modern busy world. Here I was with Randell, who was dressed as a

British soldier, hanging out with rescue animals on land where a large, gruesome battle was fought. Like so many things in life, it was great example of the many dichotomies we encounter. I asked Randell about what it felt like to grow up here.

"It's kind of daunting. As a child, I heard stories about the battle and people talking about all these different things that happened here. It's hard to fathom. As I got older and people started to really tell the stories, I got to visualize it for myself. I started wearing the clothes as a reenactor. It became very powerful," Randell said. "When you put on the uniforms and you hear the musket fire and all the cannons and the smoke and the yelling, it's the best way to interpret and experience history. It's so powerful—gives me goosebumps."

The spot where we were standing, across the street from the farmstand and alongside the country lane was a high point above the area where the British troops had set up their artillery defenses during the battle. Thornbury Farm was the site of the final troop engagements during the battle. This was a battle with heavy hitters from both sides of the conflict participating. The British side was led by Generals William Howe, Charles Cornwallis, and Wilhelm von Knyphausen. The American forces were under the leadership of George Washington, the Marquis de Lafayette, Nathanael Greene, Alexander Hamilton, "Mad Anthony" Wayne, John Sullivan, William Alexander, Adam Stephen, and Casimir Pulaski. We were literally walking in the footsteps of these historical giants in the combat zone.

"My ancestors were in the 2nd Pennsylvania Regiment here on the farm fighting for the Continental Army, but by being able to dress up as a British soldier, I also learn history a little bit better, because history a lot of times is written by the winners," Randell said.

He explained that by looking at both sides of the story, one can often obtain a clearer picture of what might have really happened.

I had met a lot of reenactors over many years of researching and learning about past battles and historical events. Most of them, though, didn't live on a site where the important historical events took place. It really did provide a perspective with a whole other level of depth.

Randell said there were more full-sized horses to meet down the country lane towards the 1709 farmhouse, where much took place during the Battle of Brandywine. We walked down the paved road lined with fences and fields on each side to the old stone house in the valley. I looked up to see the date of 1709 on one of the stones near the roof. To the left of the farmhouse was a barn and series of paddocks where horses milled about. More were grazing in the expansive backyard, which rose up to a hill where trees lined the top of the knoll.

At the time of the battle, a Quaker farmer named Davis, a blacksmith by trade, was living in the home. He found himself in the middle of the chaos. The family did everything they could to survive and help the wounded, setting up a makeshift hospital in their home. The family removed shutters from the windows to use them as tables.

I looked up at the home's façade. There were two small glass-paned windows on the top of the older 1709 side of the home. These had no shutters. On the bottom were two windows with small white shutters.

During the battle, up on the hill we had just walked from was where the British had set up their defense. In front of us now, behind the home was where the Americans would have been positioned in the woods at the top of the far hill. The home was smack in the middle of the two opposing forces.

"There were some thirty thousand troops at the Battle of Brandywine, more than in Philadelphia at the time where Congress was stationed," Randell said. "The battle was so large that Congress could hear the cannon fire from Brandywine all the way in Philadelphia."

The home that we saw today had had various additions over time. It looked like two distinct houses pasted together. The darker serpentine-stone right half was built in 1740 and reminded me in style of Independence Hall in Philadelphia. On the left, the original 1709 portion was made of the lighter-colored quarried stone.

Randell now rents out the home to help cover the many expenses of the farm, so we couldn't go inside, but he said that the interiors still have the old wooden beams, the natural pine floors, and that big old fireplace that would have been used for cooking. There are even leather straps in the ceiling where the original owner would have hung his musket. Randell himself had tested out the straps.

"So, I actually put my musket in the straps," Randell said with a smile. "My grandmother used to tell stories about what it must have been like to live back then and be able to cook everything over a fire. My aunt remembers a story about 1942, when the farm lost power for over a week and they melted snow in the fire and used that same fireplace to make all their meals."

The old home was like a time capsule. It was wild to think that it was still lived in and appreciated, surrounded today by the serene grounds. Horses milled about in the pastures, and just beyond the pastures was the quarry in the back woods.

The house, located in the middle of the fighting, sustained significant cannon fire. Randell led me around the side to see the damage. I could tell where various stones had been replaced to repair the damage.

There were no windows on this side of the stone home, only a tall, thin white doorway about six feet up. The doorway was suspended on the side of the home with no stairs to meet it. Randell said it was a so-called coffin door, a name coined after the colonial era.

During colonial times, most wakes or funerals were held inside homes. The deceased often were viewed in their beds by a window or in the parlor. It's thought that these doors were created as a way to get coffin boxes out of the home rather than having to maneuver them through the narrow hallways and winding staircases. Coffin boxes could be moved through these special openings on the houses and then loaded right into a hearse wagon.

Though called coffin doors, these openings were also likely created for other practical uses like ventilation or to be able to get bigger furniture items in and out of homes. The term *coffin door* arose out of legend or folklore that persisted as an oral story. I marveled at the fact that it was still being told to me today.

Many colonial people were superstitious about death, and it's thought that many installed these coffin doors so that the dead wouldn't leave from the same front door the inhabitants entered and exited from each day. Some people were said to fear the spirits.

"We don't plan to use it anytime soon," Randell joked. "We don't have that kind of excitement on the farm anymore."

With much hand-to-hand combat amongst the thirty thousand troops being part of the Battle of Brandywine here on Thornbury Farm, it was a significantly macabre day.

"One of the streams here on the farm was said to run red with blood because there were so many casualties," Randell said. "People fell dead into the stream. It was a horribly gory battle."

I was seeing the farm and the battle today through so many lenses. I could now understand better what it had been like for Davis's family, who, like so many families living quieter lives on rural farms during the Revolution, were thrust into gore and madness. Through Randell's descriptions, I could understand better the contrast of the well-trained British militia against American soldiers, some of whom had never fought or been trained and had to courageously try to fight amid Thornbury's woods, meadows, and valleys.

Those who were lucky enough to survive the bloody combat surely would have experienced post-traumatic stress on a level I couldn't comprehend. I continued to wonder what drove Randell to keep sharing these stories, good and bad, with the greater community. He had a lot on his shoulders—sharing the grisly details of a landmark battle, helping rescue animals, and feeding the public, all the while keeping this farm viably running.

Randell regularly hosts large-scale reenactments at Thornbury Farm and invites the public to also relive history in this way. I had asked him at the beginning of our time together about what it felt like to continue this legacy and what it meant to share this history, but I wanted to ask again, having learned so much from him in such a short amount of time.

"You've researched the history and know it very well," I said. "What's it like to live at this site that has this history?"

"It's powerful. It's daunting," he repeated as before. "I'm actually the steward of this history. I feel I don't live here. I don't own it. All I do is try to maintain it and make it something for tomorrow…. With technology and archeology, we're able to pull artifacts out of the ground that we thought would be gone forever. We've been doing an over-ten-year study here with GPS coordinates and using LiDAR and all kinds of new technology to try and learn what's here, so we can continue to share it with future generations."

We need these stewards of open space and history, so that we can all better appreciate and learn from the past. With each traveler or community member picking up a pumpkin at Thornbury's farm store and perhaps taking the time to read the historical marker or hear from Randell, more people are learning about the past, making us better stewards of this important historical site.

Birmingham Hill and The General Warren: Lafayette and a Tavern's Legacy

The Battle of Brandywine covered a large area of rolling hills, farmland, and ravines. Thus, visitors who want to truly experience the various aspects of the battle need to hop in a car to drive to various important sites. I drove about ten minutes from Thornbury Farm to Birmingham Hill, where a big focus of this part of the battle was Marquis de Lafayette. Prior to the battle's culmination at Thornbury Farm, Birmingham Hill was the location of the first and second defensive lines of the Continental Army. Today, Birmingham Hill is both hallowed ground and a preserve of over 110 acres open to the public for exercise and reflection.

It's where I spoke with Bruce Mowday, an area journalist who has written twenty-six books, including two on the battle. He would help to further interpret this site where Lafayette was wounded but continued to lead American troops even before receiving the care he needed to survive.

Wearing a wool fedora-style hat, peacock blue button-down shirt, casual zip-up navy jacket, and light-toned khaki pants, Bruce had a practical but polished, classic style that reminded me of my father's. My dad would rarely be seen without a hat, both because of his loss of hair and because he just looked good in hats. Some people are hat people. Bruce was a hat person. Now in his mid-seventies, Bruce recently got married at Thornbury Farm, a detail that gave me a bit of joy to learn. Bruce also guides travelers on tours of the area, including to Birmingham Hill and dinner at the General Warren, both on our list today.

Birmingham Hill's preserved verdant rolling fields and trails are popular places for locals to recreate. I saw a few people out walking in pairs or solo. From the parking lot, beside which is a Friends Meetinghouse cemetery, there are interpretive signs that provide an overview of the basics of what happened at this location.

I looked out to the sprawling acres of open, undulating fields. There were only two houses in the distance. Located in the central Birmingham Township in Chester County and just a stone's throw from the historic Birmingham Friends Meetinghouse, which was used as a hospital during the battle, the preserve is within the Birmingham Township Historic District and the greater ten square miles that are designated as a National Historic Landmark. The Battle took place throughout more than ten square miles or around 350,000 acres. Standing with Bruce overlooking the open spaces here at Birmingham Hill gave me a greater sense of the scope of the large swaths of land where the soldiers fought and perished and where today people live, recreate, and visit to learn about the past.

I asked Bruce how he got into leading tours and writing so many books related to history. Bruce relayed that he was first paid to write at the age of seventeen, covering sports for a daily newspaper and eventually went over to hard news and later true crime and some paranormal stories. One of his books, *Lafayette at Brandywine: The Making of An American Hero*, underscores the significance of the French aristocrat and general's heroism here at Brandywine and on Birmingham Hill.

As we began to walk out into the open field, Bruce went into greater detail on the various troop movements during the battle. Here at Brandywine, Washington was unfortunately not getting accurate information from his scouts. This lack of reputable information, confusion, and the fact that the Americans were totally outmatched as far as training and battle skills would contribute to the significant loss of life that day.

"I read some of the reports and memoirs written by British officers, and they said if they had another two hours of daylight, there wouldn't have been a George Washington's army left," Bruce said.

We walked up the hill along a mowed trail to the left of the parking lot. The hill crested along a strand of woods. Bruce said that Lafayette was wounded on top of the hill behind us and would eventually head to the woods in front of us to seek treatment. He was shot through the calf.

It was unlucky. It was Lafayette's first American Revolution battle. Washington had not wanted him to fight, but Lafayette had insisted. Eventually Washington ordered him into battle under the command of Major General John Sullivan. Lafayette had only arrived in South Carolina a few months earlier, in June of 1777, at the age of nineteen. He had purchased his own ship from Spain for the voyage, which his father-in-law opposed.

Perhaps this major life incident and his upbringing in France influenced him to make the bold move to cross the ocean and take up arms to fight the against the British. On his voyage to America, he learned English and studied battle tactics.

Bruce researched using Lafayette's memoirs, including interviews with the American Friends of Lafayette and letters that Lafayette wrote back to his wife, which are now at Lafayette College in Pennsylvania. I asked Bruce more about the transatlantic voyage.

"He wrote a letter to his wife," Bruce said. "He had forgotten to tell her he was leaving!"

Once in America, Lafayette befriended General Washington and was assigned to work on the commander's staff. Though wounded at the location where Bruce and I were walking, Lafayette continued to fight that day until the Continental Army finally retreated. Washington cited Lafayette for his courage.

Lafayette was a French officer before coming to America, but he had never been in combat. On the field where Bruce and I were standing, Lafayette tried to rally General Conway's troops, who were breaking under the assault of the British coming up the hill.

"He didn't have to. He was a general. You know, he could have directed people, but he actually got off his horse, in front of the men, and tried to make a big bayonet charge. When he was shot, that was the defining moment. And that really helped us win or our freedom because it made him the hero," Bruce said. "As soon as he shed his blood, he started on the road to become the American hero. Without Lafayette, we wouldn't have had as much support from France, and without France's support, we would have never defeated the British, so this spot was very important in American history."

Bruce continued to explain that when George Washington heard that Lafayette was wounded, he told his doctors to find him and treat him as if he was his own son. Lafayette would heal from his battle wounds in Bethlehem, and later head to Valley Forge, participating in further skirmishes around Valley Forge. In 1779, he returned to France a hero, meeting with King Louis XVI and calling for further support for the American cause. He would venture back to America in 1780 with French reinforcements, once again meeting up with George Washington. The two became very close friends—so close, in fact, that Lafayette would later name his only son Georges Washington de La Fayette, in honor of George Washington.

I asked Bruce how Lafayette felt in the aftermath of this battle and more about his personality. He described Lafayette as a humous and personable guy—who seemed to take things in stride.

"He wrote back to his wife in France and said *I received this wound, don't worry about it. If you had to be wounded, this was the type of wound to have,*" Bruce said. "*And, anyway, I've been here three months, and this is the first time anybody ever shot at me.*"

While Lafayette took his personal injury in stride, perhaps a little naively, it was part of the sequence of events that would lead to the end of the war and a favorable outcome for the Americans.

The loss at Battle of Brandywine had led the Continental Congress to flee Philadelphia a few days later. They would venture to Lancaster and then further west to York, bringing me full circle here at Brandywine to where I started my Pennsylvania journey.

Visiting battlefields like this is so much more than dates, troop movements, and facts—it's gaining a greater perspective on the personalities, emotions, and nuances that accompanied these major turning points in American history. By speaking with people who have spent years and sometimes a lifetime, like Randell, immersing themselves in the past, you can gain a more complete picture of what happened—with a dash of local legends and color commentary.

Before my visit to Brandywine, the whole battle seemed like a distant, impersonal event, but being on location with Randell and Bruce gave me a better sense of the true struggles, challenges, and ramifications of the people involved, both soldiers and everyday citizens.

Travelers who want to dine or stay in a historic property while visiting Brandywine can either drive an hour east to Philadelphia, an hour and forty-five minutes west to York, or just thirty minutes north to Malvern, Pennsylvania, to the General Warren Tavern. Bruce Mowday often takes his tours to this historic tavern for dinner. It's where Bruce and I would visit to end my time in Pennsylvania.

This inn and restaurant, located off the Old Lancaster Pike, has welcomed travelers since 1745. It was one of around sixty taverns on the Philadelphia-Lancaster Turnpike between 1792 and 1881. During the American Revolution it served many guests, but more recently it has elevated the experience offering with fine dining and renovated rooms. You can still dine just as they did centuries ago—only now with a few modern comforts. The inn includes eight guest rooms, 150 indoor dining seats, and ample room to dine outdoors, too. Owner and chef Patrick Byrne, who has been running the restaurant and inn for thirty-eight years, renovated the structure by taking the original smaller inn rooms and joining them together to create more spacious accommodations for modern travelers.

Bruce shepherded me to the inn and introduced me to Patrick out front of the beautiful Georgian two-and-a-half-story inn. Patrick was wearing a three-quarter-length zip-up navy polo sweatshirt with a button-down shirt underneath. He gave a bright smile, flashing his perfect white teeth. He told me he'd been a TV chef and had done radio work over the years, and I could visualize that from his confident, yet to-the-point answers and appearance. Patrick's father had been an area horse trainer who didn't want him to get into horses, because it was a seven-day-a-week job. Yet, Patrick laughed, he'd ended up running a restaurant and inn, which is also a seven-day-a-week job, as well as a labor of love, especially one involving a historic property.

I studied the seven-bay building with its gable roof. The General Warren was constructed of stone with stucco and had received various additions over time. Accented with displays of pumpkins and flowers with the colors of fall by its front door, the entrance included a historic placard detailing some highlights from its long history. Patrick said that the tavern had been expanded over time. His most recent additions were in 1985, 2005, and 2015: all years that end in fives. A coincidence, he said! The original 1745 construction was the eastern side of the inn.

The original owner was William Penn's son, John Penn. Following the Revolution, the Penn family liquidated their holdings and returned to England. Casper Fahnestock ended up purchasing the inn. Locals wouldn't do business with Fahnestock because the tavern was named after two British naval heroes, so he renamed it after an American hero, General Joseph Warren.

"It had previously been named after Admiral Warren, so he was able to keep the Warren name in his new name, but now he was making amends with the Americans," Patrick said with a smirk. "So it was all about marketing."

Fahnestock was successful, keeping it in the family for half a century as a relay stop for stagecoaches and the area's first post office. During the American Revolution, the tavern and surrounding area was the site of much activity. On September 15, 1777, New Jersey Continentals from Washington's army camped here before the Battle of the Clouds. Lord Cornwallis's division from General Howe's army passed by on September 18 and on September 20 in 1777. British forces again passed by the site on their way to the Battle of Paoli, which was fought just one mile south of the property.

"If you were British, it was known as the Battle of Paoli. If you were an American, it was known as the Paoli Massacre, because American civilians were killed during the battle, which was not the norm in that era of warfare, so it was quite a major turning point in the local area," Patrick said.

Part of the Philadelphia Campaign, the Battle of Paoli occurred after the Battle of Brandywine. It was a nighttime surprise attack by the British on the camp of General "Mad Anthony" Wayne, who we learned about in York.

We walked down a small hill to the side of the inn and into a manicured and landscaped open grassy area. In the distance were the old stone ruins from the stables where they used to house Conestoga wagons and their horses at night from later eras of travel. With Philadelphia to the east and Lancaster to the west, Conestoga wagons were constantly hauling materials and cargo from factories in Philadelphia and bringing produce from Lancaster to Philadelphia. The side area had beautiful bright red burning bushes, fountain grasses, and American arborvitae, a verdant, feathery, and conical evergreen tree.

Patrick told me another story about the British marching past this inn in 1777 on their way to capture Philadelphia.

"The British allegedly captured the local blacksmith at the house on the corner, which is still here to this day. You can see it at the stop sign. They brought him over to the inn and they tortured him to try to make him give up the location of the encampment of Mad Anthony Wayne, which was just about a mile south of here. Whether it's true or not and whether he gave it up or not, we're not sure, but it's a good story," Patrick said.

At a tavern and inn that has survived over so many centuries, there are bound to be lots of stories and legends, including those about ghosts. Patrick said that a lot of his staff and customers have experienced ghostly interactions. There have been numerous paranormal investigations over the years, and all have come up with similar results—the General Warren is likely haunted.

We ventured inside the cozy, yet apparently haunted, inn's well-appointed dining room, where we found white tablecloths and oil paintings featuring horses, a fox in a snowy forest, and other country scenes. There were flowers in the middle of our table, where an exquisite meal of continental American cuisine was being laid out for us. My colorful plate had grilled Scottish salmon with a cauliflower mash, haricot verts, and caramelized onions. Bruce would enjoy a large oven-roasted lump crabcake over sweet potato puree served with warm brussels sprouts and maple remoulade.

I toasted Patrick for keeping this inn and tavern, with all its history, alive for travelers to experience. There are not a lot of places like this that date and predate the founding of our nation for travelers to experience.

It was a fitting end to another chapter of Revolutionary travels, where history comes alive in challenging and delightful ways.

REFERENCES

Chapter I

Tomlinson, Brett. "The Continental Congress at Nassau Hall." *Princeton Alumni Weekly*, 13 Aug. 2018, paw.princeton.edu/article/continental-congress-nassau-hall.

"President's House (Maclean House at Princeton University)." New Jersey Slavery Records, Scarlet and Black Research Center at Rutgers University / Rutgers–New Brunswick, item 7097, https://records.njslavery.org/s/doc/item/7097.

"Nassau Hall Faculty Room." *Princeton MediaCentral*, Princeton University, https://mediacentral.princeton.edu/id/1_cn41 srzk.

Tomlinson, Brett. "The Continental Congress at Nassau Hall." *Princeton Alumni Weekly*, 13 Aug. 2018, paw.princeton.edu/article/continental-congress-nassau-hall. Accessed 25 Nov. 2025.

Levin, Anne. "Yankee Doodle Tap Room Reimagined Around Painting by Norman Rockwell." *Town Topics*, 8 Mar. 2023, https://www.towntopics.com/2023/03/08/yankee-doodle-tap-room-reimagined-around-painting-by-norman-rockwell/.

Achenbach, Joel. "Einstein at Princeton." *Princeton Alumni Weekly*, 22 Apr. 2021, paw.princeton.edu/article/einstein-princeton.

"Princeton Battlefield State Park." New Jersey Department of Environmental Protection, nj.gov/dep/parksandforests/ parks/princetonbattlefieldstatepark.html.

Chapter II

"Denmark Vesey, Abolitionist Is Hanged." *African American Registry*, The Registry, https://aaregistry.org/story/denmark-vesey-hanged/.

Commonwealth Museum, Massachusetts Secretary of the Commonwealth. *Sarah and Angelina Grimké (1792–1879)*. Massachusetts Secretary of the Commonwealth, n.d., sec. state.ma.us/divisions/commonwealth-museum/exhibits/ online/suffragist/PDFs/4-Grimke.pdf.

McIntyre, Jennifer Berry Hawes. *"How a Grad Student Uncovered the Largest Known Slave Auction in the U.S." ProPublica*, 16 June 2023, https://www.propublica.org/article/how-grad-student-discovered-largest-us-slave-auction.

"Discover the Stories Within the Stories Gardens." Middleton Place, Middleton Place Foundation, https://www.middletonplace. org/explore/gardens/.

Hamilton, Alexander. *"Alexander Hamilton to Major General Nathanael Greene, [12 October 1782]." Founders Online*, National Archives, founders.archives.gov/documents/ Hamilton/0103020090. *The Papers of Alexander Hamilton*, vol. 3, 1782–1786, edited by Harold C. Syrett, Columbia University Press, 1962, pp. 183–184.

Butler, Nic, PhD. *"Buried Alive in Early Charleston." Charleston Time Machine*, Charleston County Public Library, 25 Oct. 2018, https://www.ccpl.org/charleston-time-machine/buried-alive-early-charleston.

"List of Places Named for Francis Marion." *Wikipedia: The Free Encyclopedia*, Wikimedia Foundation, last modified 5 Sept. 2025, https://en.wikipedia.org/wiki/List_of_places_named_for_Francis_Marion.

Chapter III

"Saratoga Surrender Site." *National Park Service*, U.S. Department of the Interior, www.nps.gov/places/saratoga-surrender-site.htm.

Baroness von Riedesel and the American Revolution: Journal and Correspondence of a Tour of Duty, 1776–1783 Riedesel, Friederike Charlotte Luise, Freifrau von. *Baroness von Riedesel and the American Revolution: Journal and Correspondence of a Tour of Duty, 1776–1783*. Edited by Marvin L. Brown Jr., Omohundro Institute of Early American History and Culture and University of North Carolina Press, 2012.

Pace, Caroline. "Friederike Charlotte Luise Riedesel (Baroness Riedesel)." *Voices of the American Revolution*, Smith College, https://sites.smith.edu/voices-of-the-american-revolution/friederike-charlotte-luise-riedesel-baroness-riedesel/.

Levin, Anne. "Controversial Statues and Monuments Around the World." *Reader's Digest*, https://www.rd.com/list/controversial-statues-and-monuments-around-the-world/.

Chapter IV

Lewis, J. D. *The American Revolution in South Carolina.* *Carolana*, www.carolana.com/SC/Revolution/home.html. Accessed 22 Nov. 2025.

"WATCH: Ceremony held for remains of Revolutionary War soldiers as their remains make their way back home to

Camden." *YouTube*, uploaded by *SCarolinaAmRev250*, 22 Apr. 2023, www.youtube.com/watch?v=gDxH9iIrThM.

Miklos, Mark. *"The Camden Burials: A Travelogue." InsideGMT*, 2023, insidegmt.com/the-camden-burials-a-travelogue/.

Richardson, Katherine H., and Good, Rickie. *A Guide to Historic Sites: Kershaw County Historical Society's Historic Sites of Camden, South Carolina*. Camden Archives & Museum, 2023, *Experience Camden SC*, experiencecamdensc.com/wpcontent/uploads/2024/10/KCHS_guide_book2023_web.pdf.

Chapter V

Parker, Mariah. *"Thomas Garrett." Quakers & Slavery*, Haverford, Swarthmore & Bryn Mawr Colleges, web.tricolib.brynmawr.edu/speccoll/quakersandslavery/commentary/people/garrett.php.

"The Green or Market Plaine." Historical Marker Database, CeraNet / HMdb.org, www.hmdb.org/m.asp?m=3423.

Dallabrida, Eileen Smith. *"This Old, Old House." Delaware Today*, 9 July 2008, delawaretoday.com/uncategorized/this-old-old-house-2/.

"New Castle, 1891." Historypin, Shift Collective, https://www.historypin.org/en/new-castle-1891/geo/39.659715,-75.563045,5/bounds/26.001355,-84.857479,51.071677,-66.268611/paging/1/pin/151890.

"An 'Unsurpassed Soldiery' – The Delaware Regiment During the American Revolution." Delaware Public Archives, State of Delaware, archives.delaware.gov/events/an-e2-80-9cunsurpassed-soldiery-e2-80-9d-the-delaware-regiment-during-the-american-revolution/.

"Papers of George Washington." *University of Virginia Press*, University of Virginia Press, upress.virginia.edu/series/pgw/.

Schwartz, Ryan. *"History Was Made Here: The Dover Green." History, Division of Historical and Cultural Affairs, State of Delaware*, 12 May 2021, history.delaware.gov/2021/05/12/dover-green/.

"Dover, Delaware." *Preserve America Community*, Advisory Council on Historic Preservation, www.achp.gov/preserve-america/community/dover-delaware.

"Old State House." *Harriet Tubman Byway*, Shift Collective, harriettubmanbyway.org/38-old-state-house.

Tom Irvine. *"Which Side of Black History Is Delaware On?"* ACLU Delaware, 11 Feb. 2022, www.aclu-de.org/en/news/which-side-black-history-delaware.

Eichmann, Mark. *"Juneteenth Did Not Mean Freedom for Delaware Slaves."* WHYY, 19 June 2020, whyy.org/articles/juneteenth-did-not-mean-freedom-for-delaware-slaves/.

"John Bell House." *National Park Service*, U.S. Dept. of the Interior, www.nps.gov/places/john-bell-house.htm.

Deseret News. "Restored John Bell House Reflects Del. History." *Deseret News*, 3 Apr. 2011, www.deseret.com/2011/4/3/20182937/restored-john-bell-house-reflects-del-history/.

"About." *Battell and Read Chapter, NSDAR*, BattellAndReadDAR.org, www.battellandreaddar.org/about/.

"John Dickinson, 'Penman of the Revolution.'" *National Park Service*, U.S. Dept. of the Interior, www.nps.gov/people/john-dickinson.htm.

Chapter VI

"David Schenck (1835–1902, J111)." North Carolina Department of Natural and Cultural Resources – Blogs, 10 Jan. 2024, www.dncr.nc.gov/blog/2024/01/10/david-schenck-1835-1902-j-111.

"Park Archives: Guilford Courthouse National Military Park." NPSHistory.com, National Park Service, npshistory.com/publications/guco/index.htm.

"Guilford Courthouse." American Battlefield Trust, www.battlefields.org/learn/revolutionary-war/battles/guilford-court-house.

"Visit the Hoskins Farm." National Park Service, U.S. Dept. of the Interior, www.nps.gov/thingstodo/visit-the-hoskins-farm.htm.

"Guilford Courthouse National Military Park: Hoskins Farm." National Park Planner, npplan.com/parks-by-state/north-carolina-national-parks/park-at-a-glance-guilford-courthouse-national-military-park/guilford-courthouse-national-military-park-hoskins-farm/.

"Morehead and Schenck." National Park Service, U.S. Dept. of the Interior, 12 Dec. 2022, www.nps.gov/places/morehead-and-schenck.htm.

"African Americans at the Battle of Guilford Courthouse." National Park Service, U.S. Department of the Interior, www.nps.gov/guco/learn/historyculture/african-americans-guilford-courthouse.htm.

Pebbles, Andrew. *Pension Application S38297*. Southern Campaigns American Revolution Pension Statements & Rosters, 11 May 1818, revwarapps.org/s38297.pdf.

"Citizen Archivist." National Archives and Records Administration, www.archives.gov/citizen-archivist.

"Women of Guilford Courthouse." National Park Service, U.S. Dept. of the Interior, www.nps.gov/guco/learn/historyculture/women-of-guilford-courthouse.htm.

"Dolley Madison." Virginia Museum of History & Culture, virginiahistory.org/learn/dolley-madison.

"Greensboro History Museum Offers Rare Revolutionary War Artifact and Lecture." Greensboro History Museum, 7 Mar. 2017, greensborohistory.org/news/rare-revolutionary-war-artifact-and-lecture/.

Dodson, Jim. *"Beloved Possessions: The Liberty Cap." O.Henry Magazine*, 27 May 2022, ohenrymag.com/beloved-possessions/.

"Arthur Forbis and Crown Forces Monuments." National Park Service, U.S. Dept. of the Interior, 10 Oct. 2024, www.nps.gov/places/arthur-forbis-and-crown-forces-monuments.htm.

"Halifax and the Revolution." Historic Halifax State Historic Site, North Carolina Historic Sites, historicsites.nc.gov/all-sites/historic-halifax/history/halifax-historic-district-importance/halifax-and-revolution.

"Josiah Martin (D89)." North Carolina Department of Natural and Cultural Resources – Blogs, 11 Dec. 2023, www.dncr.nc.gov/blog/2023/12/11/josiah-martin-d-89.

"Historic Halifax's McMahon Spotlights Black Soldiers' Role in the Revolution." The Daily Advance, dailyadvance.com/features/local/historic-halifaxs-mcmahon-spotlights-black-soldiers-role-in-revolution/article_c66f159e-62e6-11ee-bae2-cb0f701da016.html.

ACKNOWLEDGMENTS

A book like this doesn't happen without thousands of miles on the road. My close-knit production team—my road family—helped make those miles fly by. Greg Barna, Chad Davis, Evelyn Kwan Green, and Janice Selinger, thank you for seeing the world with me and helping me share the world with others.

A book like this also doesn't happen without countless hours steeped in history. To the storytellers who guided me at each site featured in this book, your passion for history is ultimately what inspired me to help you preserve it. You keep these stories from passing out of time and memory, and I'm honored to help ensure future generations will still remember who helped America become America.

I'm similarly grateful to Bradley Lennie, Scott Culclasure, and Joe Mathews for taking the time to read my early drafts. Your keen eyes and curiosity for the smaller details of history were invaluable in shaping this work, as was the support of Andy Nichols and Adrianna Senior. Thank you for shepherding a visual storyteller through the fields of literary publishing.

Finally, thanks to my mom—a truly imaginative soul—who loved to write and coaxed us to create stories, dances, songs and plays. And to my dad—an original road trip warrior—who drove across America several times (in a Prius no less) and was a great travel companion.

arley Newman is an award-winning host, producer, author, and travel expert recognized by *Forbes* for building a "PBS media empire." She's blended world-record feats with purposeful storytelling—from leaping off the world's highest commercial bungee in Macao to riding horses across Botswana to interviewing civil rights witnesses and small business owners in rural America. As the creator and host of *Travels with Darley*, *Equitrekking*, and *Look Up with Darley*, she combines travel, history, and narrative to uncover hidden gems across the United States and around the world. A trusted, authentic voice, her series and podcast reach dedicated fans on PBS, Amazon Prime, iHeart, and internationally in more than eighty-five nations. Darley has earned multiple Emmy Award nominations for hosting, writing, producing, and directing. She's been honored with the North American Travel Journalist Award, Inspiring Woman

Credit: Chad Davis/Travels with Darley

Award, two Telly Awards, and induction into the Taste Awards Hall of Fame. Having filmed her series in destinations as close to home as New York City and Los Angeles and as far afield as Seoul, Uruguay, and Dubai, she inspires audiences to explore beyond their comfort zones. She is a graduate of The George Washington University.